transforming education

Also available from Bloomsbury

Transforming Schools: Creativity, Critical Reflection, Communication, Collaboration by Miranda Jefferson and Michael Anderson

Transforming Organizations: Engaging the 4Cs for Powerful Organizational Learning and Change by Michael Anderson and Miranda Jefferson

Effective Teacher Development: Theory and Practice in Professional Learning by Bob Burstow

Perspectives on Educational Practice Around the World edited by Sue Hammond and Margaret Sangster

Picture Pedagogy by Paul Duncum

Reflective Teaching in Schools by Andrew Pollard

Sustainable School Leadership: Portraits of Individuality by Mike Bottery, Wong Ping-Man and George Ngai

Transforming Teacher Education: Reconfiguring the Academic Work by Viv Ellis and Jane McNicholl

Transforming Teacher Education with Mobile Technologies, edited by Kevin Burden and Amanda Naylor

Transforming University Education: A Manifesto by Paul Ashwin

Why Do Teachers Need to Know About Child Development?: Strengthening Professional Identity and Well-Being edited by Daryl Maisey and Verity Campbell-Barr

Why Do Teachers Need to Know About Diverse Learning Needs?: Strengthening Professional Identity and Well-Being edited by Sue Soan

Why Do Teachers Need to Know About Psychology?: Strengthening Professional Identity and Well-Being edited by Jeremy Monsen, Lisa Marks Woolfson and James Boyle

Why Teaching Matters: A Philosophical Guide to the Elements of Practice by Paul Farber and Dini Metro-Roland

transforming education

reimagining learning, pedagogy and curriculum

Miranda Jefferson and Michael Anderson

BLOOMSBURY ACADEMIC
LONDON • NEW YORK • OXFORD • NEW DELHI • SYDNEY

BLOOMSBURY ACADEMIC
Bloomsbury Publishing Plc
50 Bedford Square, London, WC1B 3DP, UK
1385 Broadway, New York, NY 10018, USA
29 Earlsfort Terrace, Dublin 2, Ireland

BLOOMSBURY, BLOOMSBURY ACADEMIC and the Diana logo are trademarks of
Bloomsbury Publishing Plc

First published in Great Britain 2021

Copyright © Miranda Jefferson and Michael Anderson, 2021

Miranda Jefferson and Michael Anderson have asserted their rights under the Copyright, Designs and Patents Act, 1988, to be identified as Authors of this work.

For legal purposes the Acknowledgements on p. xi constitute an extension of this copyright page.

Cover design by Charlotte James
Cover image: Rhythm No.3 decoration for the Salon des Tuileries by Robert Delaunay
© Photo 12/ Universal Images Group via Getty Images

All rights reserved. No part of this publication may be reproduced or transmitted in any form or by any means, electronic or mechanical, including photocopying, recording, or any information storage or retrieval system, without prior permission in writing from the publishers.

Bloomsbury Publishing Plc does not have any control over, or responsibility for, any third-party websites referred to or in this book. All internet addresses given in this book were correct at the time of going to press. The author and publisher regret any inconvenience caused if addresses have changed or sites have ceased to exist, but can accept no responsibility for any such changes.

A catalogue record for this book is available from the British Library.

Library of Congress Cataloging-in-Publication Data

Names: Jefferson, Miranda, author. | Anderson, Michael, 1969– author.
Title: Transforming education : reimagining learning, pedagogy and curriculum / Miranda Jefferson and Michael Anderson.
Description: New York : Bloomsbury Academic, 2021. | Includes bibliographical references and index.
Identifiers: LCCN 2020047649 | ISBN 9781350130081 (hardback) | ISBN 9781350130098 (ebook)
Subjects: LCSH: School improvement programs—Cross-cultural studies.
Classification: LCC LB2822.8 .J44 2021 | DDC 371.2/7—dc23
LC record available at https://lccn.loc.gov/2020047649

ISBN:	HB:	978-1-3501-3008-1
	PB:	978-1-3501-3007-4
	ePDF:	978-1-3501-3006-7
	eBook:	978-1-3501-3009-8

Typeset by RefineCatch Limited, Bungay, Suffolk
Printed and bound in Great Britain

To find out more about our authors and books visit www.bloomsbury.com and sign up for our newsletters.

Contents

List of Figures vii
List of Tables ix
Acknowledgements xi
List of Abbreviations xiii
Foreword *by Yong Zhao* xv

1 **Transforming education for the infinite game** 1
2 **Transforming complexity through capabilities** 13
3 **Transforming values: Guides for transformative action** 33
4 **Transforming learning: The power of agency** 51
5 **The Learning Disposition Wheel** 75
6 **Transforming pedagogy: Curating learning** 103
7 **The Pedagogy Parachute** 123
8 **Transforming curriculum: Connecting education to students and their contexts** 151
9 **Transforming teacher education: Experience, reflection and inquiry** 179
10 **Transforming leadership: Shared action and agency** 201
11 **Transforming education: Putting the pieces together** 227

Glossary 237
Notes 239
Index 259

Figures

1.1	Crafting infinity, Wahiba Sands, Oman.	4
1.2.	Curricular and co-curricular learning is a false dichotomy.	5
1.3	A steam train: working in some old paradigms is like perfecting steam train technology – comforting but pointless.	7
1.4	'Aerosol words' vanish when you try and get hold of them.	9
2.1	The 'monster' of Gévaudan.	14
2.2	Pieces of the capability jigsaw describe the capabilities of transformation enabled by the 4Cs.	20
2.3	The Creativity Cascade coherence maker.	23
2.4	Collaboration Circles coherence maker.	25
2.5	The Critical Reflection Crucible coherence maker.	26
2.6	The Communication Crystal coherence maker.	28
3.1	Global Climate protests in London, 20 April 2019.	35
3.2	4C Transformative Learning in action.	39
3.3	Students co-lead a learning bazaar on a 4C network day.	42
4.1	Greta Thunberg speaking at a climate rally.	52
4.2	At 19 years old, the entrepreneur Boyan Slat created the non-profit organization The Ocean Cleanup, which has designed a massive plastic-catching device to clean up the Great Pacific Garbage Patch.	53
4.3	The OECD Learning Compass.	56
4.4	The Learning Disposition Wheel.	65
4.5	Students discussing their learning using the Learning Disposition Wheel.	68
5.1	The 'evolution' of the wheel.	76
5.2	A pre-Columbian toy dog with wheels.	77
5.3	Interpersonal domain of the Wheel.	81
5.4	Cognitive domain of the Wheel.	87
5.5	Interpersonal domain of the Wheel.	94
5.6	Students at Ecole 42 in Paris, France.	100
6.1	Tunnels and chambers at MONA (the Museum of Old and New Art) in Tasmania, Australia.	104

Figures

6.2	The technology device called 'The O' gives visual and aural information about the artworks at MONA.	105
6.3	A diagram illustrating the relationship between general pedagogical knowledge, pedagogical content knowledge and content knowledge.	111
6.4	The Deep Noticing and Action Eye.	114
6.5	Students at Learnlife, Barcelona.	118
7.1	Leonardo Da Vinci's sketch of a parachute, 1514.	124
7.2	Veranzio's Parachute, 1615.	125
7.3	Garnerin's use of frameless parachute in 1789.	125
7.4	The Pedagogy Parachute.	129
7.5	Martin and Rose's (2005) adaptation of Basil Bernstein's matrix of pedagogical theories and approaches (1990).	131
7.6	The periodic table for chemical elements.	133
7.7	Developing pedagogic practice.	134
8.1	9/11 Memorial and One World Trade Centre.	152
8.2	A lino cut from the Te Rito Toi project by Charlotte Prebble.	159
8.3	Templestowe College has transformed education for their students.	161
9.1	Lake Champlain near the United States/Canadian border.	180
9.2	Experience, reflection and inquiry are interdependent processes enabled by the 4Cs.	186
9.3	Hurstville Public School, established 1876.	191
10.1	New Zealand's Prime Minister, Jacinda Ardern, comforts a member of the community after the Christchurch massacre.	202
10.2	The Leadership Wheel.	203
10.3	Going for the ball at a line out; the All Blacks national rugby team in Wellington, New Zealand.	205
10.4	Migratory birds such as magpie geese fly in an emergent V formation, illustrating the natural phenomenon of emergence in a complex system.	211
10.5	A framework for leading transformation also known as 'eggs in a basket'.	214
10.6	Transforming School Structures diagram.	215
10.7	The tension of transformation in schools, adapted from John P. Kotter's diagram of acceleration stalled.	218
11.1	The infinity symbol.	228
11.2	The puzzle of transformation.	229
11.3	The Transformation Tangle.	231

Tables

1.1	The 4Cs: coherence makers for creativity, critical reflection, communication and collaboration.	11
2.1	Differences between simple, complicated and complex problems.	18
4.1	A student rubric for motivation adapted from the continuum of self-determination according to motivation and self-regulatory behaviour by Ryan and Deci (2000).	63
4.2	Learning dispositions oscillating between the personal and the public, from Buckingham Shum and Deakin Crick (2012).	66
6.1	The diverse methodologies at the school LearnLife in Barcelona, Spain.	119
9.1	Dewey's approach to inquiry reflected through the Critical Reflection Crucible.	188
10.1	Comparison of three different perspectives of shared and active leadership, adapted from Barbara Simpson (2016).	212
11.1	How the phases of transformation are enabled by capabilities.	233

Acknowledgements

We would like to acknowledge the following colleagues who contributed to the development of *Transforming Education*.

Carol Anderson
Daniel Bell
Hon Boey
Tanya Bowd
Luke Bristow
Caroline David
Mike Dicker
Alison Duff
Jamie Gerlach
Paul Ginns
Peter Howes
Mary Ann Hunter
Constantine Loucopoulos
Olivera Mateski
Clare Matthews
Kirsti McGeoch
Antonia Mitsoulis
Jayne Muir
Susan Orlovich
Alison Rourke
Stephen Smith
Mark Steed
Giovanna Trenoweth
Amanda Whitfield
Anastasia Yule

The following figures are the property of 4C Transformative Learning and are used here with their permission: Figures 2.2, 2.3, 2.4, 2.5, 2.6, 4.4, 5.1, 5.3, 5.4, 5.5, 6.3, 6.4, 7.4, 7.7, 9.2, 10.2, 10.5, 10.6, 11.2 and 11.3. All of the design elements (icons) in chapters 5 and 7 are also the property of 4C Transformative Learning and are used here with their permission.

Abbreviations

4Cs	Creativity, Critical Reflection, Collaboration, Communication
4CTL	4C Transformative Learning
CCV	Collaborative Classroom Visit
COP	Community of Practice
CRC	Conventions on the Rights of the Child
DNA	Deep Noticing and Action
GERM	Global Educational Reform Movement
LDW	Learning Disposition Wheel (the Wheel)
OECD	Organisation for Economic Co-operation and Development
PBL	Problem-Based Learning or Project-Based Learning
PIRLS	Progress in International Reading Literacy Study
PISA	Program for International Student Assessment
TIMMS	Trends in International Mathematics and Science Study
UNESCO	United Nations Educational, Scientific and Cultural Organization

Foreword
The Change We Need

Yong Zhao

Education needs to change. Few would argue against this simple statement because it is clear that education as practised now in schools does not serve us well. On the one hand, education does not work equally well for all students. There are too many students who suffer from the education we have and live on the other side of the achievement gap. On the other hand, education does not work for all students. The world has changed and will continue to change. The changed and changing world requires a set of new capabilities for students to thrive.

There have also been many different efforts to change education. The massive changes have been launched by governments. Typically, their focus has been on standardization – standardization of curriculum, pedagogy, assessment and ultimately learning. This effort can be seen in the rise of national curriculum such as the Australian National Curriculum and the Common Core State Standards Initiative in the United States. It is also evident in the adoption of standardized exams to hold schools and teachers accountable. Governments have additionally been working on promoting certain pedagogies such as direct instruction as well as school marketization.

The government-led changes have attracted tremendous amounts of investment. They have forced behaviour changes of teachers and schools. For example, the majority of schools and teachers have succumbed to the pressure of national standardized assessments, which have led to the acceptance of these assessments in students and parents. Their efforts have also created a different culture of education – viewing test scores as the measure of quality of education and capability of students.

However, these efforts have not addressed the problems of education: equity and excellence. Even using the traditional measures of educational success, test scores in a few subjects such as mathematics and reading, the progress in education has been very limited. International test scores have not improved much, and wide gaps remain among different groups of students. The same is true for national assessments. By and large, scores did not rise significantly, and the achievement gap has not been closed.

These reform efforts have done even less to prepare students for the changing world. As the world moves into the Fourth Industrial Revolution, technological changes will undoubtedly further displace human workers, collapse industries and create new possibilities for work and life. To avoid direct competition with smart machines and take advantage of new possibilities, future citizens of the globalized society need to be creative, entrepreneurial, socially responsible, globally competent and environmentally ethical. These and other related capabilities have been written and articulated in various documents and policies, but they have rarely been implemented in schools because schools have been mistakenly driven by the desire to improve test scores.

Fortunately, there have been other efforts to change education. These efforts have not been the mainstream or supported by government policies. They have generally been initiated, implemented and sustained by individual education leaders, schools and organizations. They have been by and large grassroots efforts, waiting to be recognized and adopted by governments.

In *Transforming Education: Reimagining Learning, Pedagogy and Curriculum*, Miranda Jefferson and Michael Anderson describe such an effort. This effort is drastically different from government-led reform efforts. Instead of using standardized curriculum, pedagogy and assessment to homogenize school experiences for all students, this effort aims to transform education by reimagining curriculum, pedagogy and assessment. This book is about true transformation of education and attempts 'to explain the why and then provide the rationale, the research and some of the frameworks (coherence makers) for "how" we might transform education'.

The book considers education as an infinite game that keeps all involved 'participating and engaged in the game, no winners, no losers, just participants'. This is a powerful vision for educational change. 'This vision for education requires teachers, students and school communities to reimagine the capabilities for transformation: values, learning, pedagogy, curriculum, teacher education and leadership. An education system that can achieve these reimaginings has potential to build a better and more equitable society.'

This vision is ambitious and courageous. To build not only an education system for the students, but also a system that is more equitable and is able to cultivate students as citizens who can build a better society, is no small task. But the book does an excellent job explaining the process of transformation, backed with evidence and historical artefacts. It explains 'the big picture' purpose of education by inviting the reader to reimagine what schools can and should be, to make it relevant to students. The book guides the reader to almost every aspect of education that can have a broad impact on the experience of students, from values to learning, from pedagogy to curriculum, and from teachers to leadership.

The book rightly recognizes that transformations like this are 'unlikely to be initiated by governments, systems or politicians'. The best thing governments and systems can do is not to stop the effort and possibly create space for such effort to survive and thrive. But these efforts, given enough time, could lead governments and systems to change, ultimately.

What struck me most in this book is the authors' message that 'transformation begins when educators collaborate and ask the simple question: what do students need to survive and thrive and how can we make that happen?'. The purpose of educational transformations is to create a better experience for all students. Thus, we, as the people who are responsible for creating such experiences for all students, must develop a clear understanding of our students, our society and the various changing factors of our society, a deep appreciation for the process and mechanisms of transformation, and a clear vision of the human purpose of education. This book is a great resource for us to develop such an understanding, appreciation and vision!

Yong Zhao
School of Education, University of Kansas
Melbourne Graduate School of Education, University of Melbourne
September 2020

Transforming education for the infinite game

1

A thought experiment...
Transforming Education 2

Who is this book for? 3

Finite and infinite games 4

Developing infinite education 5

Transforming Education 6

What is successful
transformation? 7

What are coherence makers? 8

The 4Cs enable transformation 10

Transforming schools 12

A thought experiment... Transforming Education

If you could reimagine the education system from the ground up what might that look like? Could we:

- imagine deep learning enabled by creativity, critical reflection, communication and collaboration?
- imagine values that drive and guide deeper transformative learning?
- imagine coherent learning that builds agency through intrapersonal, interpersonal and cognitive dispositions for lifelong learning?
- imagine an agile curriculum that connects learners to their world?
- imagine pedagogy that is broad, deep and contextually developed and fosters agency for students and teachers?
- imagine teacher education that is sustained and focused on each teacher's needs and context through reflection, experience and inquiry?
- imagine leadership as collaborative and creative?

This 'imagination experiment' helps us to understand our priorities and consider what features of education go to the heart of the reason for education. Imagination gives us the power to aspire to something beyond what we have at the moment, to think creatively about what schooling could be. Our ability to reimagine what schools and education can be is the first step in making the changes required to ensure our community has the education system it needs to face the challenges of the present and the future. This book is a work of educational imagination with a twist. *Transforming Education: Reimagining Learning, Pedagogy and Curriculum* responds to these imaginings but explores how we move from imagining to reimagining to reality. The twist is, unlike this imagination experiment, it is not possible to begin from a blank sheet of paper. We can't magically uninvent centuries of education practice and policy. The complexity of education has long been bemoaned, discussed and sometimes used as an excuse not to change anything. We want to consider how we might reimagine and transform education given the existing resources and challenges.[1]

In 2017 we wrote *Transforming Schools*, where we laid out our blueprint for transforming schools based on our experience with schools over decades. Since that book we have generated long-term partnerships with more than fifty schools on creating sustainable transformation through an organization we formed called 4C Transformative Learning.[2] In 2019 when we wrote *Transforming Organizations*, we took our understanding of transformation in places of learning (such as early learning centres, schools and universities) and applied it to organizational contexts. Our approach is focused on learning not training, agency not hierarchies and inquiry not transmission.

In this book, *Transforming Education*, our ambition has broadened. How do we imagine an ecosystem of education that meets the needs of our citizens and our community in uncertain times? Instead of considering education in its component parts, our work here considers the transformation of education through building capabilities in our students, teachers and school communities. Our research and experience have taught us that by communicating across, between and over silos in education (including age, stage, culture, space and modality), we enrich rather than constrain discussions. Context is critical (and we have more to say about that), but there are key features of a reimagined education system that connect everyone interested in deep and authentic learning throughout education.

Who is this book for?

In a book called *Transforming Education*, you can expect a substantial discussion of what needs to change in education. Up front we want to acknowledge that teachers, school leaders and students have been involved in the transformation of education over many years. We are not suggesting here that deep learning and transformative pedagogy is nowhere to be seen. On the contrary, we could only write a book like this if these practices were evident. We have referred throughout this book to examples of practice around the world that evidence this. Our aim in this book is to provide examples from this practice, academic research and our own work as an insight into the *how* of transformation. In that sense this book is the third of a trilogy. If you would like to learn more about the why and the centrality of the 4Cs – creativity, critical reflection, communication and collaboration – *Transforming Schools* is a good place to start. If you would like to understand how educational transformation might enrich organizations and leadership inside and outside education, the second in the trilogy, *Transforming Organizations*, might serve as an introduction. This book is for those who are convinced that the 4Cs are critical for learning and are ready to be challenged. It is for those who are up for the challenge of reimagining the capabilities for transformation in education including:

- values,
- learning,
- pedagogy,
- curriculum,
- teacher education, and
- leadership.

Before we discuss more of the 'how', let's look at the big picture of education through the metaphor of games.

Figure 1.1 Crafting infinity, Wahiba Sands, Oman.

Finite and infinite games

Theologian James P Carse[3] uses the metaphor of finite and infinite games to explain how he thinks the world (including education) works. A finite game has a winner and a loser. An infinite game has no ending, no beginning, no winner and no loser. The aim of the infinite game is to keep the game going and to keep everyone participating actively in the game. Corporate leadership expert Simon Sinek, who recently popularized the discussion of infinite and finite games in business, claims that there are examples everywhere of finite mindsets distorting infinite games. He argues:

> When we lead with a finite mindset in an infinite game, it leads to all kinds of problems, the most common of which include the decline of trust, cooperation and innovation. Leading with an infinite mindset in an infinite game, really does move us in a better direction. Groups that adopt an infinite mindset enjoy vastly higher levels of trust, cooperation and innovation and all the subsequent benefits.[4]

Examples of infinite games include health, education and international diplomacy. Finite games include cricket, football and, in the educational context, standardized tests. Paradoxically, infinite games often have embedded finite games. These finite games often have great value when they support the infinite game. The damage is inflicted in education when we don't realize when finite games detract rather than strengthen the infinite game. What happens when a finite game takes over the infinite game and all our energy is taken by a spelling test or a numeracy exam rather than deep learning? Fundamentally, education should be about learning in its broadest possible sense. If this is the case, it has deep implications for the way we 'do' curriculum, pedagogy, teacher education and leadership at all levels of education including early childhood, primary, secondary and tertiary (especially teacher education).

On one level, that seems like a completely uncontroversial argument. However, ask many leaders or teachers what takes precedence: learning or the endless pursuit of finite games? If we are truly to understand that learning is an infinite game, we need to rethink and reimagine our education system and each of the pieces within it.

Developing infinite education

For transformation to be a reality in our education communities and not just a buzzword, we need first to understand our 'why'. We must then engage our innate human capacities of creativity, critical reflection, collaboration and communication (the 4Cs) to enable capacities that drive deep learning in schools and organizations. For schools and school leaders, this means questioning everything through the prism of deep learning. For instance:

- Do values lead to transformative action?
- Is learning deep and authentic and focused on our students?
- Is assessment focused on learning?
- Is agency a feature of the learning environment?
- Is the pedagogy focused on the needs of the learners?
- Are the curriculum, leadership and organization focused on learning or are they focused on other factors such as logistics and bus timetables?

For example, when we think about learning, is there a division between formal and informal learning in the curriculum for no good reason? There is as much potential for deep learning about collaboration and communication in basketball, football and the dance ensemble as there is in mathematics, science and history, yet schools arbitrarily divide learning into 'curricula' and 'co-curricular'. In 'co-curricula' learning, students learn through combining strategy, agility and embodiment. When

Figure 1.2 Curricula and co-curricular learning is a false dichotomy

schools silo these activities off from the curriculum, they potentially miss out on valuable and transferable learning. Schools also miss out when they arbitrarily partition learning into discrete subjects without connecting areas of knowledge (such as history to music and mathematics).

In secondary schools, deep learning is possible in transdisciplinary contexts but the politics of established disciplines and faculties with their knowledge silos leads to inbuilt disincentives for widespread integrated learning (e.g. interdisciplinarity, or multidisciplinarity or transdisciplinarity). There are some who argue that teaching integrated curriculum through the 4Cs (discussed in chapter 8) will lead to the disintegration of the disciplines (such as English, history, mathematics and so on). This is a false dichotomy. Deep disciplinary understanding allows students to apply the 4Cs and create links within and between disciplines. We can, and for the sake of our students must, engage with both subject depth and interdisciplinarity to create deep learning that supports students in their own 'infinite games' (relationships, health, engagement with community, work and so on). To make education into an infinite game we need to bring coherence to the critical concepts for learning. But more than that we need to reimagine everything about schools to make them responsive and ready to our shifting world and the problems those shifts throw up.

Transforming Education

We included 're-imagining' in the title of this book as it is critical for transformation. Education researcher Sanne Akkerman defines imagination as 'a process of making sense that extends the "here and now" to the "there and then"'[5] – in other words, thinking about something (such as curriculum or pedagogy) in relation to but beyond our present concepts, contexts and understandings. As philosopher Ziauddin Sardar argues, imagination is mandatory, 'Because we have no other way of dealing with complexity, contradictions and chaos. Imagination is the main tool; indeed I would suggest the only tool, which takes us from simple reasoned analysis to higher synthesis. While imagination is intangible, it creates and shapes our reality; while a mental tool, it affects our behaviour and expectations.'[6] We have included in the title of this book 'Reimagining Learning, Pedagogy and Curriculum' to emphasize the power and usefulness of imagination as a starting point for transformation.

We use the term *transformation* to indicate two qualities of change. Transformation, when effective, is a deliberate process that moves people and organizations beyond their current realities to new practices and approaches. This entails a fundamental reimagining of educational structures including student and teacher learning, pedagogy, curriculum and leadership. This process necessitates the second quality of change, the unlearning of old practices and the reform of outmoded structures to create new structures to suit new realities. Doing better with old thinking is akin in our view to perfecting steam train technology – nice to do, but hardly an effective response to a world that has long ago moved away from steam to power transport. In many places of

Figure 1.3 A steam train: working in some old paradigms is like perfecting steam train technology – comforting but pointless.

learning, we still rely on old practices because like steam trains they are familiar and we have an affection for doing things the way we have always done them. Steam trains have outlived their practical usefulness as a means of transport, and so have many educational practices outlived their relevance, but educators often cling to them.

Transformation is not simply making what exists slightly better – this is sometimes called school improvement. We are not arguing for school improvement, rather we are proposing revolution at an evolutionary pace. Transformation retains and adapts what is effective and useful for learning, but reimagines and re-establishes several of its components through transformative capabilities in education.

We use the term *education* in the title of this book to emphasize the connectedness of early learning, primary, secondary and tertiary learning as a system. Transformation can only be successful if the whole system transforms so students can have a consistent expectation of deep, coherent and connected lifelong learning throughout their education. Relying on status-quo or 'improvement' practices will not generate the changes our students need. Our education structures and systems require transformation.

What is successful transformation?

How do we measure success in education? At the moment, and for a fair while, we have measured success through a benchmark score, standardized testing and a system that often pits individuals against one another and schools against schools. The result is less like comparing apples with oranges, and more like a system to rank the relative worth of a fingerprint. While fingerprints are useful, they don't tell us all there is to know about ourselves. And our modern testing regimes certainly don't tell us all we need to know about student progression and what's working and how it is working in schools, universities and other organizations.

As education researchers and teachers, we often find ourselves in discussions with educators about how we might reimagine our schools to embed deeper learning. Recently we were in a school talking about the capacity for the 4Cs – creativity, collaboration, communication and critical reflection – to fundamentally transform not only schools, but the way we view learning across education. We had a fairly receptive audience and the educators present engaged with perception and depth to the discussion. Yet there was a lingering objection from quite a few leaders and teachers including the principal which amounted to: 'What about our standardized tests? What about our university entrance tests?' This story, which is common across education, reveals the kind of dichotomy that we encounter in many sites in our education systems. Put brutally, the objection is: 'We don't have time to learn deeply because we have to maximize our test scores.' We spend so much time thinking about the 'what', we fail to consider the 'why' of schooling.

We think the disconnection from the 'why' is one reason some schools are resistant to deep and sustained transformation. Until we get the *why* of education focused, the *how* is not particularly meaningful. We first should understand why we do school – why do we require students to spend in some places more than 520 weeks in school? The confusion is understandable. For instance, high-stakes testing, typically imposed from above, creates great stresses on schools, students and teachers to 'win' the rankings games driven by league tables, but to what end? If rankings are the answer, what is the question? Is it: 'How can we ensure our students take tests most effectively?' In the end, the testing loop becomes a self-sustaining system that feeds itself, with little reference to the learning needs of students.

The problem is, while schools and students are focused on how their test scores look compared to those of the school down the road, we miss the opportunity to make deep learning central to what our schools and universities do. We miss the opportunity to focus on the kinds of learning that engage and prepare students in their present and their future. Educators who realize this can lead and refocus our profession, unlearn irrelevant practices and reimagine schools as student-centred places of deep, authentic and connected learning.

In education we can suffer from tunnel vision when we habitually repeat old practices. This has a tendency to limit our educational imagination. This has caused our focus to drift from the potential of deep learning and towards the finite games of testing and compliance. To sharpen our focus we can transform our schools, making them places that engage and empower our young people through the 4Cs, pedagogy, learning, curriculum and leadership. To support schools understand these concepts, we have devised coherence makers to structure and clarify these sometimes vague concepts.

What are coherence makers?

Coherence makers are designed to bring meaning and structure to critical concepts in education. They are schemas (discussed in chapters 6 and 7) that organize knowledge. They are also metacognitive devices that help educators consider deeply the quality and effectiveness of their processes and strategies in learning, curriculum, pedagogy and leadership. Our coherence makers are schemas that organize knowledge, skills and understanding for educators. We identify several coherence makers that we have created for our work with schools and organizations including:

- the Creativity Cascade (chapter 1),
- Critical Reflection Crucible (chapter 1),
- the Communication Crystal (chapter 1),
- Collaboration Circles (chapter 1),
- the Learning Disposition Wheel (chapter 5),
- the Pedagogy Parachute (chapter 7),
- the Leadership Wheel (chapter 10), and
- the Transformation Tangle (chapter 11).

Some of these words or concepts that the coherence makers are based on have become vague and undefined, becoming buzzwords or, as we call them, 'aerosol words' (figure 1.4). For them to become useful and powerful again, we need to bring meaning and coherence to them so educators can understand them and put them into practice.

Figure 1.4 'Aerosol words' vanish when you try and get hold of them.

For instance, the 4Cs creativity, critical thinking, communication and collaboration have become 'aerosol words'; they are sprayed around, they smell pleasant, but quickly vaporize into nothing. Perhaps due to their overuse, the 4Cs as concepts have lost their meaning. Coherence makers bring structure to understanding the 4Cs to make them 'teachable' and 'learnable'. Learning is complex, and coherence makers as conceptual schemas provide order to complexity. The paradox of a coherence maker is that in its simplicity to make ideas clear, it also opens up ever greater complexity. A coherence maker should not make thinking reductive, limited or procedural. For example, the simple and the complex are evident in the theorems and equations of mathematics. $E=mc^2$ (energy = mass × speed of light squared) is a seemingly simple algebraic formula that make coherence of a profound relationship between energy and matter. While our coherence makers are not equations, nor as profound, they attempt to reveal and address the complexity of processes in education through simplicity.

Coherence makers in learning support and challenge teachers and students to develop a deeper proficiency in the processes of learning, and allow for 'emergence'.[7] By emergence (Chapter 2) we mean that coherence makers encourage teachers and students to build new and unpredictable knowledge about learning itself. For instance, the Pedagogy Parachute coherence maker we introduce in chapter 7 supports an understanding of the possibilities of pedagogy. Rather than mandating what pedagogy is, it supports a bending, breaking and blending approach to pedagogy so teachers can experiment with novel approaches in collaboration with their students. Coherence makers are designed to open up complexities through simplicity, not reduce or close down deeper understandings about phenomena. We have developed 4Cs coherence makers to open up and support a response to the complexity of transformative learning in schools education. So what are the 4Cs and why are they so prominent in our work and in this book?

The 4Cs enable transformation

The acronym 4Cs (table 1.1) is shorthand for developing the capacities for creativity, critical reflection, communication and collaboration. The 4Cs are somewhat of a paradox. They are inherent in each of us. Yet we need to develop and engage with them in our context to ensure we grow in our ability to apply them. Like a muscle, the 4Cs need exercise to strengthen. As we discuss in the prequel to this book, *Transforming Schools*, humans are all capable of and depend upon creativity, critical reflection, communication and collaboration to navigate our lives, whether we know it or not. Yet our ability to understand the 4Cs and enact them individually and collectively determines the success or otherwise of our endeavours individually and in our communities.

The 4Cs are even more critical in post-normal times of chaos, contradiction and complexity.[8] In these times they provide the foundational capabilities that allow us as individuals and communities to respond with agility as challenges arise. In other words, rather than narrow skills, the 4Cs provide the core skills that can be adapted

Table 1.1 The 4Cs: coherence makers for creativity, critical reflection, communication and collaboration

Creativity engages our imagination to iteratively and collaboratively design and enact new approaches and processes in response to complex challenges. The Creativity Cascade coherence maker provides a schema for learning[9] creativity and includes Noticing, Asking why, really why?, Playing with possibility, and Selecting and evaluating.	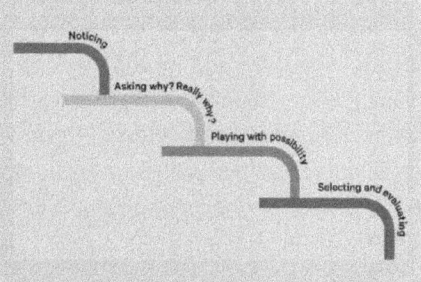
Critical reflection is to analyse experience, relationships and power dynamics. Critical reflection seeks to question, elaborate and develop action based on analysis and reflection. The Critical Reflection Crucible provides a schema for learning critical reflection and consists of Identifying assumptions, Why this? Why so? Contesting, elaborating and adapting, and Re-solving.	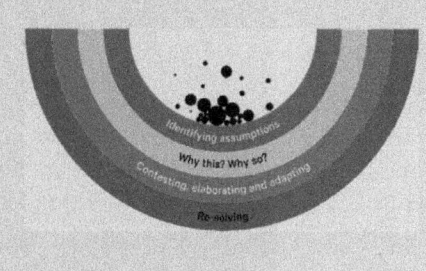
Communication creates messages that lead to action. Effective communication enables all participants to agentically convey meaning and purpose. The Communication Crystal provides a schema for learning communication and includes: Alert to messaging, Enabling voice, Conveying meaning and purpose, and Generating action and agency.	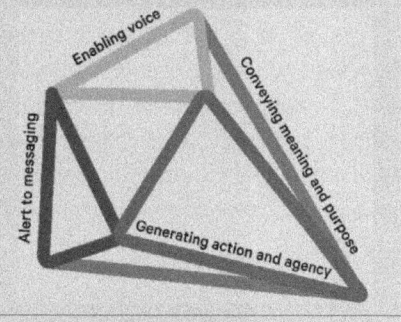
Collaboration is a process of trustful co-construction and openness to challenge and being challenged to create shared ideas and actions. The Collaboration Circles coherence maker provides a schema for learning collaboration and includes: Offering, Yielding, Challenging, evaluating and extending, and Advancing co-construction and connections.	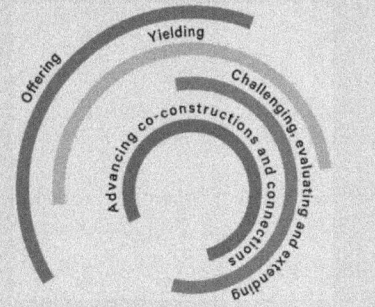

to any emergent or insoluble problem. How we respond to and transform out of crises will rely on our ability to communicate, collaborate, create and critically reflect.

When we work with schools, their ability to enact and engage with the 4Cs determines their capacity to imagine, enable and enact transformative change. Making coherence and meaning of these processes is vital and yet we expect our young people, our schools and our teachers to know what the 4Cs are and how they can be used almost by accident. An understanding and ability to enact the 4Cs can shape, unify and transform education. In short, the better we understand the 4Cs, the more effective our transformative efforts will be. Table 1.1 outlines the coherence makers for the 4Cs.

Transforming schools

The Covid-19 pandemic that began in 2020, like many of the pandemics before it, generated massive changes in our communities. These changes limited our movement, curtailed our freedoms and for many cut lives short. The flux the pandemic generated caused schools in many countries to transform their teaching and learning within a matter of days. For us, this disproved the myth that our schools can't change. They did and they can. The pandemic was an existential threat. There is, however, another existential threat that, while not as sudden and dramatic as a pandemic, still threatens our schools. It is the threat of wasted potential from schools that have become irrelevant and do not enable students to understand their present and create their future. The process of transformation that we detail in this book seeks to reimagine learning, pedagogy, curriculum, teacher education and leadership as agentic, democratic and innovative processes that are focused on our students first. Our approach to transformation is like Elliot Eisner's, not improvement and not revolution. He argued:

> I am not thrilled with the array of values and assumptions that drive our pursuit of improved schools. I am not sure we can tinker towards Utopia and get there. Nor do I believe we can mount a revolution. What we can do is to generate other visions of education, other values to guide its realization, other assumptions on which a more generous conception of the practice of schooling can be built.[10]

If we believe that learning is for all, that our schools can rise to the challenge of the infinite game, then we have no choice. We must transform education.

In chapter 2, we begin our discussions of the 'how' of transformation by exploring the capabilities that can make educational transformation a reality.

Transforming complexity through capabilities

2

- The myth of the monster and the silver bullet 15
- Why transformation? 16
- Complexity theory 17
- How does complexity theory frame educational transformation? 19
- A capabilities response to complexity 20
- Capabilities to respond to complexity 21
- How do capabilities enable transformation? 22
  - The 4Cs enable transformative capabilities 22
  - Creativity enables transformative values 23
  - Collaboration enables transformative pedagogy 24
  - Critical reflection enables transformative teacher education 25
  - Communication enables transformative leadership 27
- Capabilities for transforming education 28
- Concluding reflections 31

You have probably heard the term 'silver bullet'; it refers to a quick-fix solution to a problem. For instance, in 1928 when penicillin was discovered by the Scottish biologist Alexander Fleming, it was hailed as a silver bullet solution to bacterial infection and has saved the lives of countless patients worldwide since. It is difficult to say for certain where the term 'silver bullet' emerges from. One popular theory relates to a mythical, monstrous werewolf that terrified villagers in the province of Gévaudan in the Margeride mountains of south-central France between 1764 and 1767.[1] The folklore of the times tell of a ferocious and terrifying monster that roamed the villages attacking people within a 50–55 mile (80–90 kilometre) radius. The villagers imagined the monster was a supernatural being. According to one expert on French history and folklore, Jay Smith: 'The beast aroused sustained fascination because its actions seemed to signal the presence of a mysterious being: a witch, an agent of divine justice, an unknown hybrid, a werewolf, a creature from Africa, a wolf of extraordinary type. In the Gévaudan, tragic events provided sufficient fodder for continuing speculation about strange monsters through the end of December 1764.'[2] The beast (or more likely groups of beasts) that were, depending on who you believe, a wolf, a dog or a wolf-dog hybrid, had huge terrifying talons and a massive tail. In 1765 alone the 'beast' killed and feasted on sixty villagers and created

Figure 2.1 The 'monster' of Gévaudan.

widespread panic in Gévaudan and the surrounding districts.³ Jay Smith argues: 'The story of the beast of the Gévaudan is dramatic and absorbing, and its unfolding reveals human responses to crisis in all their many facets: fear, urgency, courage, humor [sic], compassion, cynicism, desperation, confusion.'⁴ The beast, according to legend, finally met its end when a local 'trickster', Jean Chastel, fatally shot the 'monster' with a bullet – a 'silver' bullet. Whether the bullet was silver and whether it was the actual monster or just a garden-variety wolf minding his or her own business is still debated.

The myth of the monster and the silver bullet

We have devoted the opening of this chapter to this legend because it introduces some ways that we often think about problems (monsters) and solutions (silver bullets) in education. The story also sheds some light on the reasons humankind creates monsters in the face of complex problems. In education and especially discussions around transformation, we often hear discussions about the monstrous enormity of transforming schools. Like that original monster, people confronted by transformation also respond with fear, urgency, courage, humour, compassion, cynicism, desperation and confusion.

We argue in this book that the challenges of transformation are complex. Transformation is, however, achievable if we recognize and build capabilities to respond to complex problems. Like the citizens of the Gévaudan, educators can fall into the trap of thinking problems in schools and other places of learning can be fixed with silver bullets.

The silver bullet that the trickster Jean Chastel used probably wasn't silver (most likely lead) and probably killed a wolf that may or may not have been part of the problem. In education too, we often reach for the silver bullet solution to complex problems that can often do more harm than good. Frequently we hear policy makers and educational leaders search for 'quick fix' solutions. Headlines such as *The Guardian*'s 'Top of the class: Labour seeks to emulate Finland's school system'⁵ and the seemingly endless attempt to find the right 'effect size'⁶ to solve a school's problems suggest we are hooked in education on the simple, quick and uncomplicated adoption of solutions. Educators Steve Lewis and Anna Hogan, commenting on the tendency to apply 'quick fix' solutions from one context to another, suggest: 'in spite of the seemingly obvious alignment between fast policies and a fast social world, [it seems likely] that good policy might come from slower and more complex processes, where education is not a problem to be fixed but a way to a better future for our particular children in our particular education systems'. While there is something to be learned from effect sizes and Finland, applying them acontextually reflects a misunderstanding of the complexity of the transformation challenge.

In terms of transformation, we can heed the mistakes of the legendary silver bullet. We can understand the nature and complexity of the challenge before developing actions that go beyond the simplistic to make transformation possible. Let's consider now why transformation of the complex systems in education is required.

Why transformation?

Transformation can break the recurring patterns of metaphorical 'monsters' and 'silver bullets' in education policy and practice. As we argued in *Transforming Schools*, the world is changing rapidly and educators are frequently called on to respond to complex, chaotic and often contradictory challenges. These challenges generate persistent mismatches between policy and practice that we identified as the pedagogy/policy gap.[7] These policies push transformation (e.g. more twenty-first-century skills) while not providing sufficient guidance (the how) to make sustainable change possible. Understanding the 'how' of transformation closes that gap. Meanwhile our education system continues with the status quo including often pointless testing regimes, siloed curriculum and frequently outmoded and ineffective approaches to learning, pedagogy, curriculum and leadership.

More hopefully, we are seeing in our work a widespread and growing realization suggesting educational transformation is not an option – it is crucial to make schools relevant for our young people. In our own work partnering with schools, we see transformation in action through our 4C network in dramatically different contexts. We see it in diverse and varied contexts including: schools in remote areas, schools in hospitals, large schools, small schools, primary schools, secondary schools, new schools, long-established schools, progressive schools, distance education schools, early childhood settings, traditional schools, private schools and public schools, universities and organizations beyond education. We are an emerging network but there are plenty more like us.[8]

All of these partnerships make the case for transformation. They understand transformation is a complex challenge. To meet that complex challenge, we work in partnership with schools to build transformative capabilities enabled by the 4Cs. For these educators transformation becomes more than an aspiration. Transformation becomes a reality through developing capabilities in reimagined values, learning, pedagogy, curriculum, teacher education and leadership that places deeper student learning first.

In this chapter, we discuss the complexity challenges inherent in transformation and how we can understand them. We then outline the challenges and opportunities of transformation as a 'complex' problem. The development of capabilities enabled by the 4Cs underpins effective responses to the unpredictability of complex challenges. The capabilities for transformation fit together like pieces of a jigsaw puzzle (see figure 2.2) to make transformation possible.

These capabilities are:

- values
- learning
- pedagogy
- curriculum
- teacher education
- leadership.

While these terms may seem familiar, we argue that they require reimagining and reframing to make them drive transformation. Rather than silver bullets, the capability approach to transformation enabled by the 4Cs has the potential to provide a map and a process to transform education at every level. Capabilities focus on building agency in school communities to enable educators to design and activate transformation in their own complex contexts. Complexity theory can help to frame the nature of our challenge in educational transformation.

Complexity theory

Complexity theory deals with complex problems that differ from other problems we see in the world. Let us consider how we might think about the kinds of problems we face through a process of *problem finding*. Often we rush to the solution without thinking carefully about the type, shape and dimensions of a problem. This may be why we sometimes seek silver bullets. As Einstein observed, 'the formulation of a problem is often more essential than its solution'.[9]

Complexity theory helps us to understand the different types of problems that occur as we look to engage with them. In essence, we can categorize problems into three types: simple, complicated and complex.[10] Table 2.1 summarizes the features of simple, complicated and complex problems based on Sean Snyder's work for the OECD.

A simple problem has a set of steps that when followed will lead to the same (or similar) outcomes every time. For instance, putting together a self-assembly book case is a simple problem that can be solved if the instructions are followed. A complicated problem is more difficult as it requires expertise and the ability to explore trial and error to solve that problem. For instance, building an electric car that can be mass-produced requires multiple areas of expertise such as physics, chemistry and design; however, when the problems are solved, the same approach can be used repeatedly for a similar outcome. Complex problems (which complexity theory addresses) feature many unknowns and there are very few simple cause and effect relationships. Climate change is a good example of a complex problem that features many unknowns, flux and unpredictability.

The nature of problems matters because when considering transformation in education, we begin by understanding the type of problem we are facing before we

Table 2.1 Differences between simple, complicated and complex problems[11]

Simple problem e.g. building a book case	Complicated problem e.g. building an electric vehicle	Complex problem e.g. managing climate change
Instructions required	A set of principles can be applied.	Application of principles may assist but do not assure success.
Process can be repeated	Building a prototype that works will ensure with a high degree of certainty that it will work next time.	Solving one issue does not predict that a similar problem can be solved the same way.
No or little expertise needed	Expertise is needed across a range of fields (chemistry, maths, design, etc.).	Expertise is useful but does not assure success.
Produces the same outcome every time	High levels of similarity between different vehicles (i.e. principles can be applied across models).	Each issue is approached understanding the factors that relate specifically to that issue.
Following the instructions and following a process leads to the best outcome	Once the problems are solved and a prototype created, it is likely that the process can be replicated.	Even when problems are addressed, uncertainty remains.

attempt a solution. As researcher Sean Snyder argues in an Organisation for Economic Co-operation and Development (OECD) report:

> What works for one child, teacher, district or system is not guaranteed to work for another. Indeed, what works for one element of one system may not work for other elements even within the same system. This makes the problem of educational governance complex rather than complicated since solutions are not necessarily replicable and transferable. . . Flexibility and feedback are necessary to manage successfully in a complex system. . . Policies must move from one-size fits all solutions to iterative processes derived from constant feedback between all stakeholders.[12]

On one level this is well understood by many educational leaders that we talk to, but 'one size fits all' policy approaches are pervasive in education. Perhaps this response reflects the somewhat naïve hope that solutions will be simple. Transformation relies on educators in their school's context, understanding and responding to complexity rather than expecting 'quick fixes' to bring sustainable change.

Each school has unique contextual factors such as demography, socio-economic status, expectations and attitudes of the community that shape the complexity of each school. What works in one place will not work in another. The schools we see that are transforming take account of their contextual factors and employ reimagined capabilities (such as, pedagogy, curriculum and leadership) to shape transformational action that responds to, rather than ignores complexity. These local school solutions (called 'emergence' in complexity theory) are working because they understand contextual factors and apply transformative capabilities. So how do we understand and respond to the nature of the problems we are facing in education, and how might complexity theory help us to frame the problem effectively?

How does complexity theory frame educational transformation?

To understand complexity theory,[13] we can break it down to its features.

- Complex problems involve large numbers of *interacting elements*. There are many moving parts or variables in a complex system (e.g. a school) such as students, teachers, leaders, systems, etc. All of these interacting elements are in relationship with each other.
- *Interactions are nonlinear* and changes can produce disproportionately major consequences. Small decisions can have unexpected effects. For instance, a change to school start and finish times might have implications for everything from travel logistics to student engagement.
- The system has a *history, and the past is integrated with the present*; the elements evolve with one another and with the environment; and evolution is irreversible. In complex systems, history cannot be ignored as it influences culture. For schools, if teachers and schools have historically not had any agency in decision-making, that will influence their attitudes to leadership proposing change. The past, present and future should be considered as interacting in a complex system.
- Though a complex system may, in retrospect, appear to be ordered and predictable, *hindsight does not lead to foresight* because the external conditions and systems constantly change. What may have worked in the past may not work in the future as the conditions shift. For schools, a pedagogical approach that worked a decade ago may not suit the current context.
- *Nodes are persistent features of complex systems* that connect with each other. The behaviour of one node influences others depending on the strength of their connections. Finding and developing key nodes of influence (such as the 4Cs and the capabilities we describe in this book) create rich feedback

loops in complex systems. Targetted attention to the right nodes can cause a 'ripple effect' and impact a school's complex system.[14]

- *Emergence* occurs because 'solutions' cannot be imposed. Responses to complexity arise from differing circumstances. Each school could consider its context and develop local transformative solutions to their local challenges.

Complexity theory helps educators to understand that transformation can never be 'one size fits all'. If we understand schools as complex places with many parts that interact and influence each other in sometimes unpredictable ways, we have begun to understand the shape and dynamics of the challenge. Emergent responses enable dynamic, unique responses in each context. In our work with schools we build capabilities enabled by the 4Cs to help each school respond dynamically to their own complexities. If we accept transformation in education is a complex challenge, problem or set of problems, how might we respond to the challenge?

A capabilities response to complexity

If we reject the myth of 'silver bullet' solutions, we need a theory of change that helps educators deal with the complexity of transformation. Figure 2.2 summarizes our approach to building capabilities in complex education contexts through the

Figure 2.2 Pieces of the capability jigsaw describe the capabilities of transformation enabled by the 4Cs.

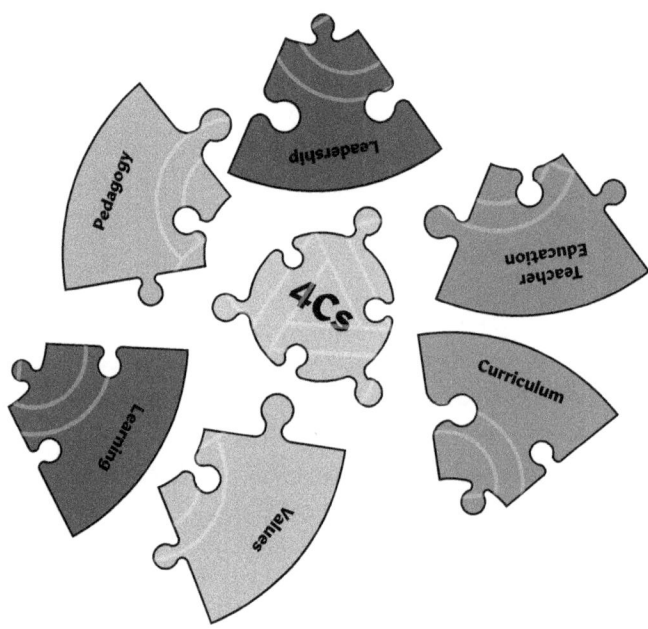

metaphor of jigsaw pieces. Capabilities enable what people are able to do and to be, and the kind of life they are effectively able to lead. Capabilities allow people to achieve a sense of being and functioning in the world.

The first thing to notice in the jigsaw (figure 2.2) is that the 4Cs are the centre piece enabling and connecting the capabilities of values, learning (student and teachers), pedagogy, curriculum, teacher education and leadership. Without the 4Cs the transformative capabilities cannot be understood or effectively implemented. The 4Cs in this model are enabling capabilities, as they provide core understandings and skills that make transformative capabilities possible. For instance, in transformative leadership (see chapter 10), educators require creativity to imagine new ways of operating when schools are transforming, and collaboration to ensure that students, teachers and the community all have agency in the transformation process. Transformative leaders also require effective communication capabilities to convey the meaning of the innovations inherent in transformation and critical reflection to understand the most effective way to influence the implementation of those innovations. A capabilities approach allows educators to respond to complex challenges by providing them with the skills, tools, approaches and frameworks to respond flexibly.

Capabilities to respond to complexity

The capability approach pioneered by philosopher Martha Nussbaum[15] argues that we should understand each person's agency in their context to achieve freedom and dignity. Freedom and dignity are made possible when people have control over their own decision-making (agency) and the capabilities to navigate their lives unhindered. To achieve this, people require opportunities to access and build capabilities individually and in groups.[16] In schools, this means supporting teachers to lead lifelong teacher education (professional development) to develop and grow capabilities in values, learning, pedagogy, curriculum and leadership. Education in all its forms when focused and effective is a place where capabilities can be developed. Nussbaum argues that education is critical in helping people reach their potential through the development of capabilities:

> At the heart of the capabilities approach since its inception has been the importance of education. Education. . . forms people's existing capabilities into developed internal capabilities of many kinds. This formation is valuable in itself and a source of lifelong satisfaction. It is also pivotal to the development and exercise of many other human capabilities: a 'fertile functioning' of the highest importance in addressing disadvantage and inequality.[17]

Nussbaum is arguing that the development of capabilities in individuals and groups enables ongoing and sustainable change. Capabilities in this sense contribute to professional, personal and collective growth over time.

Educators Emilia Szekely and Mark Mason contend that the capability approach creates action in the face of complexity for schools. Szekely and Mason argue that an understanding of agency and then a capability response is a right for our whole community including our teachers and students. They claim:

> The capability approach asks about the real opportunities with which society has provided individuals to choose and lead the lives they have reason to value: their capabilities. These real opportunities provided by society mean much more than just the right to education, for example. They entail the physical and meaningful provision of the wherewithal through which people might realize their right to education.[18]

In this book, we argue that the 4Cs are the enabling processes that drive change and develop transformative capabilities.

How do capabilities enable transformation?

Transformation is not made possible through silver bullets. It requires the slow and sustained development of capabilities in individuals and teams to meet complex challenges. An approach to transformation that recognizes schools as complex builds local capabilities to respond to contextual factors. Rather than a 'top-down' set of strategies mandated from a system, this approach recognizes and values the agency of individual students, teachers and schools (individually and in networks) to build capability to drive collaborative action. In other words, those who know their context best should have the agency to co-create education in their context. This does not mean the system has no role, rather that schools should have the agency to collaborate with their school community to design learning that emerges from their students' needs.

The 4Cs enable transformative capabilities

In the capability jigsaw (figure 2.2), the 4Cs have the potential to connect and enable the transformative capabilities in each school's context. Creativity, critical reflection, communication and collaboration enable transformation as they provide the core skills and knowledge to do the 'heavy lifting' of transformation. As we discussed in *Transforming Schools*, the 4Cs are necessary to:

- connect,
- extend, and
- mobilize understanding and drive learning.

The same is true of the transformation process. The 4Cs connect, extend and mobilize transformation. We require these capabilities to enable transformation as an active, agentic emergence that connects and engages educators with diverse and sometimes conflicting views. For instance, the process of developing transformational values requires everyone to have agency in their formulation. To illustrate, we have explained how one of the 4Cs enables a transformative capability.

Creativity enables transformative values

In chapter 3 we discuss the values of transformation that are critical to frame and anchor transformation. Values are an expression of individual and/or group preferences for action that directly considers the aspirations, purpose and mission of organizations. For schools, transformation often requires a creative framing of their aspirations, purpose and mission to establish and propel transformative agendas and actions. When schools collaborate to develop transformative values, we sometimes ask the following questions based on the Creativity Cascade (figure 2.3):

- What do you notice as distinctive about your context (school, university, etc.)?
- Why? Really why? Is that distinctive?
- What possibilities could we play with to make that distinctive feature integrate with transformative values?
- From those possibilities, which values can we generate that are consistent with transformative values?

If this process were undertaken without creativity, it is likely that values would not rise beyond a set of platitudes. In this case we need everyone to imagine how the

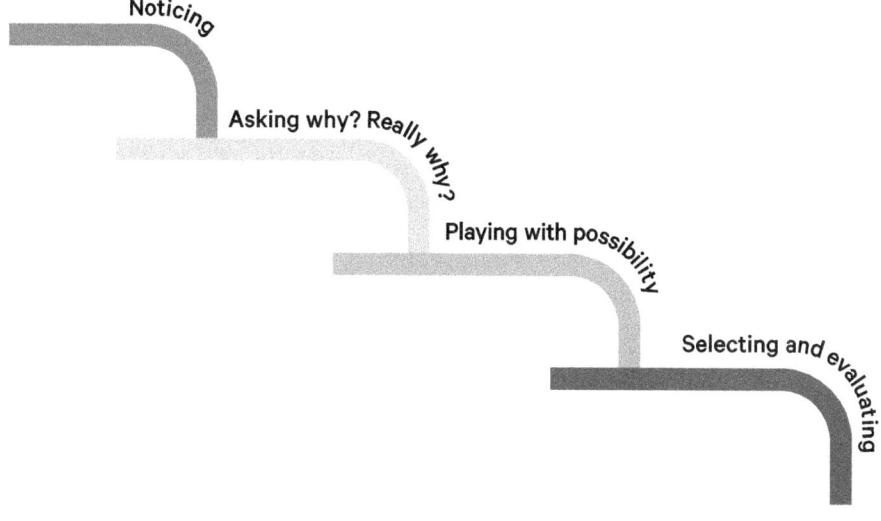

Figure 2.3 The Creativity Cascade coherence maker.

distinctiveness of the context and the values of transformation can be integrated to imagine a different way of 'being' as a place of learning. In this way, the 4Cs (in this case creativity):

- connect local values to transformative values,
- extend the concept of values from a set of potentially meaningless platitudes to guiding principles, and
- activate by allowing everyone ownership over the values and offers a series of critical principles to guide, measure and understand the process of transformation.

Collaboration enables transformative pedagogy

We recently visited a school that has championed the use of co-teaching in their programmes for more than a decade. Co-teaching (also known as team teaching) is not particularly common, but this school has a deep commitment to co-teaching. Their teachers were resistant at first, but now report their passion and commitment to this approach. For this school, co-teaching makes possible collaborative planning that engages several perspectives on the design and curation of the learning. Co-teaching allows teachers to structure learning experiences flexibly, allowing for greater differentiation for students. It also allows teachers to rethink pedagogy as a collaborative endeavour opening up space for pedagogical creativity and a reimagining of classroom learning.

In our view this approach has substantial untapped potential to support transformation by fully realizing the opportunities collaboration provides to reimagine pedagogy as a 'team sport' rather than an individual pursuit. The Collaboration Circles coherence maker provides a structure for understanding collaboration as an enabling capability for pedagogical transformation. Here are some key framing questions based on the Collaboration Circles coherence maker (see figure 2.4):

- What can each teacher *offer* to the design of collaborative teaching? (Approaches to pedagogy, experiences, resources, etc.)
- How are teachers *yielding* (giving and taking) to other ideas and approaches to create authentically collaborative learning?
- How is the pedagogical design process *challenging* our existing approaches, evaluating alternative models and extending all of these beyond what might be possible if teachers worked individually?
- How are teachers advancing *co-construction and connections* with other educators to ensure a pedagogically rich, diverse and effective approach?

Figure 2.4 Collaboration Circles coherence maker.

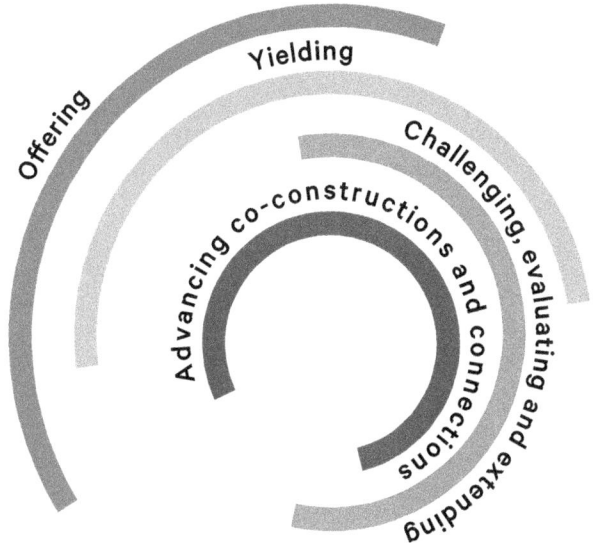

Collaboration enables transformative pedagogy by changing the default from the individual teacher to a group developing a shared practice through a shared 'affair of the mind'.[19] Collaboration enables transformative pedagogy as it:

- *connects* different perspectives and expertise to generate learning that moves beyond silos (e.g. faculties, stage teams, primary educators, secondary educators),
- *extends* beyond an individual perspective to generate communities of pedagogical practice, and
- *activates* teams to engage collaboratively and work constructively.

Critical reflection enables transformative teacher education

Teacher education that is grounded in critical reflection can support professional growth over the career, as we argue in chapter 9. Ironically lifelong teacher education (also known as professional development or professional learning) has often been delivered in ways that do not respect the agency and professionalism of educators as leaders of learning. Typically this approach sees experts provide a seminar to large groups that rarely takes account of the contextual factors that are critical in complex systems like schools and universities. Critical reflection enables a space for considering the contextual factors such as the social, political and other dimensions of the context. By using that reflective process, schools can formulate wise collaborative action that takes account of those factors to design and enact context driven learning.

Critical reflection enables educators to analyse their context. It enables collaborative approaches to transformation that create emergent transformation (focused on each school's context) rather than 'bolt on' or silver bullet responses. We have developed lifelong (ongoing) teacher education programmes with our education partners using guiding questions framed by the Critical Reflection Crucible (figure 2.5), including:

- What assumptions can we identify about the way we currently do teacher education? Why do we do it this way? Why do we use the same methods we've always used if nothing is changing in our practice?
- Can we do things differently and if we did what would they look like?
- What are some approaches that might work in our context?
- What options? How can we reimagine and re-solve to make lifelong teacher education drive transformation?

If critical reflection and the other Cs are present, high-quality teacher education can be achieved. In this context, critical reflection:

- *connects* teacher education to the dynamics and characteristics of each individual context,
- *extends* practice by encouraging educators to deeply interrogate taken for granted assumptions and creates new more contextually aware responses to teacher education, and

Figure 2.5 Critical Reflection Crucible coherence maker.

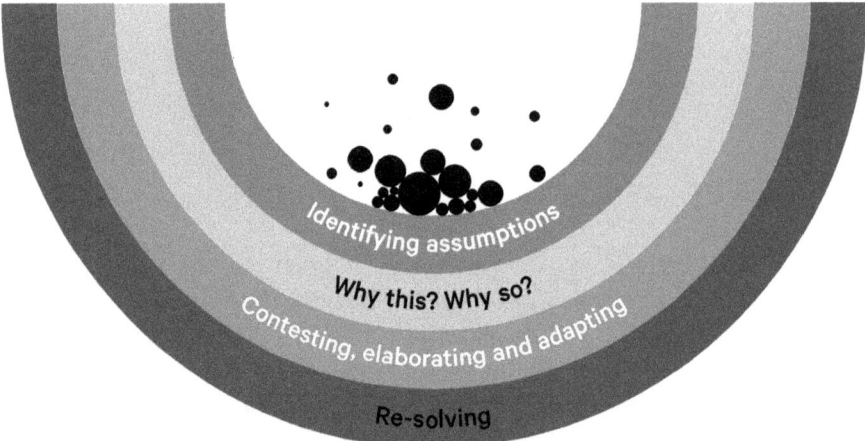

- *activates* educators to consider the effectiveness and relevance of their own learning and then reshapes it based on the needs of their students.

Communication enables transformative leadership

As we discuss in chapter 10, leadership is a capability that every educator needs to develop. Communication enables transformative leadership by creating clear messages that support beneficial and agentic change and reduces anxiety and misinformation. As the story of the 'monster' that opened this chapter illustrates, anxiety in the absence of effective communication becomes hysteria. Clear communication builds leadership that is alert to the messages and narratives that are circulating about transformation. We frequently hear that transformation is 'too hard' or 'another fad', etc. Leaders need to communicate clearly the rationale and evidence for transformation. They then need to listen to ensure the messages they receive back are understood. Collaborative leaders enable voices throughout their organization so all views are heard and considered. Collaborative leaders do not discourage dissonant voices, but rather listen to divergent views and encourage a diverse conversation. 'Robust conversations' are encouraged to ensure everyone has agency to contribute. The Communication Crystal coherence maker (figure 2.6) can provide a framework for this process.

We can use the Communication Crystal to interrogate this process:

- How can leaders be alert to the sometimes conflicting messaging occurring in their school, and how can their messaging respond constructively to a diversity of voices?
- How can we convey meaning and purpose to articulate the values and rationale for transformation?
- How can we provide a clear rationale to motivate engagement with transformation at every level of the organization?
- How can those leading transformation generate action and agency in others to begin and sustain the transformation journey?

Communication enables leaders to build agency and clarity as they develop the case for transformation. As the process generates momentum, communication:

- *connects* ideas and diverse voices in an agentic conversation that helps inform and build capability for transformation,
- *extends* ideas and approaches to transformation by generating discussion across the organization leading to a broader consensus for transformation, and
- *activates* strategies through clear and coherent messaging to all in the organization.

Let's now consider how these capabilities can grow transformation.

Figure 2.6 The Communication Crystal coherence maker.

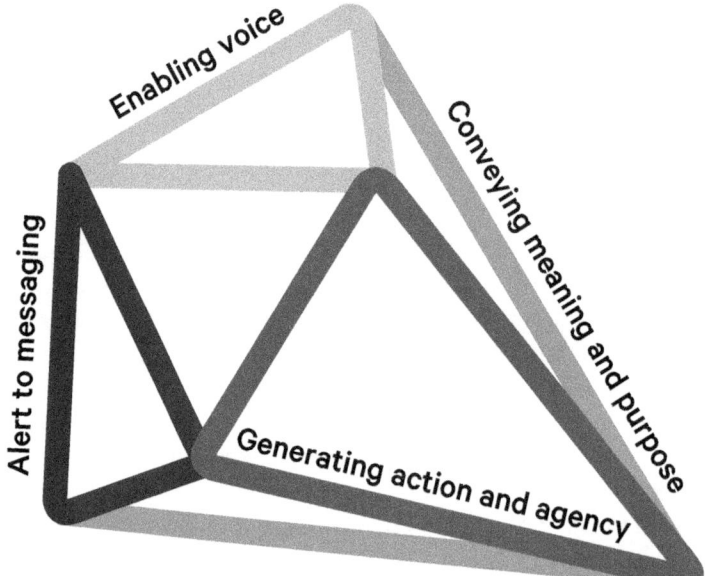

Capabilities for transforming education

As we mentioned at the opening of this chapter, our best response to complexity is not to wish it away or simplistically respond with 'silver bullet' solutions. A more generative approach is to understand the nature, shape and context of the complex problem. Rather than imposing a 'solution', a capability approach builds capacity in students, teachers and schools to design and generate transformative action. In the next part of this chapter and throughout the book, we will discuss and analyse each of these capabilities for transformation and how the 4Cs are critical for their successful development. The first capability for transformation is values.

1 *Transformative values*

   Values are essential to anchor transformation. In chapter 3 we discuss a set of values that have been effective in the schools with which we have worked. The values we have identified include:

   - critical hope,
   - wisdom,
   - unlearning,
   - imagination,
   - explicit learning,
   - deep learning,

- agency,
- reimagined pedagogy,
- connected and coherent learning,
- collaborative partnerships, and
- praxis.

These values frame and drive transformation by providing a set of governing principles. In complex systems it is difficult to predict what will come next; however, values provide a framework to set expectations and then develop and guide decision-making and transformative action.

2 *Transformative learning*

The first step in developing transformative learning is developing agency, which is the ability and will to influence positively your life and the lives of others. A key process in building agency is developing the dispositions to learn so our students can exercise agency in their learning and their lives (discussed in chapter 4).

Understanding the core dispositions necessary for learning is a critical component of the transformation journey in our partnership schools. The nine dispositions identified through international research[20] form the basis for learning how to learn. Mapping, unpacking and applying these dispositions is a deep and sustained learning process for schools that can take years. In *Transforming Schools*, we introduced the Learning Disposition Wheel[21] (discussed in chapter 5). The Wheel divides learning into interpersonal, intrapersonal and cognitive domains, although in practice these domains are interdependent and overlap. The Learning Disposition Wheel has been used by educators to organize learning by providing a common metalanguage.

3 *Transformative pedagogy*

There has rightly been a renewed focus on the learner over the last few decades. The learning relationship between students and teachers in transformation is critical to the success of any transformation process. Yet in our experience deep knowledge about pedagogy and the elements of pedagogy, its theoretical origins and applications are lacking in many places. Pedagogy is critical to effective learning. Teachers in all parts of education require a deep understanding of the origins, elements and impact of elements of pedagogy to curate and facilitate deep learning in their students. We have devoted two chapters (6 and 7) to discuss pedagogy and developed a coherence maker (the Pedagogy Parachute, chapter 7) that identifies and defines the theoretical perspectives, elements and applications of pedagogy. Like any effective coherence maker, the parachute can lead to discussions across ages, stages, systems and subjects about the elements of the art and science of teaching, allowing for a common language. This coherence maker also provides the opportunity for school communities to map their pedagogical approaches to understand what elements of pedagogy they emphasize and where the opportunities lie to engage with underutilized elements of pedagogy.

4 *Transformative curriculum*

Curriculum constitutes everything that is learnt at school, whether that is intentional or not. A reimagining of the possibilities of curriculum can contextualize learning for the needs of students in each school's context. Rather than thinking of curriculum as being equivalent to syllabus, we argue in chapter 8 that transforming schools can reimagine all of their activities as learning. This includes the way schools arrange timetables, the way students are spoken to by teachers or the subjects they are offered. Curriculum can create powerful learning for the benefit or sometimes detriment of students and as such requires renewed attention to achieve transformation.

Status quo curriculum reinforces outmoded and irrelevant practices and has the tendency to entrench disadvantage and irrelevance.[22] In chapter 8 we argue for transformative curriculum that puts the student and their context at the centre of the learning. This approach considers how knowledge, skills and understandings can be curated most effectively to suit the current and future needs of learners, teachers and the whole learning community.

5 *Transformative teacher education*

Teacher education has two main components: foundational teacher education (also known as preservice) and lifelong teacher education (also known as in-service). In chapter 9 we argue to achieve transformation in schools, we urgently need to reform teacher education. A transformative approach to teacher education founded on John Dewey's concepts of inquiry, reflection and experience, enabled by the 4Cs, has the potential to provide agency for teachers to transform their classrooms and their schools collaboratively. In chapter 9 we propose a coherent continuum of teacher learning that begins the first moment educators enter foundational teacher education and continues throughout their career.

In chapter 9 we also discuss the need for lifelong teacher education to change from an 'injection model' – a one-day jab of training to a sustained, contextualized and coherent set of strategies driven by inquiry and reflection on experience.

6 *Leadership*

Leadership is a frequently misunderstood capability. Our conceptualization of leadership[23] is diametrically opposed to 'hero leadership' narratives we see constantly. In chapter 10 we conceive leadership as a capability required for everyone transforming education. In our experience, transformation cannot be established successfully unless and until leadership with transformational values and agency emerge in each setting.

Concluding reflections

The twenty-first century challenges faced by our education system and our society aren't uncomplicated or insignificant; they are complex. To respond to these challenges, the first step is to understand how to respond to complexity. Education, historically, has been beset by 'silver bullet' solutions that routinely fail. As we know from the stories from eighteenth-century France, people often replace deep analysis and effective responses with reductive hysteria. When we consider the problems of educational transformation, we would do well not to let our pessimistic imagination override experience and evidence. Building capabilities recognizes that schools have within them the experience, skills and dispositions to respond to a shifting world. When we trust schools to reimagine values, learning, pedagogy, curriculum, teacher education and leadership in their own context, transformation is not only possible, it is likely.

We need to act swiftly to transform our complex and sometimes outmoded education system to meet the needs of our students in a complex, contradictory and sometimes chaotic world. When we resort to silver bullets to slay (often) mythical monsters, as our education system so often does, we frequently miss the target and can do more harm than good. Education is complex. But we have a choice. Our communities and societies can continue firing silver bullets into elusive or mythical monsters and watch our schools drift into irrelevance. Or we can place faith in school communities (including teachers and students) by building their capabilities to transform education by reimagining schools as places of imagination, agency, relevance and deep learning.

In the next chapter, we will discuss how we begin transformation by generating values to anchor and guide transformation.

Transforming values

Guides for transformative action

3

Values that create transformation 34

Values that drive action 34

What are values? 36

Why values matter 36

Values in education 37

Transformative values in education 38

Example of practice: 4C Transformative Learning 39

Transforming schools 39
The 4C Network 42

What are the values of transformation? 43

Critical hope 43
Unlearning 44
Wisdom 44
Imagination 45
Explicit learning 45
Deep learning 46
Agency 46
Reimagined pedagogy 47
Connected and coherent learning 48
Collaborative partnerships 48
Praxis 49

Concluding reflections 49

Values that create transformation

Atlassian is an international software company founded in 2002 by Mike Cannon-Brookes and Scott Farquhar. The company has more than 3,500 employees internationally and has a market value of more than US$30.66 billion dollars.[2] It makes software that helps teams to collaborate. We would like to focus here on how Atlassian as an organization live their values, and how that leads to transformative action that forms culture. Atlassian founder Mike Cannon-Brookes explains his rationale for values:[3]

> Culture is the thing that can't be manufactured so much as it's a combination of characters of all the people that live in the building. Our values are an attempt at making sure that we're hiring the types of people with the right attributes we want, whilst at the same time understanding their skills will change, their job roles will change but fundamental base attributes of how those people treat the world, treat other people and treat their customers won't change over the lifetime of the company.

Critically, Cannon-Brookes connects values to an organizational culture in a constant state of transformation. At Atlassian, transformation is baked into the values that drive their culture. In other words, they are building a transformative culture. Their values include:[4]

Open company, no bullshit
Build with heart and balance
Don't #@!% the customer
Play, as a team
Be the change you seek

These values reflect fine sentiments and yet without action they are just more 'white noise'. The action of this company is the test of whether values actually have any meaning. What actions are driven by values at Atlassian?

Values that drive action

In 2019 a series of global climate strikes brought to heightened public attention the climate emergency (also known as climate change). These series of 'strikes' were aimed at provoking change in government policy. Figure 3.1 is an image from one of these strikes in the United Kingdom. On 20 September 2019, Cannon-Brookes joined the protest and encouraged everyone employed at Atlassian and across the community to do the same.[5] A few weeks later he flew to New York to commit his company to net zero emissions by no later than 2050.[6] This action is entirely consistent with Atlassian's values and in particular 'Be the change you seek' which the company explains as follows: 'All Atlassians should have the courage and resourcefulness to spark change – to make better our products, our people, our place. Continuous improvement is a shared responsibility. Action is an independent one.'[7]

Figure 3.1 Global climate protests in London, 20 April 2019.[1]

Their values and the actions they inspired made Atlassian a prominent voice for change in the corporate sector, generating influence in national and international political spheres. There are key differences between the technology industry and education. Atlassian can recruit whoever it likes and partially build culture through that process, whereas in education, we often need to work with old paradigms and legacy practices. However, in schools we can build values through leadership that changes mindsets and culture over time. Transformation does not happen through values alone; however, a foundation of authentic values and wise, strategic leadership can create starting points to enable action and culture change.

In this chapter, we argue values are capabilities that frame and drive schools to achieve and sustain transformation. Philosopher Amartya Sen argues that capabilities are social arrangements that promote freedom through each individual's agency to achieve functionings they value.[8] Extended to schools, values are devised and driven by collaboration to create a robust set of transformational values. These values influence, inspire and guide beneficial action. We argue that values are an expression of individual and then group preferences for action. They are usually based on critical reflection, that directly considers the purpose and mission of organizations.

The transformation of values provides clear directions to drive decisions and action. In this chapter we explore the values of transformation and how they can make action possible in education. We discuss how values can be more than just a series of pointless platitudes. Values can set up the attitudinal conditions across educational settings to shift culture and make transformation possible. We then discuss an example of practice from our organization, 4C Transformative Learning, to explain how values can inspire and sustain transformation.

What are values?

Values are the qualities that we (as an individual or group) use to anchor and guide an organization. Values can be defined as 'a set of acceptable and expected norms for the individual members of an organization'.[9] Values are a set of attitudes which help to provide guidance for leadership, strategy and decision-making as we saw in Atlassian's case at the opening of the chapter. Dispositions (see chapters 4 and 5) are the inherent qualities that under the right conditions all humans possess to be able to learn. They are interdependent with values as we need dispositions to ensure our values become action. Grit, for instance, helps us implement and sustain our values. When we consider educational transformation, a focused set of values can support action by providing a common understanding of the expectations of everyone in the organization. This chapter explores and considers why values matter in the process of transformation.

Why values matter

The concept of values has been significantly devalued in recent times. We have seen over and over again where an organization's stated values are irrelevant or inconsistent with their actual behaviour. For instance, consider the following values:[10]

- Enterprising spirit – We pursue growth passionately, all the while accepting the entrepreneurial risk that comes with it. We're bold and strive to overcome challenges.
- Freedom through responsibility – We always strive to do the right thing for society. And we use our freedom to act in the best interest of consumers.
- Open minded – We're a forward-looking company. One that takes on board social changes and different perspectives. So we're always open to new ways of doing things.
- Strength from diversity – We respect and celebrate each other's differences. We enjoy working together. And we value what makes each of us unique.

Can you imagine what kind of company might hold these kinds of values? You might opt for a modern, responsible organization that works to incorporate social change as they strive to build a diverse community and society. Think again. These are the stated values of British American Tobacco (BAT), which makes some of the most toxic and destructive products on the planet – cigarettes. The World Health Organization reports that tobacco-related disease is the leading worldwide cause of preventable death. Seven million people die annually due to cigarette smoking. Smoking-related health problems cost US$300 billion in the US alone.[11] Values becoming inconsistent with actions give rise to widespread cynicism about their usefulness. While many organizations such as BAT erode the credibility of values, they can be critical in clarifying organizational goals and framing transformative action. They can be a useful way to establish and sustain educational transformation when implemented with integrity.

Values in education

Research into the values evident in schools reveals some predictable albeit worthy themes. An Australian study[12] found there were similarities in the themes schools reported. The themes that most frequently appeared were 'academic achievement, mental health promotion, school belonging, personal characteristics, teacher support, other support, environment, Christianity, future, and individual needs'. While these are all worthy aspirations and in many cases complementary to transformation, many of them do not aspire to anything more than maintaining the status quo.

Educational leadership researchers Keith Gurley and colleagues investigated the impact of values in schools with educational leadership students. They claim: 'Organizational and educational experts agree that articulated values, or shared commitments, are fundamental to the process of organizational improvement. These statements are not merely a set of words or platitudes. When commonly developed, adopted, and lived, organizational values actually drive the daily practice of individuals within the organization'.[13]

In our view, values can create a set of shared understandings beyond mere moral expectations or codes of conduct such as 'we act with integrity'. Values, and especially those focused on transformation can define and frame a process of how education is done. These values can then lead to a shared set of actions. Gurley and colleagues' research reflects a poor understanding and application of values by educators. They report:

> . . . among school leaders, there exists a lack of understanding of exactly what mission, vision, values, and goals statements are and the value such foundational statements offer to the development of shared commitment among stakeholders to the process of school improvement. . . The results from the current study confirm these findings and combine to suggest a disturbing lack of understanding of the purpose and value of developing and stewarding mission, vision, values, and goals statements among graduate-level, educational leadership students.

There are some caveats here. This is a North American study and the authors are not addressing transformation. They are considering 'school improvement', which we argue is a limiting approach to school change. In our work with educators, we notice similar patterns of values being ignored, irrelevant or ineffective. This research and our experience points to a disconnect between values and their application. As Gurley and colleagues report, 'Data from this study indicated a nearly universal absence of articulated values or organizational commitments in schools represented by study participants.'[14] Given this disconnect, how might we employ values to galvanize transformation?

We will consider how transformative values can connect the process of change with values to create unified and engaged action. We have looked at our own work with schools and derived some critical values for transformation. Again, the values themselves do not cause transformative action but they do make the aspiration and qualities of the process clear. In Atlassian's case, just identifying the value 'be the change you seek' on their website could be as hollow as British American Tobacco's value 'We always strive to do the right thing for society'. It's not the statement that matters, it's the action that the statement enables that counts. In Atlassian's case, the actions of influencing the political process and reducing their own emissions have the potential to make actual change and could lead to less scepticism around the usefulness of values.

Transformative values in education

As we mentioned earlier, educational institutions (such as schools or universities) often have very worthy 'business as usual' values. Transformation, however, requires different mindsets, behaviours and ultimately a renewed culture and therefore a different set of values. In other words, if educators wish to generate and inspire transformation, values will reflect and drive transformation. These values are in no particular order and as with most transformative processes, these values are interdependent. They are:

- critical hope,
- wisdom,
- imagination,
- unlearning,
- deep and explicit learning,
- agency,
- reimagined pedagogy,
- connected and coherent learning,
- collaborative partnerships, and
- praxis.

Before we explain these in depth, we thought we would use an example of practice of our own work to exemplify how these values enable transformative action. This example of practice tells the story of 4C Transformative Learning (4CTL). We will italicize each of the values (for instance, *agency*) as we move through the example of practice.

Example of practice: 4C Transformative Learning

Transforming schools

In early 2017, after *Transforming Schools: Creativity, Critical Reflection, Communication, Collaboration* was published, we were contacted by several schools in Sydney, Australia asking about the *how* of transformation. For many schools, the arguments for urgent change in *Transforming Schools* resonated. These requests from schools made us wonder what might be possible if we started our own organization that was not driven by the impulses of a system or a government's political preoccupations. An organization that viewed transformation as a series of beneficial changes to generate deep, connected and coherent learning. An organization where *deep learning* permeated everything educators do, from teaching to student well-being to leadership and administration. What we knew from our work in schools over several decades was that individual schools were the starting point for this kind of transformation. Sometimes individual teachers want transformation in their schools but in our experience, unless the whole school ultimately engages, through leadership first, then through a (usually) small group of early adopters engaging in *collaborative partnerships*, transformation rarely gets out of the starting blocks.

Another problem that obstructs transformation is the interference of systems. Large educational bureaucracies can easily become hostage to short-term political agendas. Systems have a critical enabling role to support innovation and transformation in schools rather than obstruct beneficial change. In other words,

Figure 3.2 4C Transformative Learning in action.

systems that provide agency for schools to make their own decisions based in their own contexts are more likely to see transformation occur. Schools that are allowed sufficient *agency* can work with their community to transform their schools. They achieve this by developing and enacting pedagogy and curriculum that directly meets the needs of their students and builds a consensus for transformation.

One of the first schools we worked with was Casula Public School. All of our 'early adopter' schools exercised *critical hope*, whether they knew it or not. *Critical hope* for Casula was demonstrated through their attitude to transformation. They knew that transformation was possible and achievable when the process was enabled by patience, *wisdom* and strategic *collaborative partnerships*. Casula Public School gave us the space to begin imagining what might be possible in *collaborative partnerships.* We partnered with the staff at Casula to *reimagine pedagogy* and then allow that capacity for *imagination* to permeate everything the school did. This co-constructed partnership sat in contrast to other relationships we formed in the early days.

In the first few years, we sometimes accepted partnerships and work that was not founded on true and authentic collaboration. We learnt several lessons from those early experiences. Firstly, authentic *collaborative partnerships* are only possible when the partners both contribute to the process of transformation. When we allowed the partner to dictate the terms of 'partnership', we found that transformation slowed or stopped and we became less useful.

This is part of the growing *wisdom* that we gained through our successful and unsuccessful relationships. We grow wise in the transformation process by learning in response to our experiences and applying *deep learning* and *imagination* to the ongoing *praxis* of our work. In many senses, the *wisdom* gained from unsuccessful experiences helps us to learn as much as our successes. From our successes and our less successful experiences, we developed an approach that generates authentic *collaborative partnerships* where we work with schools to *imagine*, design and develop transformative approaches that are suited to each context. We spend time understanding the school with the leadership, discussing the unique prevailing conditions in each educational context.

At Casula and with our other partner schools, we engage first with leadership (in a series of learning workshops) and work with a group we call the 'innovation' team. The 'innovation' team is formed from those who volunteer to engage with the learning. They are usually a mix of experienced and beginning staff from across the school with leaders also engaging with this willing and able group. One of the key principles when we begin this work is that no member of staff is forced to participate. If we value *agency*, it is critical that all staff have the opportunity to engage *imaginatively* and enthusiastically, and that rarely occurs when educators are compelled to participate.

The learning focuses on the capabilities and processes of transformation and developing a whole school language for transformation. Our approach begins with the Learning Disposition Wheel[15] (see chapter 4, figure 4.4) that we introduced in *Transforming Schools*[16] and we discuss in chapter 5 of this book. In our experience, many partners take twelve to twenty-four months to understand the implications of the wheel for transforming pedagogy, curriculum and school organization. The

Learning Disposition Wheel challenges many of the assumptions we have in schools and requires substantial *unlearning* and reflection. A deep dive into the Learning Disposition Wheel often prompts partners to re-engage with all aspects of their organization to focus on student-centred *deep learning*.

We often begin our discussion with leadership by using the Learning Disposition Wheel as a diagnostic tool. We encourage our partner schools to identify their strengths and areas for development on the wheel individually, in teaching teams and across the whole organization. This is a *wisdom* building process that asks teams to notice deeply what is happening and not happening in their context. This process is also designed to de-silo educational organizations by providing a common language focusing on the kinds of capacities required to be a successful learner (or teacher, or leader).

The professional learning also focuses on the coherence makers for the 4Cs including; the Creativity Cascade, Communication Crystal, Critical Reflection Crucible and Communication Circles that we discuss in detail in *Transforming Schools*. After we understand the basic needs of each context, we use this sequence to begin the transformation design in each setting. To understand each context, we initiate critically reflective discussions to engage with the joys, opportunities, anxieties and challenges related to transformation. Our initial discussions with schools often engage with their anxieties such as:

- 'What will happen to our standardized test scores?'
- 'What if parents complain?'
- 'What will my director/supervisor think?'
- 'What happens if staff don't want to engage?'
- 'How can I work on this alone?'
- 'We are already doing (e.g. Curious Schools/Growth Mindsets). Won't this work conflict with what we are already doing?'
- 'How can I start this work if I can't understand the 4Cs approach completely?'
- 'How can I commit to something that will take so long?'
- 'What is the evidence that this works?'

The work with our *collaborative partners* is an *imaginative* co-creation where problems and challenges arise and we work together to develop a response. Our approach is not to provide answers or even expert advice, but rather to support our partners as they consider how to transform their practices and approaches through the 4Cs. The approach drives *deep learning* by focusing on inquiry and reflection on experience to build understanding. This demands that educators focus on their context and reflect deeply on their practice and the culture of the school, and imagine how practices might change to enable transformation.

We now have more than fifty collaborative partnerships (at the end of 2020) with schools and other education settings across Australia. These schools meet regularly to share and support each other through 4C network events to drive learning through reflection on their experience of 4C transformation.

The 4C Network

In June 2019, about 190 teachers and leaders from primary and secondary schools met for a network professional learning day at a primary (elementary) school in Sydney, Australia. Nothing remarkable there, but as figure 3.3 shows, there were a few distinctive features of this day. You may notice in this picture two kindergarten students, a 6-year-old boy and a 5-year-old girl, speaking with the group of teachers. These students are collaborating with teachers to lead the professional learning session with their teachers on understanding and enacting influence. The value *agency* was facilitated in this process for teachers and students alike. This day could have been designed to use 'experts' providing lectures, but if we value agency, having students and teachers at the centre of the learning is critical.

This approach values *collaborative partnerships* to generate understanding. On that day, more than thirty sessions were led by students and teachers facilitating active and engaging workshops on transformation. This collaborative approach asks the educators to inquire and reflect on their own experience. This process values each participant's *pedagogical imagination* and allows multiple voices to contribute to the transformation discussion. Rather than relying on one or two experts, this work was designed to bring everyone's perspectives to the learning. These are not one-offs. These network days help our schools understand what *agency* can look like and how *collaborative partnerships* generate deep learning. This approach to growing and

Figure 3.3 Students co-lead a learning bazaar on a 4C network day.

supporting each other requires patience as we build and grow these generative collaborations. The 4C network reinforces and inspires our schools to learn more deeply from each other as they navigate their own transformation.

Transformation is a slow process and we are now in our third year of work seeing transformation occurring. Our approach is distinctive as it rejects the 'one shot' model of professional learning that fills you up like junk food but is rarely sustaining. Our *collaborative partnerships* are *praxis* based (the blending of research and practice). Philosopher Paulo Freire describes praxis as a reflection and action upon the world in order to transform it.[17] A *praxis* approach ensures school transformation has strong foundations (from theory and research) and is applied effectively to each school's context and practices.

We value deep and trusting relationships that respect the *agency* of the leaders, students and teachers to make transformation possible. Our team of nine will need to grow as the need for transformation nationally and internationally expands. There are many challenges ahead as we think strategically about how this work can be strengthened rather than diminished, as it scales to include more schools. What we know after three years of engaging with educational transformation is there is a passion in our schools for *pedagogical imagination* through *deep learning*. There are also many able leaders and teachers who are *critically hopeful* and ready to face the joys and the challenges of transformation.

These schools are not disengaging from their own systems; rather they are transforming their own practice and sharing their knowledge into their own systems and, by doing so, generating growth in an innovative network. The work is frequently challenging but growth and progress towards transformation is deeply rewarding for all involved in our organization.

Critically these schools are living proof and exemplars that transformation is possible. Their examples present a series of working models and light the path for others excited by the possibilities of educational transformation. Having considered our own case, we will consider in depth the values of transformation to understand how they cohere and inspire transformative action.

What are the values of transformation?

Critical hope

Critical hope strives to transform structures, processes and practices while simultaneously understanding barriers, challenges and opportunities in each context. Paulo Freire argues that 'hope is something shared between teachers and students. The hope that we can learn together, teach together, be curiously impatient together, produce something together, and resist together the obstacles that prevent the flowering of our joy.'[18] As Freire suggests, education is fundamentally hopeful but not naïve. The 'critical' in critical hope looks to examine power relationships and inequities in systems (like schools). As educators Devita Bishundat and colleagues argue, 'Traditional conceptualizations [of hope] cannot create the type of change that is so desperately needed in society because they lack the necessary critique and understanding of inequities.'[19] Critical hope addresses power structures with the ultimate aim of developing agency in all participants in a system.

Critical hope provides the opportunity for educators to collaboratively discuss, imagine, plan and act for a better future while simultaneously understanding the history, constraints and opportunities in each context.[20] For instance, in our work with transformation we understand the current influence (and for some students damage) that standardized testing regimes exert. This knowledge frames our approach to learning and assessment. Our approach encourages growth and learning rather than the current disconnect we see in the education system. Unlearning old practices and attitudes enables hope to thrive by building innovative practice and transformative action.

Unlearning

Unlearning is a process of questioning assumptions and previous practices, beliefs and approaches and reconsidering them in the light of new understanding. This frequently requires the development or growth of capabilities (e.g. pedagogy, leadership). Unlearning is required when irrelevant, outmoded and sometimes damaging policies and practices become taken for granted. Unlearning gives us the opportunity to revisit and reimagine these practices to meet the needs of our students.

One of the classic unlearnings we often see is the 'hands up' to answer questions in the classroom. This practice reduces student agency and does not encourage noticing. Unlearning this practice requires educators to develop other processes for answering questions and running whole group discussions that encourage more than four or five students' participation. When we work across schools, and particularly with secondary schools outmoded beliefs such as 'hands up' often prevail. As we consider school transformation in secondary schools, we often facilitate a process of pedagogical renewal where teachers consider the depth and range of their pedagogical approaches (see chapters 6 and 7). This pedagogical reimagining often calls for teachers to unlearn their approach to pedagogies and re-engage with approaches they had not previously considered such as creative iteration or collaborative inquiry. Unlearning requires grit, focus, courage and a measure of wisdom.

Wisdom

In our view, wisdom is the capacity to learn from experience. We learn wisdom through processes such as inquiry and reflection on experience as we come to understand 'what works' and why. Wisdom is a key part of critical reflection as it encourages analysis rather than passive acceptance. Educational researcher Robert Stenberg argues that wisdom is critical to creating a better world: 'With a world in turmoil, perhaps we need to turn our attention in schools, not only to the identification and development of knowledge bases, nor even of intelligence, narrowly or broadly defined. Perhaps we need to turn our attention to the identification and development of wisdom. If there is a key to a better world, this may be it.'[21]

If wisdom is an organizational value, challenges will be evaluated and analysed on the basis of past experience and an application of evidence from other places. Wise action is often slower but usually results in more reliable and sustainable results. In our collaborative partnerships, we encourage educators to reflect on the practices that have become endemic in education. Some of these practices are useful but some are at best irrelevant and at worst destructive. The application of wisdom allows educators to test old and new practice against evidence and experience, and to generate transformative action that is suited to their context.

Imagination

Imagination is the capacity to develop a vision for a reality that does not yet exist. Imagination requires the bending of *what is* and *what might be*. In our work, rethinking pedagogy is critical if we are going to transform schools. The Pedagogy Parachute in chapter 7 was developed by the 4C Transformative Learning Team and trialled in our partnership schools. That process required imagination for our partners and ourselves to wonder what might be possible if pedagogy were reimagined. This is true for much of the work we do in schools. One of the biggest leaps required in school transformation is the ability to see beyond the known and to imagine education differently and particularly the school differently. Entrenched practices and approaches tend to limit the imagination and can lead to inertia.

When we imagine a new way to do pedagogy, timetabling, curriculum, assessment and teacher education, more powerful possibilities become apparent. Without a vibrant educational imagination, educators and their institutions can become stuck in undynamic and irrelevant practices. When we have gone through a process of unlearning, we can reconsider our practice supported by explicit and deep learning.

Explicit learning

In chapter 1, we described 'aerosol' words. These are the concepts that require explicit definitions and understanding to create structures and frameworks that allow learning to take place. In our partnerships with schools, we focus on explicit learning through the development of coherence makers. For us, coherence makers provide accessible schemas that allow educators to understand how concepts can translate to the classroom.

Effective coherence makers make sense of complex or dense concepts, rendering them understandable and teachable. These coherence makers may seem simple at first glance but open up the complexity and multidimensionality of each concept. For instance, in the Creativity Cascade that we outlined in *Transforming Schools* the processes are deceptively simple in some ways. It is only as you dig deeper you begin to realize the complexity and the possibilities of creativity. As we work with educators, the interconnections between the 4Cs become evident and obvious, which again unfolds complexity and possibility. We often describe coherence makers as being like the poetic form, haiku. On the face of it, the haiku is deceptively simple. It has only seventeen syllables, in three lines of five, seven and five. Yet often as a well-written haiku is studied in depth, it can open up remarkable complexity. This haiku makes meaning from topics as dense and difficult as climate change[22]

> Forty years from now
> Children will live in a world
> Shaped by our choices

Explicit learning requires explicit teaching. Explicit teaching seems to have become a euphemism for transmissive teaching or what is sometimes called 'chalk and talk'. In our view, explicit teaching is not transmissive. It requires a deep understanding of pedagogy and a deliberate approach to the content of the learning. It is not sufficient just to tell students what creativity might be in vague terms. Explicit teaching requires a coherent understanding of concepts such as creativity (in all its complexity) taught with the most effective pedagogical approach (see chapter 7). Explicit learning enables deep learning.

Deep learning

As we discussed in *Transforming Schools*, deep learning (also known as deeper learning) forges connections and transfer between disciplines. The US-based National Research Council defined deeper learning as 'the process through which an individual becomes capable of taking what was learned in one situation and applying it to new situations (i.e. transfer)'.[23] For instance, learning in persuasive writing in English could be transferred to science through persuading classmates to take action based on empirical evidence from a science experiment. As educator Parker Palmer argues, 'Good teachers possess a capacity for connectedness. They are able to weave a complex web of connections among themselves, their subjects, and their students so that students can learn to weave a world for themselves.'[24] These connections are difficult, but they are critical for deep and authentic learning. Also critical is the development of an agentic culture for educators and students.

Agency

In organizations inside and outside of education that are successfully transforming, agency is a critical feature of the culture. By agency, we mean that capacity to exercise a positive influence over decisions in the context of changes to practice, policy and approach. Agency does not mean that individuals have unfettered rights to say and do what they like. On the contrary, it is understanding of how to engage respectfully and wisely in discussions and to provide others in organizations with the space to speak and collaboratively engage in decision-making. In organizations that are not agentic, we often see disempowered and dispirited teachers and students who feel they have no say, control or rights to engage in decisions that directly involve them.

When agency is present in culture, we see students communicating confidently and understanding their rights and exercising appropriate responsibility for decisions in collaboration with other students, teachers, leaders and the community. This creates a very different cultural expectation. Agency generates a feeling (and reality) that students, teachers, leaders and the community not only have a say in what goes on but also are able to provide space for others to express agency. Agency can generate consensus on the vision, practices and policies of an organization.

Recently in one of our network schools, we observed agentic practice in action with kindergarten students (5–6-year-olds). Instead of using the command and control method of 'hands up', students learned how agency works in practice by waiting for an appropriate moment to speak and then speaking while noticing the need for others to contribute. Other examples include:

- students co-leading professional learning for and with teachers,
- students supporting learning and teaching processes through peer mentoring, and
- students and community engaged in discussions around curriculum, timetabling, etc.

These practices are not easy, nor do they happen without thought. In our experience when they are embedded in the culture they lead to new imaginings of what might be possible as everybody contributes. Agency also allows everyone access to imagine a different way of doing pedagogy.

Reimagined pedagogy

One of the key themes of this book is understanding how we can reconnect, re-engage and reimagine pedagogy. Reimagined pedagogy allows educators and leaders to connect, combine and create learning with diverse pedagogical elements to generate a range of teaching approaches. In some cases, pedagogy can become mired in old habits, shutting down possibilities. In reimagined pedagogy, a palette of pedagogies is developed, and the impact of each is explored. The need for reimagined pedagogy became apparent to us recently when we led some professional learning for a new partnership school. We asked participants to identify and map their pedagogical approaches and the likely impact of the pedagogies on learners. The principal observing their responses returned despondent, reporting that a few of her teachers in a staff of 120 were able to identify elements of pedagogy or their impact on student learning. An understanding of pedagogy can open up the possibility of curating deep learning (see chapter 6) for students. This can drive a culture for deep learning in schools and other educational settings.

For learning to be effective, educators could see pedagogy as more than jargon and engage deeply with all the possibilities of understanding pedagogical depth, connections and range. Reimagined pedagogy extends the range and enhances the depth for more effective learning and teaching to become a reality. Pedagogical imagination is vital to creating connected and coherent learning.

Connected and coherent learning

Connected and coherent learning seeks to connect domains (subjects) and stages (ages) of learning. This kind of learning retains domain depth, which is critical to deep learning but seeks connections to authentic problems in the real world which, by necessity, connects domains of knowledge. For instance, as students consider global food shortages they could consider history, economics, health education, food technology and geography. As we discussed earlier, education tends to silo around contexts and domains, but a connected and coherent approach engages with the 4Cs to deepen and connect learning. This approach is sometimes called transdisciplinary, multidisciplinary or interdisciplinary learning, and we will discuss how this might be possible in chapter 8. In essence, learning should not be bound by silos, and teachers can actively seek coherence and connection within and between subject domains. Un-siloing is also crucial in our partnerships.

Collaborative partnerships

Transformation is rarely (if ever) possible without vibrant and engaged partnerships. These partnerships need to be established on solid 4C foundations with shared values such as those we are articulating here. Aligning collaboratively requires a common language that leads to a diverse yet shared approach. In the 4C network we described in the example of practice, there are shared values and purposes across schools. For transformation to be enabled, there is a set of common structures and languages. The use of the Learning Disposition Wheel, the Pedagogy Parachute and the other 4C coherence makers anchors the work in a common set of understandings and provides a shared language. The 4C Network (figure 3.2) has become a community of practice.[25] In educational researcher Etienne Wenger's approach, there are three features of a community of practice[26] (COP):

- *Mutual engagement*: in this process, community members work together to establish the culture of the group through the shared values, practices and principles such as the values we have outlined here.

- *Joint enterprise*: this is the process of working together toward a common domain goal. In the case of the 4C network, the shared domain goal is the transformation of education.
- *Shared repertoire*: this describes the tools, frameworks and processes that are applied to the domain task. In our 4C networks, this begins with the Learning Disposition Wheel (see figure 4.4) and then builds on that understanding with other coherence makers (see 4C bazaar in the example of practice, this chapter).

These features of the COP generate formal network interactions that are facilitated by network convenors. Perhaps as critical are the less formal interactions where COP members develop and share resources and expertise between them in the pursuit of the shared enterprise. Once a shared practice is developed, praxis brings research, theory, policy and practice together.

Praxis

Praxis is the marriage of theory and practice in context.[27] Praxis values equally practices, research and theory. For schools, praxis encourages the application of theory and research to local contexts in a process of inquiry and reflection on experience. Too often we see a tendency to silo off research, theory and practice. This siloing can deny schools access to the collected wisdom contained in research and theory. Conversely, applying theory and research without considering context often leads to disconnected and irrelevant approaches. Theory informed by practice provides the most promising opportunity to create an inquiry culture in schools that supports and drives transformation.

Concluding reflections

We often hear discussions in education about how crucial culture is in the transformation process. That is unquestionably the case but there is often less agreement about how culture can be changed and shaped. In Atlassian's example (which opened this chapter), the organization is actively shaping culture through a shared set of values. They not only *say* they care about the planet, they *act* to look after the planet. In a world where values have become cheapened by a lack of action, this is a remarkable demonstration of how organizations can shape culture through shared values. Values by themselves can do nothing. As British American Tobacco's example demonstrates, values without actions are worthless.

In education we can face the same lack of understanding, apathy and disinterest when it comes to values and how they might be enacted. If we allow values to be cheapened and ignored, we misunderstand their potential. Atlassian demonstrates how values can generate action, shape culture and inspire transformation. For transformation to begin and then become sustainable, we need to build values that frame and motivate high-quality transformation processes. Once values are agreed, they have the potential to establish and drive beneficial change. Values provide a way for us to measure our processes against an agreed set of principles. In our partnerships schools these values frame expectations and begin the process of communicating that transformation is not simply 'business as usual'. For our organization, 4C Transformative Learning, transformative values (discussed in the example of practice) have helped us to retain a focus on what matters and keep a metaphorical 'true north'. Values can help all organizations transform if they are devised with a view to making them frame and drive action.

Through neglect and misuse, the process of forming values has been allowed to fade into irrelevance. If we truly wish to transform education, we can begin by restoring integrity into the values process so it can create a powerful guide for our transformation endeavours.

In the next chapter, we will discuss how a renewed and reimagined approach to learning can drive transformation.

Transforming learning
The power of agency

4

What is the power of agency? Greta Thunberg's story 52

How and why should learning be a capability for agency building and transformation? 54

What is agency and how does it change learning? 57

Why develop agency in learning? 58

How does Self-Determination Theory explain agency? 59

    Competence 60
    Autonomy 60
    Relatedness 61

What does Self-Determination Theory mean for learning? 61

What is the role of motivation in self-directed learning and agency? 62

How does Self-Determination Theory inform the Learning Disposition Wheel? 64

What is a learning disposition and what research underpins the Wheel? 65

How is the Learning Disposition Wheel used? 71

Learning: a capability for transformation 72

Concluding reflections 72

What is the power of agency? Greta Thunberg's story

There are two stories to tell about Greta Thunberg (figure 4.1). The first is the story of a 15-year-old girl in Sweden who began a social movement for young people wanting action on climate change. Greta Thunberg inspired mass student rallies across the world (including the climate strikes we referred to in chapter 3), addressed heads of state at the United Nations and was nominated *Time Person of the Year* in 2019. Her story illustrates how young people can be empowered to have a voice and make a social impact. There are adults who support the young people's climate strikes and there are adult voices who argue students should be in school, not out demonstrating. An article about the Australian Prime Minister, Scott Morrison, in *The Guardian* (26 November 2018) illustrates these views:

> Scott Morrison has been labelled 'out of touch' for angrily condemning a national student strike to protest government inaction on climate change. The prime minister implores children to stay in class rather than protesting things that 'can be dealt with outside of school'. 'Each day I send my kids to school and I know other members' kids should also go to school but we do not support our schools being turned into parliaments,' Morrison told parliament on Monday. 'What we want is more learning in schools and less activism in schools.' Morrison furiously reacted to Greens MP Adam Bandt during question time about the protest, dubbed the Big School Walkout for Climate Change . . . Bandt said he had met with some of the students involved and backed their actions. 'The PM is unbelievably out of touch with young people, not only in Australia but around the world,' he said. 'These students want a leader to protect their future, but they got a hectoring, ungenerous and condescending rebuke . . .'[1]

Figure 4.1 Greta Thunberg speaking at a climate rally.

At the heart of Greta Thunberg's courageous call to action is her capacity for agency in the world. There is, however, a second story of Greta Thunberg. A book written by the Thunberg family, *Our House Is On Fire: Scenes of a Family and a Planet in Crisis*,[2] reveals that at 11 years old, Greta was bullied at school and developed an eating disorder and selective mutism. She also had undiagnosed high-functioning autism and obsessive-compulsive disorder. The family went through years of difficulty challenged by her illnesses, and not being supported by the school she attended. Her mother, Malena, describes what it was like for Greta at school:

> It's like a movie montage featuring every imaginable bullying scenario. Stories about being pushed over in the playground, wrestled to the ground, or lured into strange places, the systematic shunning and the safe space in the girls' toilets where she manages to hide and cry before the break monitors force her out into the playground again. For a full year, the stories keep coming. Svante and I inform the school, but the school isn't sympathetic. Their understanding of the situation is different. It's Greta's own fault, the school thinks; several children have said repeatedly that Greta has behaved strangely and spoken too softly and never says hello.[3]

Agency is the ability and will to influence positively your own life and the lives of others.[4] The story of Greta's treatment at this school indicates a lack of agency in the students who inflicted harm, and a lack of agency in the teachers dealing with her situation. What helped her overcome her feelings of anxiety were her family's interventions. There was, however, another significant factor that changed Greta's life. At a new school she learnt about the 'Great Pacific Garbage Patch' (see figure 4.2), an accumulation of plastic debris (nearly the size of Mexico) floating

Figure 4.2 At 19 years old, the entrepreneur Boyan Slat created the non-profit organization The Ocean Cleanup, which has designed a massive plastic-catching device to clean up the Great Pacific Garbage Patch.

between Hawaii and California.[5] It was this confronting story and others like it that affected Greta's heightened sensitivities about the effects of humans on the world. It was the peril of the planet that motivated Greta to take action.

Every Friday from August 2018, she staged a personal school strike about inaction on climate change outside the Swedish parliament. From this small action, Greta Thunberg became a worldwide phenomenon, galvanizing students in Sweden and from around the world to support her campaign. Through an authentic experience, she activated the voices and agency of young people, and she activated her own voice and agency. It is this activation of personal expression and sense of purpose that helped Greta to develop a healthier and stronger sense of self. The two stories of Greta Thunberg illustrate the power of agency as social influence, and the power of agency at a personal level. Greta had developed the agency to influence positively her own life and the lives of others. Agency was something she learnt, and it transformed her sense of well-being. Her story demonstrates the capacity of agency to transform, both socially and personally. We argue that learning can be a capability that enables agency and transformation.

In this chapter we explore how learning can generate and enable agency in relationships, classes and schools. The complexity, chaos and change of the twenty-first century have brought into sharp focus the need for 4C capabilities (creativity, critical reflection, communication, collaboration) and the development of well-being and agency.[6] These capabilities (or processes) for human flourishing can be integrally linked in a powerful way through learning. This chapter discusses how these processes converge and are made coherent through the capability of learning, and more specifically through the Learning Disposition Wheel introduced at the end of the chapter (see figure 4.4). The Learning Disposition Wheel describes innate capacities that can be developed and fostered for self-direction in learning, well-being and agency. Learning in and through the Wheel dispositions supports students to transform their learning potential and their sense of self and agency.

We use Self-Determination Theory[7] to explain agency and how it changes the conditions and environment for learning. Self-Determination Theory underpins how skills in the Wheel develop a disposition for learning and transform learners to be self-directed and self-regulated. We discuss research informing the development of the Learning Disposition Wheel and how the Wheel is used as a powerful tool to inform pedagogy and curriculum development. To begin, we consider how and why learning should be a capability for agency building and transformation in education.

How and why should learning be a capability for agency building and transformation?

In response to the complex and unprecedented social, economic and environmental challenges of a rapidly changing world, the Organisation for Economic Co-operation and Development (OECD) released the *Future of Education and Skills 2030* project[8] in 2019. The *2030* project argues:

Now, in the face of deep and widespread changes that are transforming our world and disrupting the institutional status quo in many sectors, there is a growing recognition of the need to re-think the goals of education, and the competencies students need to thrive. Global trends like digitalisation, climate change, and advances in artificial intelligence, to name just three, pose fundamental challenges to both the goals and methods of education.[9]

The OECD *2030* project aims to develop a common vision and language for education that advocates the critical importance and building of:

- student agency (the ability and will to influence positively their own lives and the world around them),
- core foundations (cognitive, health and well-being, social and emotional),
- transformative competencies (create new value, reconcile tensions and dilemmas, take responsibility),
- the anticipation-action-reflection cycle (iteration and thinking reflectively towards long-term goals),
- theoretical and practical knowledge (disciplinary, interdisciplinary, epistemic and procedural),
- cognitive and metacognitive, social and emotional, practical and physical skills (to meet complex demands), and
- attitudes and values (towards individual, societal and environment well-being).

These ideas in the *2030* project are made coherent through the concept of a learning compass that students can use to navigate 'towards the future we want'[10] (see figure 4.3). The key to all these aspirations is the development of agency in students, and co-agency with the community around them. According to the *2030* project, 'The metaphor of the learning compass was adopted to emphasize the need for students to learn to navigate by themselves through unfamiliar contexts and find their direction in a meaningful and responsible way, instead of simply receiving fixed instructions or directions from their teachers.'[11]

Developing self-direction in learning leads to student agency and the ability to navigate complex and unfamiliar contexts. The *2030* project argues that two factors enable learner agency; the first is a personalized learning environment that makes connections across students' learning experiences and motivates students to design their own learning projects in collaboration with others. The second is the building of foundations that include literacy, numeracy, digital and data literacy, physical health and well-being.

The aspirations of the OECD project are aligned with our vision for learning as a capability to transform education. We agree that agency, well-being, core foundations, integrated curricula, capacities for transformation and reflected action are central to realigning and reimagining the direction of learning in the twenty-first century. The OECD's vision does state, however, that this vision can work within the existing

Figure 4.3 The OECD Learning Compass.

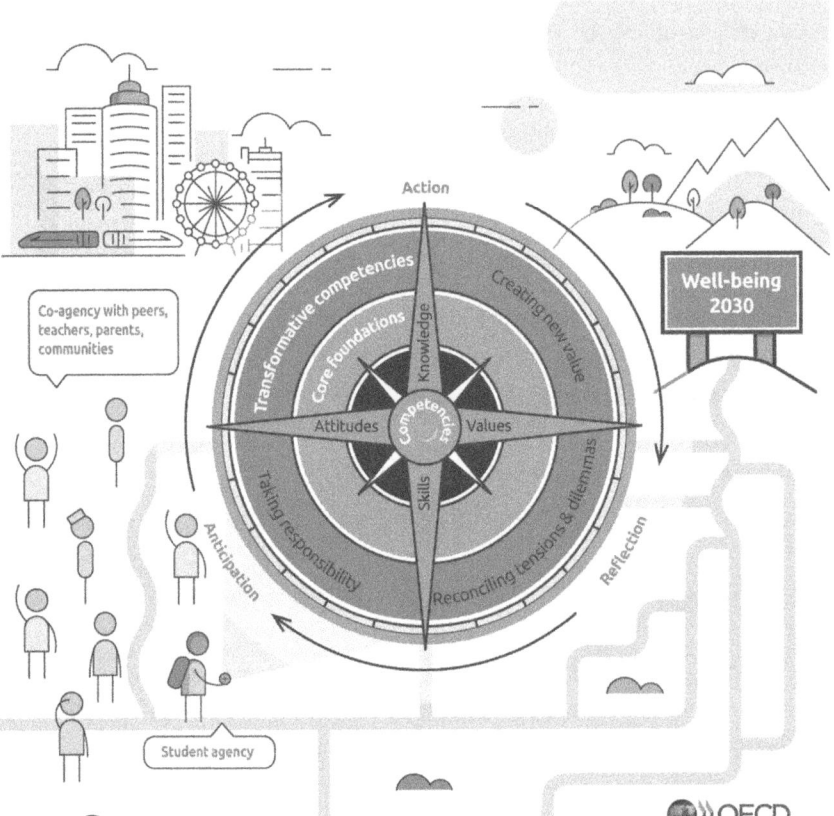

status quo of curriculum and pedagogy. For instance, when discussing the transformative competencies – *creating new value* (innovating and developing new knowledge), *reconciling tensions and dilemmas* (being comfortable with complexity and ambiguity) and *taking responsibility* (considering the ethics of action) – a *Future of Education and Skills 2030* document claims:

> The transformative competencies can be taught and learned in schools by incorporating them into existing curricula and pedagogy. For example, countries can embed the competency of 'creating new value' into such subjects as the arts, language, technology, home economics, mathematics and science, using an inter-disciplinary approach. Transformative competencies can also be acquired at home, in the family, and in the community, during interactions with others.[12]

We argue it is not enough to integrate these transformative competencies into existing structures and processes. The status quo in education reinforces and limits the building of student agency and transformation. The OECD transformative competencies could transform existing curricula and pedagogy and fundamentally change the *way* of learning. Changing the processes of *how* we learn profoundly affects *what* we learn. For instance, you cannot direct or instruct students to have agency, and you cannot just provide opportunities for students to express agency. The *how* of the learning does not serve the *what*; the learning process cannot meet the intended outcome. It is *how* skills in self-direction are learnt that affects the expression of agency in students. It is *how* students learn to communicate and *how* they experience opportunities to 'voice' their identity that impact the process of developing agency.

This can be applied to the transforming competencies named in the OECD's *2030* project. It is *how* students experience creative processes and the taking of risks with mistakes and failure that affects their learning of *creating new value*. *Reconciling tensions and dilemmas* involves learning processes that allow for ambiguity and uncertainty and the development of empathy. *Taking responsibility* involves processes that develop influence through critical reflection and collaboration. *How* these processes are facilitated and experienced can transform the *way* of learning and change the emphasis and purpose of pedagogy and curriculum. For instance, if students are to become self-directed learners, the purpose of pedagogy cannot only be instruction of subject knowledge. It has to be pedagogy that empowers skills in self-regulated learning as well. Or, if students' interests and choices inform curriculum, it changes not only the curriculum focus, but also student influence and their sense of agency in education. In these examples, the purpose of pedagogy and curriculum changes. In real world practice, agency building involves a comprehensive shift and recalibration in the way learners see themselves, and how we as educators see learners and learning. This is how learning can be a powerful capability for transformation.

What is agency and how does it change learning?

The OECD defines agency as 'a sense of responsibility to participate in the world and, in so doing, to influence people, events and circumstances for the better'.[13] It also refers to 'co-agency' as the interactive relationships students have with family, teachers, school support staff and the community to support the development of their agency. Co-agency requires everyone in the community to be a learner of agency and agentic relationships. The building of agency then is a major and profound shift in education, and it brings into sharp focus questions such as:

- How much influence do students really have on the nature of schooling, pedagogy and curriculum?
- How much freedom do students really have in education?
- Do students have an active role in shaping their education?
- Do students want an active role in shaping their education? Why not? Really why?
- Do teachers and the community have an active role in shaping education?
- Does schooling offer opportunities to act in the real world?

We hold 4C Network workshop conferences twice a year for our partnership schools (see chapter 3). The coming together of the schools is a community of praxis (see chapter 9) and an opportunity for continuing the learning as a collaborative endeavour towards transformation. It is a form of co-agency building as schools share their innovations and transformation journeys. The network days are a 'festival of agency' and the involvement of students in the teacher and leader professional learning is integral. The reaction from teachers every time they are held is that the presence of students in this setting is enlightening, profound and inspiring but also confronting. It is not what they are used to. In panel discussions (with teachers and students), teachers in the audience hear students reminding them, 'just listen to us', 'know us as people' and 'give us a voice'.

In classrooms, teachers introduce communication processes (as part of the 4C approach) to develop student confidence with voice and agency. As a response to these processes, teachers are excited by the emergence of student voice and the flourishing of student capabilities. Teachers are also challenged when these 4C communication processes reveal a lack of voice and agency in students. Teachers notice students who are afraid to talk, dominant in talk, are not motivated to talk or derail the talk of others. Teachers sometimes struggle with these communication processes in their own professional settings and learning. They struggle, like their students, with the agency and confidence to express their voice, enable the voice of others, and to notice their messaging and the messaging of others. This lack of co-agency and voice was apparent in the students and teachers at the school where Greta Thunberg was bullied and misunderstood.

Transforming learning through the development of agency means students, teachers and communities can develop the ability and will to participate responsibly in the world and, in so doing, to influence each other, other people, events and circumstances for the better. To transform learning is to facilitate skills and opportunities that develop the communication of thinking, the taking on of challenges and responsibilities, and the questioning of the prevailing norms and values in education and the wider world. There is, however, a dominant assumption that students cannot take on these responsibilities as 'they do not know what is best for them'. This assumption was evident in the Australian Prime Minister's response to the student climate strikes. With student agency comes a newfound challenge for teachers and leaders. How do we resolve the tension between the protection of young people's well-being (knowing what is best for them), and their rights to participate freely and be agents of influence in education and the world (having a voice)? We protect students in education because they are vulnerable, but that protection can deny them the opportunity to develop the agency to participate.

Why develop agency in learning?

Both protective and participatory rights are enshrined in the Convention of the Rights of the Child (CRC).[14] Education and social justice researchers Caroline Sarojina Hart and Nicolás Brando[15] argue that the protective side in a child's well-being is evident in the convention through the assurance of life, health and development, and the protection from physical or mental violence, abuse, neglect, maltreatment or exploitation. On the participatory side, they argue that the CRC promotes the child's freedom of expression and the development of 'social, spiritual and moral well-being and physical and mental health'.[16] Rather than falling into a false dualism, where one side is the restrictive control of the protection of children and the other is the permissive freedom of children's participation, a scaffolded approach from protection to participation builds children's agency and enhances their well-being.

For instance, if children want to build a treehouse to play in, adults could deter the enterprise by declaring it is too dangerous (protection). Or children could explore with adults how to build a treehouse (learning in participation). Through questions and noticings, trial and error with self-discovery, the children can learn how to build the treehouse safely and how to self-manage their play in the treehouse (participation). It is a scaffolded approach in developing the children's self-direction and self-regulation. If young people are self-directed in their learning, they can participate in a climate strike and miss a day at school. Their learning is not dependent on teachers; it depends on their will and ability to drive and own their own learning.

The CRC states that adults caring for children shall 'provide, in a manner consistent with the evolving capacities of the child, appropriate direction and guidance in the exercise by the child of the rights recognized in the present Convention'.[17] Hart and Brando[18] contend that the evolving capacities and agency of children can only be made a reality by converting these rights into capabilities, otherwise they are just a 'paper promise'. They argue social and environmental conditions that promote the learning of foundational and central human capabilities can realize the rights enshrined in the CRC and allow children to flourish.

It is the responsibility of adults to facilitate children's participatory rights and agency through the development of capabilities from the earliest possible age. This means developing agency in early learning (e.g. preschool or kindergarten) and throughout their education, so that children can exercise their freedoms as laid down in the Convention of the Rights of the Child. Educators can nurture and develop capabilities in learner agency to realize the participation rights and well-being of young people. To understand better how learning as a capability builds agency, it is useful to explore Self-Determination Theory.

How does Self-Determination Theory explain agency?

Developed in the 1980s and formalized in the work of psychology researchers Edward Deci and Richard Ryan in the 1990s, Self-Determination Theory is a macro-theory that details the origins and outcomes of human agency. The theory has been widely applied in schools and learning, parenting, health care, workplace motivation, sport and exercise, virtual worlds and other contexts. The theory assumes that human behaviour is inherently growth-oriented and proactive, and that people at their best are curious, self-motivated and striving to learn and extend themselves. In contrast to this, human behaviours can be passive, apathetic, alienated and irresponsible. The theory explains that these behaviours are determined by whether certain human fundamental psychological needs are supported or diminished by the social environment around them. The three basic psychological needs that support agency and well-being in Self-Determination Theory are competence, autonomy and relatedness. If these needs are supported by the social conditions, human agency and well-being can thrive.[19] We describe each of these psychological needs, and how they relate to learning.

Competence

In Self-Determination Theory, competence is described as the human desire to effectively master the environment we are in. Feeling mastery and competence in an environment gives us a sense of self-worth. In a classroom environment, students should feel capable and have a sense of self-worth in the learning they are doing. Teachers can create experiences that build student confidence and skills in learning. Competence as a basic psychological need suggests that teachers ask how students' feelings of effectiveness and self-efficacy can be built. Feelings of competence and worth energize curiosity and learning in students, but these feelings can be easily thwarted. According to self-determination research, competence 'wanes in contexts in which challenges are too difficult, negative feedback is pervasive, or feelings of mastery and effectiveness are diminished or undermined by interpersonal factors such as person-focused criticism and social comparisons'.[20]

Autonomy

Autonomy is the feeling of satisfaction when we experience choice and volition in our own actions. It describes being the instigator of our own thoughts and actions, rather than being controlled by something external to us. Autonomy means students can instigate learning in which they are interested and see value. Students can be motivated when they pursue what they are interested in or when teachers introduce and ignite student interest in learning that is new to them. Teachers can facilitate choice for students in the learning and develop internally regulated motivation so learners can develop the desire to choose or explore something of interest. The evidence for the role of autonomy in the growth and wellness of students is strong. Deci and Ryan argue: 'Among the more important and frequently replicated findings is that the provision of autonomy support by both teachers and parents helps students maintain intrinsic motivation for learning and develop more fully internalized extrinsic motivation for their schoolwork. In turn, autonomous motivation enhances both learning quality and psychological wellness.'[21]

Relatedness

Relatedness is the psychological need to have a sense of social belonging. It is the satisfaction that comes from feeling connected when caring for and being cared for by others. Relatedness is the influence we have on others to feel connected and significant in a social environment. In the learning context, it suggests students and teachers being aware of and considerate in how they make other students feel. To develop a sense of belonging and relatedness, teachers should know their students and their contexts as holistically as possible. Teachers might consider how well they know the students, how well the students know each other, and how they can connect and care for them. Students too can learn how to care for their teachers. Discussing how relatedness between learners and teachers makes a difference, researchers Christopher Niemiec and Richard Ryan argue:

> In the classroom, relatedness is deeply associated with a student feeling that the teacher genuinely likes, respects, and values him or her. Students who report such relatedness are more likely to exhibit identified and integrated regulation for the arduous tasks involved in learning, whereas those who feel disconnected or rejected by teachers are more likely to move away from internalization and thus respond only to external contingencies and controls.[22]

Trusting and mutually respectful relationships between teachers and students are significant for students to feel internally motivated to learn. Learning processes and environments that consider how teachers and students develop competence, autonomy and relatedness support schools to thrive and transform.

What does Self-Determination Theory mean for learning?

The three basic psychological needs of competence, autonomy and relatedness in Self-Determination Theory are inextricably interrelated and interdependent. All three needs must be developed together for students to flourish in their learning and well-being. Failing to support competence, autonomy and relatedness contributes to apathy, alienation and ill-being in students.[23] If educators can create a learning environment that supports the growth of competence, autonomy and relatedness, students are energized and engaged to achieve positive learning outcomes.[24]

We argue that developing competence, autonomy and relatedness cannot be an 'add on' or 'bolt on' programme to current pedagogy, curriculum and organizational structures in education. Supporting competence, autonomy and relatedness can be at the core of all teaching and learning, underpinning the nature of pedagogy and curriculum. For instance, *relatedness* and feelings of belonging can be developed in students if teachers have opportunities and experiences to connect with and know their students. This may mean changing the organizational structure of the school so teachers can teach collaboratively with other teachers in classrooms. Teaching across students' learning experiences also allows teachers to know their students better, as does developing opportunities and capacities for student voice.

To develop *autonomy* and self-direction, students can pursue activities that engage them, or tasks that offer novelty, challenge or aesthetic value.[25] To facilitate or enable this, pedagogy and curriculum can be flexible and adaptive to meet student needs, passions and contexts (see chapter 8 on curriculum). Students' feelings of *competence* and self-worth can be supported by pedagogy that fosters intrinsic motivation.[26] Intrinsic motivation is the capacity to exercise and extend yourself by seeking out novelty and challenge. 'Command and control pedagogy' ('I will tell you what to know and do') undermines the development of intrinsic motivation in students.[27] Pedagogy that facilitates deep noticing, questioning and positive feedback (see the Pedagogy Parachute in chapter 7) can enhance students feelings of competence and intrinsic motivation to learn. Feedback that makes students feel incompetent (for example, 'you received six out of ten' ... 'you need to do better' ... 'you should have noticed' ...) can diminish feelings of competence and intrinsic motivation.

These examples demonstrate the possibility of reimagining and reorganizing pedagogical and curriculum approaches and structures to develop competence, autonomy and relatedness. By nurturing these three psychological needs, students can develop self-direction and self-regulation in their learning and cultivate agency and well-being. Fundamental to Self-Determination Theory is understanding the role of motivation in teaching, learning and agency building.

What is the role of motivation in self-directed learning and agency?

Self-directed learning and agency in Self-Determination Theory can be explained in a continuum of motivation and self-regulatory behaviour (see table 4.1). At one end of the continuum is amotivation and an unwillingness to participate in learning. At the other end of the continuum is intrinsic motivation and being motivated by active personal commitment and satisfaction in learning. The continuum describes various stages of extrinsic motivation in between. Extrinsic motivation is being compliant or performing an activity to attain a separate outcome or reward. The continuum of self-determination describes how extrinsically motivated behaviours vary in the extent to which the regulation is autonomous. Table 4.1 describes how a student may feel in each of these stages of motivation and self-regulatory behaviour in their learning.

The continuum describes the following stages of motivation and self-regulatory behaviour:

- Amotivation (*non-regulation*) occurs when there is a lack of agency and the student does not value the learning because they believe it won't deliver them a desired result or they feel incompetent to do the learning. For example, their feelings can be expressed as 'I don't see the point of this' or 'I can't do this'.

Table 4.1 A student rubric for motivation adapted from the continuum of self-determination according to motivation and self-regulatory behaviour by Ryan and Deci (2000).[28]

Lack of motivation	Controlled motivation			Autonomous motivation		
Amotivation	Extrinsic motivation					Intrinsic motivation
Non-regulation	External regulation	Somewhat external regulation (introjected)	Somewhat internal regulation (identified)	Internal regulation (integrated)	Internal regulation	
I won't do the learning activities, or I will attempt them with minimum effort. I don't see the point of the learning, or I find the learning too hard.	I am doing the learning activities because I have been told to do them, or I will be rewarded to do them, or I will be punished if I don't do them.	I am doing the learning because I want to impress others. I want to demonstrate that I can do the activities and receive praise for doing them.	I undertake the learning challenge because they are a personal goal I have set myself. It is important for me to achieve this goal.	I am aware of the benefits of the learning challenge and believe they are important for me to do. I don't feel any particular enjoyment in doing the learning.	I am interested and enjoy the learning challenge. I feel a commitment to and sense of satisfaction in doing the learning.	

The next two stages are controlled extrinsic motivation.

- *External regulation* is when the student is compliant because of external demands in the learning such as reward and punishment. For example, 'I do the work because I don't want to get into trouble' or 'I do the work to get an early mark'.
- *Introjected regulation* is when the student is self-controlled in their learning but unconsciously adopts the ideas and attitudes of others (often teachers) as a response to show self-worth and wanting affirmation for self-esteem. For example, 'I like being praised for what I do' or 'I like to be noticed by the teacher'.

The continuum then moves to autonomous motivation and different forms of internal (self) regulation with extrinsic motivation, and then intrinsic motivation.

- *Identified regulation* is when the student consciously values the learning as a personal goal that is important to them. For example, 'I feel satisfied just to finish what I started'.
- *Integrated regulation* is when the student understands the benefits of the learning and integrates it with their personal values and needs. Unlike

intrinsic motivation, there is no inherent enjoyment and satisfaction in the learning for them. For example, 'I see value in studying hard as it will get me into a course I want to do'.

- *Intrinsic motivation* is self-regulated learning that has inherent satisfaction and active commitment. For example, 'I am really interested and stimulated to continue this learning'.

Research in Self-Determination Theory demonstrates that autonomous forms of regulation (*identified*, *integrated* and *intrinsic*) are associated with wellness, engagement and perceived competence.[29] The implication for teachers is that supporting learning experiences in agency-building facilitates the internalization of self-regulatory behaviour and more interest and enjoyment in learning. The implication for leaders is that experiences that facilitate the internalization of self-regulatory behaviours in teachers and other staff lead to greater well-being at work.[30] Agency-building experiences lead to a healthier and more productive learning and work climate. A social environment that supports the development of *competence*, *autonomy* and *relatedness* enhances the integration of internally regulated motivation. Enhanced motivation leads to commitment, effort and better achievement outcomes in education and life.[31]

How does Self-Determination Theory inform the Learning Disposition Wheel?

For the transformation of learning, teachers can consider how self-directed learning and agency-building are connected to the development of self-regulation and autonomous motivation. To gain better achievement outcomes in learning and life, how can students learn to be more internally regulated and motivated? Through praxis (research and practice) we have created the Learning Disposition Wheel (see figure 4.4) as a teaching and learning tool to support the development of skills that build agency and self-direction in students. All the skills within the domains of the Learning Disposition Wheel have the capacity to affect and strengthen a learner's disposition (inherent qualities) for learning and agency. These are the skills that Greta Thunberg learnt and strengthened through her experience with climate action.

Evident in the Learning Disposition Wheel is the connection with the basic psychological needs of Self-Determination Theory.

- The cognitive skills (*think why and how, make and express meaning, build new ideas*) support *competence*.
- The intrapersonal skills (*focus, grit, curiosity*) support *autonomy*.
- The interpersonal skills (*influence, empathy, teamwork*) support *relatedness*.

Together, they support the development of agency.

Figure 4.4 The Learning Disposition Wheel

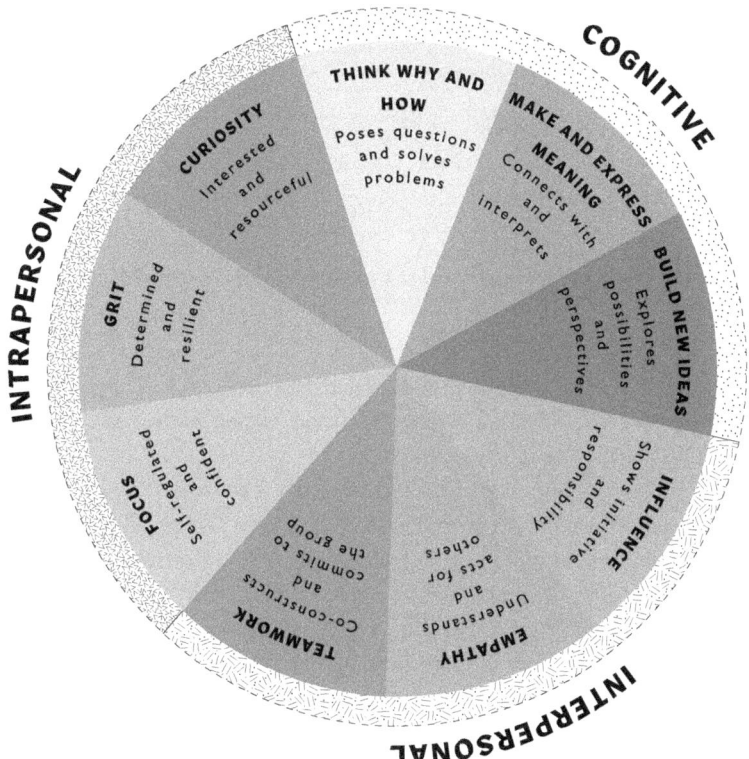

Capacities on the Wheel describe the learning dispositions that are required to develop a sense of agency and well-being. Underpinning the Learning Disposition Wheel is the assumption that human capacity is not fixed, and that capacities can be learnt as skills in the right conditions.[32] What then is a learning disposition and what research supports the Learning Disposition Wheel?

What is a learning disposition and what research underpins the Wheel?

A learning disposition is the inherent qualities that under the right conditions all humans possess to enable learning. Developmental psychologists view learner competence and behavioural development as a dynamic phenomenon. This dynamic is determined by the interplay between our innate abilities, our dispositions and the quality of our early experiences.[33] Learning analytics researchers Simon Buckingham Shum and Ruth Deakin Crick describe learning dispositions as an oscillation between the 'personal' and the 'public' (see table 4.2). The personal is our identity, personhood

Table 4.2 Learning dispositions oscillating between the personal and the public, from Buckingham Shum and Deakin Crick (2012).[34]

Self			Competent Agent
←			→
Identity Desire Motivation	Dispositions Values Attitudes	Skills and Strategies Knowledge Understanding	Competent Learner, Citizen, Mathematician, etc.
Personal ←			→ Public

and desires, and the public is our exposure to and experience of learning. The personal aspect is mobilized and scaffolded forward by the public acquisition of skills and understandings, and the public is affected backwards by personal desires and intentions.

Buckingham Shum and Deakin Crick explain how agency, motivation and dispositions are necessary for learning to learn as we go through life: 'Competence in learning how to learn requires energy, intention and desire, as well as the dispositions or virtues necessary to acquire skills, strategies and knowledge management necessary for making the most of learning opportunities over a lifespan, in the public domain.'[35] They explain how a learning disposition is the desire, or motivation to take action to learn. Someone who has a strong disposition for 'curiosity', for example, will consistently generate questions and investigate ideas. Someone who could develop their curiosity may need to learn skills in generating questions and investigating, or develop the internal motivation to want to be curious.

The National Research Council's (NRC) 2012 report, *Education for Life and Work: Developing Transferable Knowledge and Skills in the 21st Century*, argues that skills needed for a learning disposition can be learnt and taught: 'Other, more recent research, indicates that intrapersonal skills and dispositions, such as motivation and self-regulation, support deeper learning and that these valuable skills and dispositions can be taught and learned. Socio-cultural perspectives on learning illuminate the potential for developing intrapersonal and interpersonal skills within instruction focused on cognitive mastery of school subjects.'[34] A disposition for learning can be taught explicitly in and through the curriculum with mindfully selected pedagogical processes that are targeted and focused. The Learning Disposition Wheel synthesizes and makes coherent the capacities needed to build dispositions for learning and agency.

We introduced the Learning Disposition Wheel in our book *Transforming Schools: Creativity, Critical Reflection, Communication, Collaboration*, and the Wheel continues to be used in schools as a tool to transform learning, pedagogy and learners. The research in the NRC's *Education for Life and Work: Developing Transferable Knowledge and Skills in the 21st Century*[37] underpinned the Wheel's development. The National Research Council's report draws on a substantial research base in cognitive science, educational and social psychology, economics, child and adolescent development, literacy, mathematics and science education, psychometrics, educational technology and human resource development. The report identifies three broad domains for capacities in learning:

- The cognitive – the capacity to think and reason.
- The intrapersonal – the capacity to self-regulate emotions and behaviours.
- The interpersonal – the capacity to relate to others.

The NRC report developed a classification scheme to describe human competencies by aligning a content analysis of twenty-first-century skills with taxonomies of cognitive, intrapersonal and interpersonal skills and abilities from differential psychology (systems that classify human behaviour and their underlying processes). The report recognized that twenty-first-century skills are not new, unique skills that are suddenly of value today. It argues that they are competencies or skills that have been essential to realizing human potential for centuries.

From the report's research and classification scheme, we developed a metalanguage for the Wheel based on consultation with teachers, students and parents in our praxis. In the Learning Disposition Wheel, the capacities in the three domains are as follows:

- Cognitive
  - Think why and how (poses questions and solves problems)
  - Make and express meaning (connects with and interprets)
  - Build new ideas (explores possibilities and perspectives)
- Intrapersonal
  - Focus (self-regulated and confident)
  - Grit (determined and resilient)
  - Curiosity (interested and resourceful)
- Interpersonal
  - Influence (shows initiative and responsibility)
  - Empathy (understands and acts for others)
  - Teamwork (co-constructs and commits to the group)

The National Research Council report argues that the three domains (the cognitive, intrapersonal, interpersonal) are integrally interrelated, and cannot be developed without the others.[38] How we think and reason, how we regulate our emotions and how we relate to others are mutually self-reinforcing. How we develop curiosity for instance, depends upon all the other dispositions. Self-Determination Theory that informs the Wheel also illustrates how competence (the cognitive), autonomy (the intrapersonal) and relatedness (the interpersonal) are inextricably interdependent. The Learning Disposition Wheel is represented as a circle to illustrate the interconnectedness and reliance each disposition has to the other. The 4C capabilities are also evident in the Learning Disposition Wheel: creativity is inherent in *build new ideas*, critical reflection is inherent in *think why and how*, communication is

Figure 4.5 Students discussing their learning using the Learning Disposition Wheel.

inherent in *make and express meaning*, and collaboration is inherent in *teamwork*. Each disposition of the Wheel is described and explored in detail in chapter 5; however, they only make sense when they are physically experienced, practised and embedded as a continually evolving way of being in learning and pedagogy. In the following breakout box is an example of practice from Miranda North Public School, in NSW Australia. Students, a teacher and a principal describe the role that the Learning Disposition Wheel has in transforming learning in the classroom and school. In figure 4.5, students are using the Wheel to discuss their learning.

Reflections on learning with the Learning Disposition Wheel:

Daniel, 11 years old
If I had known about the Disposition Wheel when I first started kindergarten, I'd be a different person! I didn't really understand what it meant to be a learner and since we started learning about the LDW, I feel like I know what I have to draw on when I'm learning... I'm just more aware. When I'm finding something really hard, that's when I find I think more about the wheel... I look back on it and it really helps me refocus when the task is hard... like during maths when I'm solving a really challenging problem... and I have to use *grit* but also *think why and how*.

Taylah, 12 years old
Something I've really noticed since we've been learning with the Wheel is that almost all of our discussions in class make links to the wedges on the wheel. That's really different to before. I find it is really clear now and I am not so confused about what I need to be successful with my learning.

When we were first introduced to the Wheel, I was pretty unsure about what it meant for me. The little explanation under the heading on the wedge was helpful but it was when we started reflecting on our learning after an activity that I really started to connect with it. I started to understand what the dispositions were because we were actually doing them. . . that was really cool and I remember thinking 'ahhh that's what it means'.

Jake, 11 years old
One of my memories from when I was in Year 4 and new to the Wheel, was when I contributed an idea during a class discussion and my teacher got the Wheel out and made the link with what I had said. This was the first time that I really saw the link between my thinking about the learning and the Wheel. It made the Wheel really real!

Harriet, 11 years old
I think we are starting to be more aware of the Wheel outside the classroom, like when we are with friends or at home. When we are doing things together, I'm really aware of the dispositions that I need to draw on, like using *grit* when things are hard or *curiosity* if I'm doing something new with my family. I think when I go to high school, I'll be able to use my *influence* to help my friends understand more about the Wheel and how it really helps you as a learner. Kids from other schools might not be aware of the Wheel and maybe the teachers too, so it will be up to us to share what we know so everyone can be successful learners.

Antonia Mitsoulis (teacher)
I use the Learning Disposition Wheel in everything I do. In the classroom, I have it strategically placed right on the centre back wall. When I'm talking to the students, it feels like it is the core of our classroom because everything comes back to it. A simple discussion on any topic, something to do with geography, or a maths lesson, or a spelling lesson, it all comes back to the Wheel. I will move to the back of the room when we're discussing something and the students know 'she's moving to the Wheel' and then their minds focus on it. They change the conversation and say, 'That's a little bit of *influence* in what we just said.' Or 'That was *teamwork*.' I don't have to ask what part of the Wheel we were using right now.

The other day we were talking about how to put together a PowerPoint. Some children knew how to do it, others didn't know, others said, 'What's a PowerPoint?' I asked the children, 'How can we do this? How can we be a bit creative with this rather than me telling you?' And then the kids added ideas to the discussion. And I said, 'What have we just done now? *Teamwork*, we've *influenced* each other. We've *thought, why and how*?

Why do we need to do this? How are we going to do this? And together, we've *built new ideas.*'

So even an instructional lesson that I could have just stood there and said, 'OK, first step is this. . .' I decided not to do it that way, I thought, let the children take control and let them lead this learning. And all of a sudden, I had about fifteen volunteers bursting to come out in front saying, 'I know how to do this on a PowerPoint, this is how you do a transition, this is how you add voice. This is how you find a new slide.' As this was developing, more and more of the students were connecting what they were doing with PowerPoint to the Learning Disposition Wheel. When we had finished I went and stood at the back of the room beside the wheel. The students started laughing and said, 'Yep, we did everything on the Wheel!'

I sometimes talk to the kids about the wheel being our anchor, something that we're anchoring all our learning on. . . It's the heart of everything we do. And in turn, it becomes the heart of who we are. And the children really relate to that. They understand that 'for me to a complete learner or a good learner or someone that's going to be successful in life I need to have these qualities'.

I just love how these kids have grown. I've gained understanding as well on how to be a better teacher. I've learnt how to bring out the best in my students and how to make the learning really authentic to them. I ask myself, how can they connect to the learning, how can they live it. The students are passionate about what they're doing in our classrooms now. Every child in asking, 'What are we doing today?' They're just so excited about everything.

I've been a teacher for thirty-plus years and I've really enjoyed this new way of learning, this new way of being. And I can see that our students are coming through and leading our school with a sense of confidence and sense of knowing who they are. And I link it all back to the Learning Disposition Wheel and the 4Cs.

I give my students that that little bit of wisdom, that it's all about communication and collaboration and be as creative as you can be in life, reflect upon everything you do and become a better you. And that's the knowledge they leave our school with. And I carry that message in myself as well, I think my life's a lot better too!

Sue Orlovich (Principal)
As a school we understand and have engaged with how the dispositions are intrinsic to successful learners. But they're also intrinsic for good mental health and well-being and social interaction. And I think that we're now starting to really explore our well-being practices. We are starting to explore some deep questions around some of our practices of what we value or what we reinforce in terms of our well-being systems and our recognition systems. We are starting to really unpack and question some of our really ingrained practices through the lens of the Disposition Wheel. And that's a really exciting space to be in.

The students are more deeply reflective about themselves as learners and have a much broader understanding of what it means to be effective in their learning. Antonia talks about it being an anchor and you can see how deeply embedded it is in the students' responses. They are metacognitive and really able to describe the stages of their learning, particularly when the learning becomes challenging. And I guess that's what's so exciting to see in Antonia's classroom.

The students reflect on the learning and on themselves as learners. You often see in Antonia's classroom 'pause points' throughout the learning to get the students to stop, particularly when they're stuck in a challenge, and through her reflective questioning, which is always related to the Wheel, they are able to regroup, rethink and then explore.

The Learning Disposition Wheel is a tool that I think has so many uses, whether it's teacher planning, whether it's the execution of the learning, whether it's the guidance throughout the learning or whether it's the reflecting on the learning. In planning, the Wheel is used as a tool to help teachers really, really think deeply about what it is that the students need to learn.

I think as a principal, we've been challenged for a long time knowing these dispositions are essential for deep learning but it has been really hard to describe them. It's been really hard to work out how do we go about teaching them? And then how do we go about assessing whether the students have actually built these dispositions? I think the Learning Disposition Wheel goes a long way to provide an invaluable tool and resource to help us address some of these challenges.

How is the Learning Disposition Wheel used?

The Wheel is used as a diagnostic, feedback, reporting and evaluation tool where teachers can deeply notice and analyse the strengths and yet-to-be strengths of learners as a classroom cohort or as individuals. This informs and shapes pedagogy and curriculum learning design (see chapters 6 and 8). Identified strengths in the Wheel are used to build yet-to-be strengths and focusing on the yet-to-be strengths begin to develop other dispositions in the Wheel.

For instance, if pedagogy is used to develop *focus* (self-regulation and confidence), other skills such as *empathy* (understanding and acting for others) or *make and express meaning* (connecting with and interpreting) may be developed. If *teamwork* is identified as a yet-to-be strength but learning in the class reveals that lack of *empathy* is affecting their capacity to collaborate, the pedagogical focus turns to empathy to strengthen teamwork. The dispositions are taught and learnt explicitly through curriculum and pedagogy that facilitate self-direction, self-regulation and agency. Learning in the Wheel capacities is woven into curriculum and assessment. Critically, the Learning Disposition Wheel provides a common language in schools and organizations to talk about learners, learning and agency-building.

Learning: a capability for transformation

Agentic learning is a capability necessary to fulfil the charter of the Convention of the Rights of the Child. For young people to flourish, we can develop learning as a capability that generates and enables their participatory rights and agency. This can begin from the earliest years of education. Students can learn agency and co-agency with their teachers and other students, through processes that develop motivation, self-regulation and self-direction. Co-agentic relationships and processes with families and communities are also integral to the enablement and generation of agency in young people. The concept of co-agency is discussed in relationship to shared leadership in schools (see chapter 10).

Self-Determination Theory explains how fostering the optimal conditions for feelings of competence, autonomy and relatedness are critical to creating adjusted and energized learners with better educational outcomes and a stronger sense of well-being. The Learning Disposition Wheel developed from the NRC's *Education for Life and Work: Developing Transferable Knowledge and Skills in the 21st Century* report explains how cognitive, intrapersonal and interpersonal capacities can develop competence, autonomy and relatedness. These capacities can be learnt and taught through mindfully selected pedagogical processes and through a contextual curriculum.

The OECD *The Future of Education and Skills 2030* project argues the importance of agency for students to navigate and create their individual and collective futures. Agency in the OECD *2030* project is described as a sense of responsibility to participate in the world and to influence people, events and circumstances for the common good. It is in *how* learning occurs and the classroom climate it creates, that agency can be developed. Building agency and self-regulation requires paradigmatic shifts in how learning is experienced and facilitated. The development of cognitive, intra- and interpersonal skills can be nurtured through teaching and learning in the Learning Disposition Wheel. Through the Wheel, teachers and students can precisely address their strengths and yet-to-be strengths to develop their disposition to be lifelong learners and people of positive influence in the world. The Learning Disposition Wheel is a coherence maker and tool for teachers and students to explore and develop the complexity of being fully human and agentic. Learning as a capability for transformation is the endeavour of developing all students' and teachers' voices and agency through dispositions for learning.

Concluding reflections

If we consider Greta Thunberg's story, we realize that through her proactive climate change campaigning she found her voice and sense of self. She developed *autonomy* by pursuing something she was passionate about, *competence* in being an effective and disruptive communicator, and *relatedness* through a community who supported her action. Through the lens of the Wheel dispositions, Greta wondered about and investigated the state of the world (*curiosity*) and sought a way to address the pressing needs of climate change to galvanize action (*think why and how*). Her decision to organize a school strike at age 15 was a creative leap (*build new ideas*) that changed our view of how young people can be social influencers. Despite the trolling and negative responses, Greta remains positive, buoyant and committed to the collective support she receives (*teamwork*). Her passion for environmental action gives her a steely resolve to continue with her campaign (*grit*). Greta's inspiring speeches and writing (*make and express meaning*) demonstrate how she can motivate and dynamize young people and adults (*influence*) to act on the existential threat that climate change poses. The confidence that she has developed in pursuing a moral imperative (*focus*) is achieved as a response to the environmental needs of the planet and the long-term concerns for young people's future on earth (*empathy*). Greta Thunberg is developing every aspect of the Learning Disposition Wheel in her agency-building learning experience.

Our students don't have to undertake international environmental movements to be agentic. They do, however, need a sense of purpose, engagement and power to transform their personal and social worlds. As educators we can develop their capacities to achieve feelings of competence, autonomy and relatedness rather than disengagement and disempowerment in their education. Learning can be a capability for enabling and generating agency and transformation. Nothing in teaching and learning is too small to make a difference to the future of our students and the development of their voice and agency. Greta Thunberg said, 'You are never too small to make a difference.'[39] We want every student and teacher to be able to say this.

The next chapter discusses how the metalanguage of the Wheel is central to developing metacognition and deeper learning in the transformation of learning, pedagogy and curriculum.

The Learning Disposition Wheel

5

Inventing the Wheel: necessity as the mother of invention 76

What is deeper learning and why is it a necessity? 77

What is metacognition and why is it crucial for learning? 78

When do you teach and learn the Learning Wheel dispositions? 79

The Learning Disposition Wheel 80

The intrapersonal domain 81

Focus – self-regulated and confident 81
Grit – determined and resilient 83
Curiosity – interested and resourceful 85

The cognitive domain 87

Think why and how – poses questions and solves problems 87
Make and express meaning – connects with and interprets 89
Build new ideas – explores possibilities and perspectives 91

The interpersonal domain 94

Influence – shows initiative and responsibility 94
Empathy – understands and acts for others 96
Teamwork – co-constructs and commits to the group 98

An example of practice: Ecole 42 100

Concluding reflections 101

Chapter 5 The Learning Disposition Wheel

Inventing the Wheel: necessity as the mother of invention

Figure 5.1 The 'evolution' of the wheel.

Dung beetles roll their dung balls, pangolins curl into a rolling ball when attacked, and tumbleweeds break from their roots to roll and spread their seeds in the wind. Rolling exists in nature but nowhere in nature is there a wheel. The invention of the wheel was a completely human innovation. It happened, however, relatively late in human history, perhaps because it wasn't evident in nature. Where was the wheel invented and what can we learn from its invention? In pre-Columbian times a toy dog was crafted by a potter that included wheels (see figure 5.2), but there is no evidence the wheel was developed in Central America for transportation. Richard W. Bulliet, historian and author of *The Wheel: Inventions and Reinventions*,[1] argues that pre-Columbian societies thought using human strength alone (slaves and bonded labourers) was adequate to build their civilization, so the wheel remained with the toy dog. According to Bulliet, it was miners, around 4000 BC in the Carpathian Mountains of Eastern Europe, who decided that wheels for transport were a good idea. But why there, and why then?

In the late Copper Age, surface mining for copper ore was being exhausted, so mining had to go deep into mountains through vertical shafts and tunnels. Getting the copper ore out through the long tunnels for smelting was a problem. The ore was extremely heavy for human hauling, and domesticated animals used for hauling, such as oxen, could not fit in the tunnels and shafts. Bulliet suggests a miner came up with the idea that it was easier to shovel the ore into a bucket mounted on wheels and roll it through the tunnels. Fashioning a fixed axle with wheels that rotate without friction was complicated, fine work requiring metal tools. Tools made from copper were able to chisel the finely fitted holes, axles and round wheels. So, according to this theory, the wheel was born. The necessity and difficulty of extracting copper ore from underground mines was the 'mother of invention'. The Copper Age and copper tools were the required technology necessary to make the wheel.

In the previous chapter, we introduced another wheel, the Learning Disposition Wheel (figure 4.4) as a coherence maker to explore the skills needed for self-regulated learning and agency. This Wheel was developed by 4C Transformative Learning as a tool for teaching and learning. As with the evolution of the wheel for transportation (figure 5.1), necessity and technology can be applied to the development of the Learning

Figure 5.2 A pre-Columbian toy dog with wheels.

Disposition Wheel. The 'technology' required for the Learning Disposition Wheel is human potential itself. Human beings' innate disposition or inherent qualities for agency and deep learning are described in the cognitive, intrapersonal and interpersonal capacities of the Learning Disposition Wheel. These qualities have been evident since the dawn of human history and have allowed humans to adapt, flourish and innovate (and invent things like the wheel). In education, the 'necessity' for developing the Learning Disposition Wheel capacities in all learners has only recently been realized. The necessity for agentic, self-regulated learners capable of deeper learning is being heightened by today's complex, fast-changing, technological and globally connected world. This chapter focuses on describing each capacity in the Learning Disposition Wheel. Together these dispositions contribute to the necessity for self-regulation, agency and deeper learning in our students and teachers. The chapter concludes with an example of practice and a discussion of Ecole 42, a teacher-less university in France which highlights the significance of a learning disposition for deeper learning.

What is deeper learning and why is it a necessity?

Deeper learning is the ability to make connections and transfer skills and understandings from one context to another. Deeper learning occurs when skills and understandings become embedded in the long-term memory, which frees up space in the working memory to allow the embedded long-term knowledge to work with new information.[2]

Deeper learning is required to pose new questions, solve new problems and create new ideas. Inventing the wheel in the copper mines was deeper learning but so is transferring a maths formula to a new physics problem, or using an idea from one sport and applying it to another, or creating an artwork about the history of social isolation in a pandemic or how a school can sustainably reduce their carbon footprint. Rote learning and procedural learning are useful for recall and retention (learning for one-off tests), but poor for transferring knowledge. The National Research Council report *Education for Life and Work: Developing Transferable Knowledge and Skills in the 21st Century*[3] argues that if the goal is to prepare students for success in solving new problems and adapting to new situations in the twenty-first century, then deeper learning is called for.

The Learning Disposition Wheel based on research from the National Research Council's report, describes the skills that can foster deeper, transferable learning. The Learning Disposition Wheel provides teachers and students with a common language or metalanguage necessary for developing metacognition for deeper learning and agency building. Metacognition in learning plays a central role in students' ability to transfer their learning to solve new problems and learn new things.[4]

What is metacognition and why is it crucial for learning?

Metacognition is to be aware of, understand and control our own thinking so that through forethought and self-reflection, adjustments to behaviours and actions can be made. When we learn or perform a cognitive task, metacognition is our ability to select, monitor, manage and evaluate ourselves. It is being conscious of controlling our emotional, cognitive and motivational states when we learn.[5] The Learning Disposition Wheel is a metacognitive device used to explicitly teach and learn the skills of self-regulated learning and agency. The teaching and learning of these skills are best accomplished as embodied experiences when integrated with curriculum learning.[6] Teachers and students can identify, target, experience, practise and assess the skills in the Learning Disposition Wheel through strategies that build strengths and yet-to-be strengths in their learning.

Metacognition using the Learning Disposition Wheel also develops in learners a positive belief in being able to learn. As we explained in the last chapter, students' capacities in the Learning Disposition Wheel are not fixed or set in stone; they can be learnt and continually developed in the right conditions and environment. In developmental psychology, a learning disposition is explained as an oscillation between the public acquisition of skills and our personal identity.[7] The psychology of our innate capacity to learn can also be explained by the biology of our brain's neuroplasticity. Throughout our lives, our human brain architecture is developed and rewired through neuroplasticity.[8] Neuroplasticity refers to the brain's nervous system and its capacity to change its structure and function as a response and adaptation to the environment. Knowing how we can learn and why we can learn creates a positive belief or 'growth mindset', as psychologist Carol Dweck explains:

In this mindset, the hand you're dealt is just the starting point for development. This growth mindset is based on the belief that your basic qualities are things you can cultivate through your efforts. Although people may differ in every which way – their initial talents and aptitudes, interests or temperaments – everyone can change and grow through application and experience.[9]

Our learning capacity is a dynamic between innate ability and the experience and beliefs we develop towards learning. Pedagogy, curriculum and the facilitation of positive and productive beliefs through metacognition and experience are key to developing the dispositions on the Wheel.

When do you teach and learn the Learning Wheel dispositions?

The learning of the dispositions is explicit and experiential. They are not learnt in a vacuum. The learning of disciplinary (interdisciplinary or transdisciplinary) knowledge is deepened by building Learning Disposition Wheel capacities in students. The dispositions in the Wheel, however, cannot be learnt and taught without deep disciplinary knowledge in curriculum learning.[10] They are learnt when they are focused on and integrated with pedagogy and curriculum on a continuing basis. For example, there may be a group of students whose yet-to-be strength is *teamwork*. In a collaborative inquiry into carbon footprints students learn about science, mathematics and geography, and simultaneously focus on learning skills and understanding in how to work as a team. The 'content' of the learning is knowledge in inquiry (the nature of which is shaped by the subject matter), science, maths, geography and *teamwork*. This then means that feedback and assessment should address all these areas of learning, in process and as an outcome.

Another cohort of students may work reasonably well in teams but lack confidence in *think why and how* (being able to pose deeper questions and to solve challenging problems). If the curriculum learning is about how biology and lifestyle determine health factors and personal budgets, the focuses of this learning are biology, health, economics and inquiry through *think why and how*. Integrated with the subject matter learning is how to use reflection and risk-taking to probe and challenge their inquiry with questions within questions. This focus aims to strengthen the students' capacity to *think why and how*. They may use the strength of their teamwork skills to access the diverse thinking of their group to consider multiple angles to deepen their inquiry.

The Learning Disposition Wheel can also be used individually by students to work on certain areas of their learning. For instance, a student may recognize they have strengths in *think why and how* and *grit* in their literacy learning, but these same skills are not being applied to their numeracy learning. In collaboration with their teachers, the student develops strategies to develop their yet-to-be strengths and learning in numeracy. Do they have difficulties with numeracy learning? If so, what are they and why do they have these difficulties? Do they lack confidence with numeracy learning, and if so, why? Do they not see the purpose of numeracy learning, and if not, why not? Developing metacognition in students and teachers, as we have explained, is essential to learning. In this example, teachers develop skills and strategies to meet the individual needs of the student according to content knowledge and pedagogical content knowledge (see chapter 6) in numeracy, combined with general pedagogical knowledge in learning disposition capacities.

The Learning Disposition Wheel

Learning in and through the Wheel dispositions is a continual deepening of lifelong learning practices, made appropriate for any age of learning throughout life. The dispositions in the Wheel are focus, grit, curiosity, think why and how, make and express meaning, build new ideas, influence, empathy and teamwork. We discuss each disposition in the Wheel in detail and frame each with these questions:

- What is this disposition?
- How does this disposition relate to learning?
- How can you learn this disposition?
- How can you teach this disposition?
- What are some deeper questions to explore this disposition?

In 'How can you teach this disposition', we make reference to our coherence maker the Pedagogy Parachute (see chapters 6 and 7). The Parachute is a schema that describes the elements of pedagogy that teachers can use to curate learning experiences that develop self-directed learners. These references to the Parachute are in parentheses and italics. We also use our 4C coherence makers to explain approaches to learning the dispositions think why and how (the Critical Reflection Crucible), make and express meaning (the Communication Crystal), build new ideas (the Creativity Cascade) and teamwork (Collaboration Circles). Each disposition in the Wheel is interrelated to and interdependent on each other. *Education for Life and Work: Developing Transferable Knowledge and Skills in the 21st Century*[11] argues the following:

- Cognitive, intrapersonal and interpersonal dispositions can be taught in a targeted, explicit and experiential way, with guided metacognitive support and reflection.
- Targeting dispositions through scaffolded and sequenced learning can influence other dispositions and reveal other needs and achievements in students.
- Dispositions are best learnt when integrated with curriculum learning.
- Developing belief, motivation and metacognition is necessary for engaged and effective learning.
- Self-regulation and deeper learning are developed through these dispositions and contribute to well-being, agency and increased educational outcomes.

The intrapersonal domain

We begin by discussing the intrapersonal dispositions of *focus*, *grit* and *curiosity* in the Learning Disposition Wheel (figure 5.3). The intrapersonal domain is the capacity of managing our emotions and behaviours to achieve learning goals.

Figure 5.3 Intrapersonal domain of the Wheel.

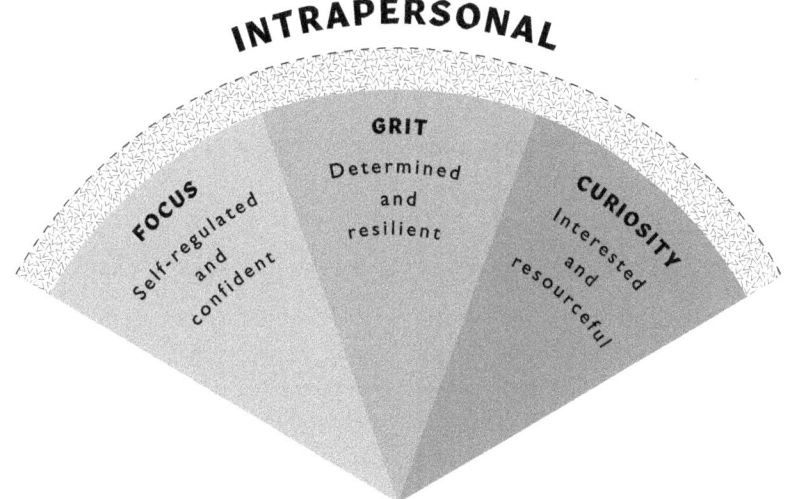

 Focus – self-regulated and confident

What is focus?

Focus is a disposition in self-regulation and confidence. Self-regulation is the capacity to self-monitor emotions and behaviours through perceptions and insights of the self. Self-regulation is developed through self-awareness and metacognition, and reflecting and directing thinking in a positive and focused way. Focus is a sense of mental and physical concentration, self-control and centredness that involves self-awareness, focusing on others and focusing on the environment and the wider world around you.[12] Focus encompasses self-efficacy and feeling positive about yourself, being confident in your abilities and having volition in what you can achieve.

How does focus relate to learning?

The beliefs students hold about learning significantly affect their learning and achievement.[13] The motivation to learn is not a fixed trait[14] – it is a dynamic affected by a learner's inner needs and drives, their goals and interests and their external circumstances such as pedagogy and the classroom climate. Self-efficacy and intrinsic motivation decrease when people lose their sense of autonomy in a controlling, autocratic classroom or school environment with imposed goals, punishments, performance pressures, competition and high-stakes testing.[15] Developing focus and self-determined motivation is associated with engagement, achievement, enjoyment, flexible and conceptual thinking, well-being and better coping mechanisms.[16]

How do you learn focus?

Metacognition supports focus and self-regulation in learners and contributes to feelings of self-efficacy.[17] Metacognition can be classified into three components: metacognitive knowledge, metacognitive skills and metacognitive experience.[18]

- Metacognitive knowledge is what we know about our knowledge, learning and behaviours.
- Metacognitive skills are how we behave or act with a given learning task.
- Metacognitive experience is how we judge our learning and behaviours.

Together, these three metacognitive components contribute to the learning of focus. Metacognition can be developed through mental strategies that support learners to create goals, monitor their progress and reflect on their strengths and yet to be strengths.[19] Generative learning strategies[20] such as summarizing, mapping, drawing, enacting, explaining, self-questioning, teaching and imagining support the development of metacognitive self-regulation. The more learners are metacognitive, the more they can self-regulate. The more learners feel confident in their abilities to self-regulate the more they can initiate and direct their efforts to learn and become active participants in their own learning.[21]

How do you teach focus?

Focus and self-regulation can be developed through pedagogy that promotes student ownership of the learning, awareness of how to learn and positive self-belief.[22] Teachers and students can stimulate metacognition through generative learning strategies,[23] thoughtful questioning and increased wait-time for thinking in classroom interactions (*motivated instruction*, chapter 7). The heightening of awareness through facilitated time in 'noticing' supports learners to monitor and self-evaluate their learning strategies, behaviours and emotions. Embodied learning experiences that involve attending to and regulating the mind with the body followed by reflective dialogue can heighten the development of focus (*reflected experience*, chapter 7). Learning to learn with focus (that is, without the external control of being told what to do) can be gradually developed by scaffolding in self-regulated learning challenges (*discovery scaffolds*, chapter 7). In these challenges, students can be encouraged and affirmed to discover their strengths and yet-to-be strengths in their focus and motivation to learn (*dynamic feedback*, chapter 7). To develop focus, self-regulation and confidence, students should have meaningful choices in the curriculum to pursue their needs, interests and goals.

What are some deeper questions to explore focus?

Using the three components of metacognition, teachers and students can address the following metacognitive questions to develop focus in all areas of learning:

- Metacognitive knowledge: In this learning, what do I already know? How does this learning make me think? How could I apply this learning?
- Metacognitive skills: What can I do to organize myself for this learning? What strategies can I use? What do I need to do to learn more?
- Metacognitive experience: What motivates me when I learn? What do I do, and what could I do when the learning is difficult?

Grit – determined and resilient

What is grit?

Grit is being determined in meeting challenges and resilient in dealing with setbacks or difficulties. Grit is more than working hard and being conscientious, it is the skill of seeking out challenges and persevering with those challenges. Psychologists Angela Duckworth and colleagues define grit as 'perseverance and passion for long-term goals. Grit entails working strenuously toward challenges, maintaining effort and interest over years despite failure, adversity, and plateaus in progress. The gritty individual approaches achievement as a marathon; his or her advantage is stamina.'[24] Grit involves overcoming adversity by finding a positive direction and making ethical choices that are in your best interests and in the interests of others.

How does grit relate to learning?

In learning, the stamina involved with grit is affected by motivation and challenges in what is being learnt. Grit refers to long-term engagement with learning challenges rather than applying short-term intensity to learning. Grit is the setting of goals as long-term objectives rather than achieving short-term goals that are neither too easy nor too hard.[25] Learning grit, however, is developed by progressing from setting short to longer-term goals. Grit describes individuals who stay the course despite disappointment and boredom; however, students can learn the benefit of grit by experiencing the 'pay-off' of persisting with smaller or shorter challenges first. Students gradually learn how to set challenging longer-term goals and how to achieve those goals.

How do you learn grit?

Being determined with a challenge demonstrates grit, but having a challenge also supports the learning of grit.[26] Approaching a challenging learning task with intrinsic, integrated or identified motivation (see chapter 4 and table 4.1) fosters a positive and energized state that evokes feelings of confidence and eagerness, which in turn is a strong motivator of task engagement and persistence. Perceiving challenges as attainable or as an opportunity is crucial for learners to develop hope and optimism[27] (also known as 'critical hope'; see chapter 3). An optimistic attitude supports active coping behaviours and positive expectations of the future when dealing with adversity.[28] Without optimism, challenges can be associated with negative emotions such as stress and anxiety. Positive emotions and experiences of success are critical for students to understand and be motivated by the long-term benefit of applying grit to challenging learning tasks. What students pursue must be of interest to them, as an individual's passion for a goal or challenge is necessary to develop and maintain long-term commitment and grit.[29]

Grit also depends on the learner's resilience. Resilience is being able to adapt positively to a situation that involves difficulties and risk-taking in learning.[30] Rather than seek an easier option, give up, or 'act out' with negative behaviours and emotions, resilience is how we manage and navigate difficulties and risk-taking through cognitive, interpersonal or intrapersonal strategies. For example, these strategies could be the applying of problem-solving to meet a challenge, or working with others to take a risk, or metacognitively knowing mistakes and failure are part of effective learning. Essential to learning resilience is the guiding and motivating of students in how to deal with confusion, frustration, mistakes and failure. Teachers can help students to understand that seeking out challenges and dealing with adversity are integral to success in learning.

How do you teach grit?

Through metacognitive learning, students can understand what motivates them and use goal setting and challenges to develop grit over time (*deliberate practice*, chapter 7). Learning to persevere with challenges and self-directed goals is supported by well-timed feedback. This allows students to experience obstacles and difficulties, and to discover how to deal with adversity by finding positive pathways (*dynamic feedback and discovery scaffolds*, chapter 7). Creativity involves risk-taking in thinking, and grit is necessary and developed in creative learning to respond to uncertainty and ambiguity when playing with possibility (*creative iteration*, chapter 7). Having an attitude of hopeful optimism and using metacognitive strategies helps students to deal with challenges. These attitudes and strategies become learning schemas or mental frameworks that support students to meet future challenges and long-term goals in life (*networked schemas*, chapter 7). To encourage students to follow their passions, the curriculum can be flexible and adaptable, and allow for differentiation so students can undertake learning challenges specific to their needs.

What are some deeper questions to explore grit?

The seeking out of learning challenges and the need for determination, grit and resilience provoke the following questions for students and teachers to consider:

- Determination – What am I passionate about, and how and why does it motivate me?
- Grit – What is my goal or challenge, and what strategies will I use?
- Resilience – What are my obstacles and difficulties to achieve my goal, and how can I overcome them?

Curiosity – interested and resourceful

What is curiosity?

Curiosity is exploring something novel and challenging, and having the resources to be able to pursue it. Curiosity is the interest and desire to explore knowledge, skills and experiences and the mindful immersion and resourcefulness to sustain that exploration. Curiosity can be stimulated by incomplete or uncertain knowledge (epistemic curiosity), by sensory stimulus and experiences (perceptual curiosity), or the social stimulants of wanting to learn more about people (social curiosity).[31] Being curious is to be excited by novelty and challenge. Through exploration of the novel and the challenging, we stretch what we know and what we can do. Psychologists Todd Kashdan and Paul Silvia explain that when people feel curious, 'they devote more attention to the activity, process information more deeply, remember information better, and are more likely to persist on tasks until goals are met'.[32] Being curious is to make meaning of life and to develop a sense of meaning in life.

How is curiosity related to learning?

Curiosity and wanting to know more in learning can motivate students to ask questions, examine images, manipulate objects, research information, seek experiences and persist with challenges.[33] Although curiosity is about seeking out new, unfamiliar and unexpected situations, it has to match a learner's perceived ability to understand those situations.[34] The intense and enduring interest driven by curiosity is dependent on competence and resourcefulness. For instance, if learners don't have noticing skills, communication skills, research skills or risk-taking skills, it is difficult to be curious. Students may need skills and resources that give them confidence to access new knowledge. Curiosity involves having an interest that motivates exploration rather than just enjoyment. In learning there can be enjoyment in doing 'busy', occupying activities, but deeper learning engagement is derived from curiosity and exploring what is challenging and complex.

How do you learn curiosity?

Curiosity is an openness to new experiences and new perspectives, and this is why being curious is to be flexible, adaptable and appreciative of diversity. Being curious about what you don't know means you have to be open to uncertainty, ambiguity and complexity. Curiosity motivates students to learn about and explore the world to challenge themselves. What can prevent learners from being curious is not having choice to find and pursue their interests, not having the resources to know how to wonder and explore, and not knowing the satisfaction and fulfilment that can be derived from being curious. Choice in the curriculum, skills in resourcefulness, and experiences in discovery (and the unexpected) can support the development of curiosity. Kashdan and Silvia argue that the benefits of curiosity are 'greater emotional well-being, perceived meaning in life, vitality, intelligence, perceived competence and control, aesthetic appreciation, tolerance and even preference for anxiety, ambiguity, and stressful challenges, and less negative emotions, authoritarianism, and reliance on stereotypes and dogmatic thinking'.[35]

How do you teach curiosity?

Pedagogy that develops students' capacities to wonder, ask questions and consider the questions and responses of others, and to seek out resources to explore knowledge, is significant in fostering intrinsic and internalized motivation in students (*motivated instruction*, chapter 7). Skills in noticing, awareness, communication and research support the development of resourcefulness. Learning to explore through collaboration is a shared approach to curiosity and can develop students' responsiveness and flexibility to others' varied experiences and perspectives (*collaborative inquiry*, chapter 7). Curiosity may be developed in learners when they have opportunities and skills to discover learning for themselves (*discovery scaffolds*, chapter 7) and when they can explore what they are interested in (*authentic connections*, chapter 7). Curiosity can be fostered through a curriculum that allows students and teachers to seek out their interests and passions.

What are some deeper questions to explore curiosity?

These questions addressing the different types of curiosity can be used to consider how to stimulate and develop curiosity in learning:

- Epistemic curiosity – How can incomplete or uncertain knowledge (for example, how things work, puzzles and mysteries) in learning stimulate curiosity, novelty and challenge?
- Perceptual curiosity – How can a sensory experience (for example, music, art, food, strange sounds and smells) in learning stimulate curiosity, novelty and challenge?
- Social curiosity – How can wanting to learn more about people (for example, seeking out people for conversation, asking questions, noticing what people do) in learning stimulate curiosity, novelty and challenge?

The cognitive domain

We next describe *think why and how*, *make and express meaning* and *build new ideas* in the cognitive domain of the Learning Disposition Wheel (figure 5.4). Cognition is the capacity to think and reason.

Figure 5.4 Cognitive domain of the Wheel.

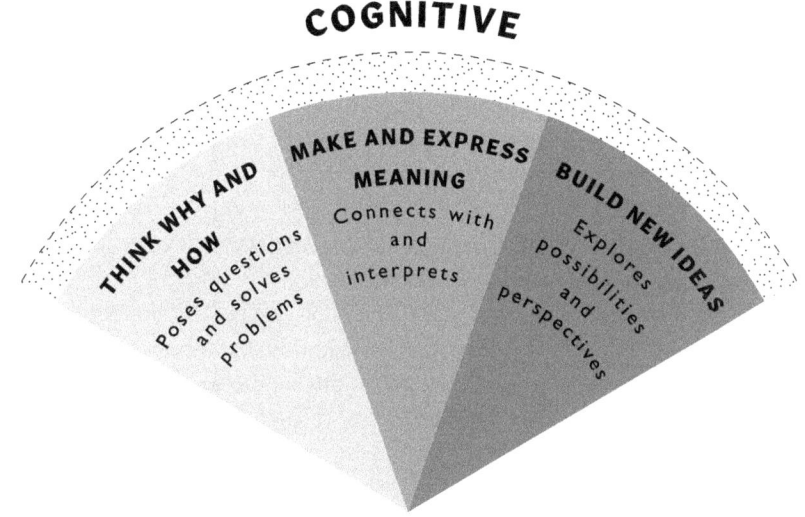

 **Think why and how – poses questions and solves problems**

What is 'think why and how'?

The disposition of *think why and how* is the ability to pose questions and solve problems. It is thinking and reasoning that is also referred to as critical thinking, critical reflection and problem-solving, and although these terms have different emphases, they all inform the disposition of *think why and how*. Educational philosopher John Dewey describes reflective thinking as 'active, persistent and careful consideration of any belief or supposed form of knowledge in the light of grounds that support it, and the further conclusions to which it tends'.[36] To think why and how is to go beyond surface, irrational or compliant thinking and use careful, goal-directed thinking requiring discipline and effort.[37]

How does 'think why and how' relate to learning?

The critical pedagogy philosopher Paulo Freire describes problem-posing in education as a means of realizing human agentic potential to influence and act in the world: 'In problem-posing education, people develop their power to perceive critically *the way they exist* in the world *with which* and *in which* they find themselves: they come to see the world not as a static reality, but as a reality in process, in transformation.'[38] To think why and how is to engage with and respond to the complex problems of life and learning. Learners are empowered to question, pose and shape the manifold issues of their personal and wider social world.

How can you learn to 'think why and how'?

For students to value and enjoy instigating thinking and working things out for themselves, their questions, observations, problems and ideas can be at the centre of learning experiences. We use the 4C coherence maker the Critical Reflection Crucible (see chapter 1) to develop thoughtful and rigorous approaches to asking questions and solving problems in learning. The metaphor of the crucible suggests critical reflection is a melting pot of ideas in the mind that interact to forge re-thinking and new thinking. The Crucible begins with the development of observational powers in close noticing and 'identifying assumptions' or suppositions that underlie what we see, think and do. This is applied to a noticing, question, hypothesis, concern, issue or problem. To identify assumptions is to realize that our perspectives and views are subjective, and often not consciously based on evidence. The seeking of evidence through critical thinking and inquiry is to find the evidence and proof to understand a question, problem or noticing. To ask 'why this?' and 'why so?' is a deeper examination of those assumptions, questions, problems and noticings. These questions can encourage complexity and reflection in thinking and challenge preconceived notions of knowledge and how it is created.

The next part of the inquiry process in the Crucible is conscious and deliberate thinking in solving problems by 'contesting, elaborating and adapting' ideas that have arisen from the assumptions, questions and inquiry. It is learning in how to ask thoughtful questions, imagine possible explanations, infer and draw conclusions, experiment, consult, analyse and judge that refines the inquiry to an understanding or solution.[39] The last part of the learning is 're-solving', suggesting that critical thinking is a continuing spiral of inquiry. Re-solving infers that to *think why and how* is a constant inquiry process to deepen awareness, reasoning and reflection to guide ongoing beliefs and actions in the world. To *think why and how* is a cognitive capacity or way of thinking that continually opens up worlds of meaning.[40]

How can you teach 'think why and how'?

Critical thinking is more effectively developed when connected to the subject matter of the learning and to the world of the learner rather than taught as a skill on its own (*authentic connections*, chapter 7). To *think why and how* can be supported by teacher modelling of questions that develop inference, analysis, synthesis, imagining and decision-making, as well as dialectical exchanges that take opposing points of view (*motivated instruction*, chapter 7). Teachers and students can consider how to ask better questions that illicit noticing, thoughtful reasoning and reflection[41] (*reflected experience*, chapter 7). The diversity of working with others when contesting, elaborating and adapting ideas can enhance the breadth and depth of critical thinking (*collaborative inquiry*, chapter 7). Working across different disciplines in integrated curricula can also promote a diversity in thinking and enrich the capacity for critical thinking.

What are some deeper questions to explore 'think why and how'?

Using the Critical Reflection Crucible coherence maker, the following questions for teachers and students can help deepen their understanding and application of *think why and how*. These questions can be applied to any learning area, such as developing literacy skills or using statistical data or exploring social justice issues or creating a music video or investigating global economics:

- Identifying assumptions – What is the learning about? What are my beliefs about this learning?
- Why this? Why so? – Why is the learning relevant, or why not? Why do I have these beliefs about the learning?
- Contesting, adapting and elaborating – How can posing questions, shaping problems and finding evidence deepen the learning and affect my beliefs about the learning?
- Re-solving – How does posing questions, shaping problems and finding evidence continue the learning and affect my beliefs about the learning?

Make and express meaning – connects with and interprets

What is 'make and express meaning'?

Make and express meaning is how we communicate and create knowledge by connecting and interpreting. Communication involves the connection and interpretation between the internal cognitive structures of the individual mind with the external social environment.[42] Communication is an expression of our identity and who we are, and how we make sense of the world. Communication encompasses the human expression of all knowledge, for instance, literacy communicates knowledge, as does numeracy, the arts, science, religion, etc.[43] Without communication we cannot make and share meaning to develop knowledge.

How does 'make and express meaning' relate to learning?

Make and express meaning is defined by psychology, education and communication researchers Tania Zittoun and Svend Brinkmann as 'the process by which people interpret situations, events, objects, or discourses, in the light of their previous knowledge and experience'.[44] This, they explain, happens at three different levels in learning – the semantic, the pragmatic and the existential. At the semantic level, students learn to communicate or make and express meaning through codes in language, signs and symbols. These different codes (literacy, numeracy, the arts, science, etc.) organize and give meaning and expression to our thinking. Communication at a pragmatic level is specific to our cultural and social practices, and this gives meaning and expression to our cultural and social identity and how we see ourselves in the world. At the existential level, communication is the means by which we develop knowledge and make meaning of our individual lives and our existence. Communication in learning should be understood and developed in all these three levels.

How can you learn to 'make and express meaning'?

We use the coherence maker the Communication Crystal (see chapter 1) to explore the learning of making and expressing meaning. The Crystal begins with being 'alert to messaging' and developing a heightened awareness of whatever is being communicated. It is to ask what is being communicated, why is it being communicated and how is it being communicated. The communication can be through speaking, writing, embodiment, numbers, scientific method, design, formulae, stories, music, etc. Being alert to messaging strengthens an awareness of *how* meaning is constructed and interpreted. 'Enabling voice' in the Crystal develops the confidence to communicate in whatever mode, through opportunity, encouragement and challenge. More meaning is expressed and made through the enabling of a diversity of student voices in the communication of learning. Enabling voice is more than an opportunity to express meaning; it is an expression of our evolving identity and self-concept as we learn with others. This is why *what* we communicate and *what* we learn has to matter to us.

'Conveying meaning and purpose' in the Crystal is to communicate with intention and clarity. The learning of skills to communicate, whether it is speaking, writing, embodiment, numbers or technology, empowers competence in the learners' abilities to make and express meaning. Being able to convey meaning and purpose develops the ability to communicate and this feeling of competence can develop self-efficacy in learners. Knowing *what* and *why* we want to communicate and knowing *how* communication affects ourselves and others are skills and understandings that underpin how we connect with and interpret the world and our place in it. The Crystal explains how making and expressing meaning are communication experiences that lead to the 'generating of action and agency', rather than generating compliance, passivity or oppression. The communication *of* and *in* learning can build positive action and voice. Our self-efficacy is connected to the efficacy of others, so to make and express meaning is to communicate and act in the world with meaning and purpose that is ethical and constructive to others. The Crystal describes how communication can lead to positive and empowering action at a semantic, pragmatic and existential level.

How can you teach 'make and express meaning'?

Efficacy in why, what and how we communicate can be developed through pedagogical opportunities in practising how we make and express meaning in all curriculum areas (*deliberate practice*, chapter 7), supported by feedback and reflection (*dynamic feedback* and *reflected experience*, chapter 7). How to interpret the world through different ways of making and expressing meaning is supported by learning schemas or frameworks that organize how different forms of communication such as literacy, numeracy, technology, the body, etc. make meaning (*networked schemas*, chapter 7). Educational theorist and psychologist Jerome Bruner argues that our culture, rather than biology, shapes our thinking and action, and how we make meaning in learning.[45] Making and expressing meaning is supported by pedagogy and curriculum that connects learners authentically with their cultural and social experiences and what they are interested in and what they are challenged by (*authentic connections*, chapter 7).

What are some deeper questions to explore 'make and express meaning'?

Using Zittoun and Brinkmann's[46] three levels of making and expressing meaning, the following questions can be considered by teachers and students across learning areas in the curriculum:

- Semantic – How does making and expressing meaning in this learning organize and affect the expression of my thinking and the thinking of others?
- Pragmatic – How does making and expressing meaning in this learning affect my participation and interactions with others?
- Existential – How does making and expressing meaning in this learning affect the way I see myself, and the way I view life and the lives of others?

 ## Build new ideas – explores possibilities and perspectives

What is 'build new ideas'?

The cognitive capacity to *build new ideas* is the creative process of exploring different perspectives and imagining possibilities. Creativity is intrinsic to human potential in everyone, every day, everywhere.[47] Building new ideas is a skill that is paradoxically both playful and disciplined in using the imagination, possibility thinking and iterative experimentation to create something new. Psychologist Lev Vygotsky explains that creativity is 'everywhere human imagination combines, changes and creates anything new'.[48] Neuroscientist David Eagleman and music researcher Anthony Brandt[49] describe the generating of new ideas as the cognitive process of *blending*, *bending* and *breaking*:

- Blending is when two or more original sources are merged.
- Bending is when an original source is modified or twisted out of shape.
- Breaking is when the whole original source is taken apart.

Possibilities and perspectives are explored through the blending, bending and breaking of ideas.

How does 'build new ideas' relate to learning?

Something new in 'everyday creativity' is when learners can go from 'what is' thinking to 'what if' thinking.[50] To build new ideas expands the learners' active participation in creating their own learning. Students can expand their experience of the world through acts of imagination to build new ideas. For learners, it is to ask, how can we bring different ideas together (*blending*) and what will it create? Or how can we alter an established idea (*bending*) and what does it create? Or how can we pull something apart (*breaking*) and what does it create? To shape new ideas in this way, learners need to develop a deep understanding of the original source being manipulated. At the same time, the creative process of combining, altering and deconstructing the source develops deeper knowledge.[51]

How can you learn to 'build new ideas'?

The coherence maker the Creativity Cascade (see chapter 1) describes a learning approach for building new ideas. It begins with 'noticing', as a new idea cannot be built without noticing the world (or knowledge) in a deep and detailed way. Noticing is more than recognizing, identifying or observing; it is making what is familiar, strange or normally unnoticed noticed.[52] It could be noticing ideas, concepts, aesthetics, patterns, problems, situations or events. 'Asking why?' in the Cascade then explores perspectives around what is being noticed. It is to ask: what am I noticing and why is it this way? The noticing can be further probed and challenged by asking: 'really why' is it this way? Noticing and asking why develops awareness, expertise and deeper engagement about something from which to build a new idea.

The Cascade describes the process of playing with possibility, which is not to seek solutions but to allow ideas to ebb and flow, emerge and submerge. Whether the ideas that arise are mundane, insightful, mistaken, on the right track, obvious, surprising, dead-ends or profound, they all contribute to the building of different perspectives and possibilities from which the best idea can emerge. From playing with possibility, ideas emerge and the most justifiable, persuasive or compelling are selected and then evaluated for its effectiveness or appropriateness. In the Cascade, this is 'selecting and evaluating'. Using feedback based on the criteria for which the new idea was built and created, the most cogent and effective idea is discerningly selected and evaluated. Creativity researcher and psychologist Mihaly Csikszentmihalyi argues that new ideas have to be recognized as valuable creations or innovations with experts in the field.[53] The new idea cannot just be fanciful, confused or random; it must be recognized as fit for purpose or contributing to the development of further new ideas in an area of the learner's knowledge.

How can you teach 'build new ideas'?

Building new ideas is active participation in knowledge-creation, not the passive receiving or spectating of learning. To engage with the creative process, learners must be passionate about the ideas they are building.[54] Pedagogy can support learners to create new ideas that matter to them (*authentic connections*, chapter 7). Pedagogy can also develop learners' efficacy to have a goal that involves imagining, playfulness and taking the risks of trial and error to allow new ideas to emerge (*creative iteration*, chapter 7). Creative collaborations support and encourage risk-taking and a diversity of perspectives and possibilities (*collaborative inquiry*, chapter 7). To deal with the unpredictability, uncertainty and difficulty of not knowing things when building new ideas, learners can have experiences where they develop the skills and confidence to discover learning for themselves. There has to be, however, a balance between their expertise in an area of knowledge and the challenge to build new ideas (*discovery scaffolds*, chapter 7). Central to the creative process is evaluation of developing ideas, so feedback is used to know whether the idea is or isn't working (*dynamic feedback*, chapter 7). For building new ideas to be developed, pedagogy in classrooms can be accompanied with curriculum structures that allow time for creative processes in learning, and assessments for learning in those processes.

What are some deeper questions to explore 'build new ideas'?

The following questions can be used to consider whether the key features of playing with possibility are evident in the creative process of building new ideas. When playing with possibility:

- Is there unpredictability and complexity in the flow of ideas back and forth?
- Is there a willingness to risk the sharing of ideas whether they work or fail?
- Is there a cross-fertilizing of ideas, but also thinking time to consider different perspectives and possibilities?
- Are there feelings of frustration with challenges but feelings of flow and enjoyment when ideas begin to emerge?
- Is there trust that the rigour, focus and time needed will allow ideas to emerge and lead to a sense of achievement?

The interpersonal domain

The next domain in the Learning Disposition Wheel is the interpersonal (figure 5.5), and this is the capacity to express, interpret and respond to others. The interpersonal dispositions are *influence*, *empathy* and *teamwork*.

Figure 5.5 Interpersonal domain of the Wheel.

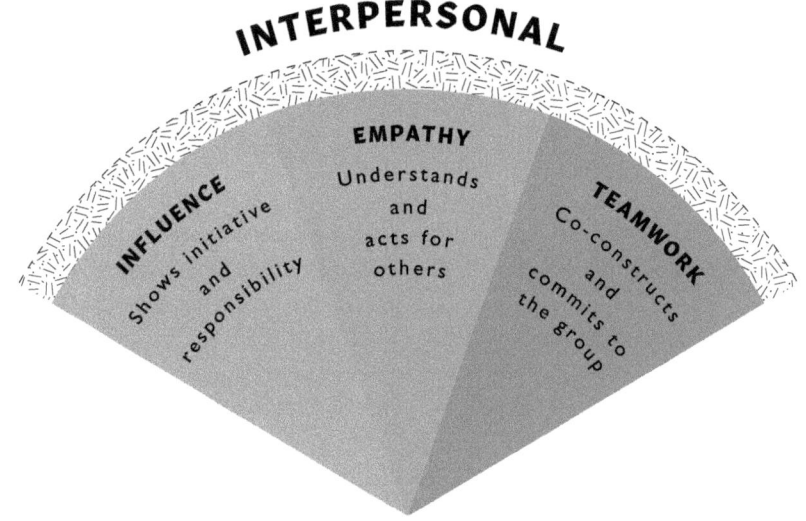

Influence – shows initiative and responsibility

What is influence?

Influence describes the positive impact we have on others through the leadership of taking initiative and responsibility. It also describes how we are positively influenced and led by others to take initiative and responsibility. *Influence* is a proactive behaviour that has an effect on the environment and other people. Being responsible is to consider the wisdom of the influence and whether it is ethical and moral. *Influence* involves a change in behaviour or belief in yourself and others. It is the empowering of the self to take action, but also the empowerment of others to take action. *Influence* is leadership and the enabling and generating of agency in the self and other people.

How does influence relate to learning?

Social ethics researcher Herbert C. Kelman developed a framework[55] to describe different processes of social influence: compliance, identification and internalization.

Compliance as influence is often only temporary, and manifests under conditions of surveillance. It is influence motivated by rewards or approval, or fear of punishment or disapproval. *Identification* as influence is adopted because of positional status and admiration or respect in a relationship. *Internalization* as influence is adopted regardless of surveillance or respect in a relationship because it is intrinsically satisfying and congruent with our own value system. Influence that builds agency in the self and others has to be internalized. Influence is the mindful consideration of agency building in others and the wider social consequences of that influence. Learning to take initiative and responsibility is integral to the development of leadership and wisdom.[56]

How can you learn influence?

Having initiative means taking an active and self-motivated approach to learning or any task rather than being passive and told what to do. Responsibility is influencing others to take an active and self-motivated approach. In learning environments, the more responsibility given to students, the more initiative is taken.[57] The more constrained students are in influencing learning, the less possibility for initiative and responsibility. Redefining students as active leaders of learning rather than passive recipients can build a positive classroom climate for influence. Personal and collective goals and aspirations created by students support the development of pro-active behaviour and initiative in learning.[58] To influence requires the building of trust in relationships and allowing others the opportunity to develop their capacity to influence. Social influence can lead to self-reinforcing dynamics within a group and create a positive classroom climate for learning.[59]

How can you teach influence?

Using collaboration as pedagogy is an opportunity to develop trust and influence (*collaborative inquiry*, chapter 7) when it is supported by developing awareness of the affect we have on others (*reflected experience*, chapter 7). Learning influence and leadership requires a supporting environment where students can create meaningful goals that allow them the flexibility to take initiative and responsibility (*discovery scaffolds*, chapter 7). Influence that builds agency is effective when communicated by questions, wonderings and modelling, rather than telling and external pressures (*motivated instruction*, chapter 7). As with pedagogy, the curriculum can be flexible and adaptive to allow space for students to influence and take initiative in the learning.

What are some deeper questions to explore influence?

To develop influence, initiative and responsibility in learning, these questions can be asked of students and teachers:

- Influence – How do my actions in the learning and the learning environment affect other people and wider social concerns beyond the classroom?
- Initiative – How can I can take action and have a positive effect on others, the learning and the learning environment?
- Responsibility – How can my actions support others to take initiative and responsibility?

 Empathy – understands and acts for others

What is empathy?

Empathy is understanding and acting for others by perceiving the feelings of someone else or imagining how someone else is feeling or experiencing a situation. Psychologists Daniel Goldman and Paul Ekman[60] argue that there are three categories of empathy: cognitive, emotional and compassionate. Cognitive empathy is when we mentally evoke the experience of someone else by imagining what they may be feeling or imagining how we may feel in the same situation. Taking the perspective of others supports our understanding of others' needs and intentions. Emotional empathy is perceiving another person's feelings by reading a person's facial expressions, tone of voice, body language and behaviour. Emotional empathy attunes us to feel another person's inner emotional world. Compassionate empathy is empathic concern that moves us to act in the interest and welfare of others.

How does empathy relate to learning?

Compassionate empathy or altruism is the motivation to act selflessly and wisely in the interests of others. Studies by researchers Daniel Batson and colleagues demonstrate that people higher in empathy are more likely to help others in need, rather than act in their self-interest.[61] Batson describes four main motives for prosocial behaviour:

1. to benefit the self (egoism),
2. to ultimately benefit the other (altruism),
3. to benefit a group (collectivism), and
4. to uphold a moral principle (principlism).

His research found that empathy-induced altruism can be genuinely selfless. The empathy-altruism relationship demonstrates that the learning of empathy enhances prosocial behaviour such as cooperation and collaboration and improves attitudes towards stigmatized groups.[62] Empathy and prosocial behaviours such as helping, generosity and acts of kindness motivate others to act in the same way and lead to a positive learning environment.[63]

How can you learn empathy?

Cognitive neuroscientist Fiona Kerr argues that humans are hardwired to connect socially, and that face-to-face contact is essential to learning and building empathy, eliciting emotion and being able to solve long-term problems. Kerr explains how learning and practice in mindful noticing and responding to empathic cues have long-term effects. Empathy, according to Kerr, 'lengthens and deepens our view switching us into discernment mode – thus shifting our perspective, changing the criteria by which we judge problems and build solutions. It minimises short-termism, forming different neural pathways which nurture foresight and wisdom.'[64] Empathy is learnt by understanding how our well-being and the well-being of others are affected by how we care for, value and act for others, and how empathy in relationships builds trust and a sense of belonging.[65]

Empathic awareness and perspective shifting are supported by learning that involves and nurtures noticing and the imagination. Arts and education theorist Maxine Greene describes the important role the imagination plays in learning empathy:

> . . . imagination is what, above all, makes empathy possible. It is what enables us to cross the empty spaces between ourselves and those we teachers have called 'other' over the years. If those others are willing to give us clues, we can look in some manner through strangers' eyes and hear through their ears. That is because, of all our cognitive capacities, imagination is the one that permits us to give credence to alternative realities.[66]

How can you teach empathy?

Developing empathy through face-to-face contact, embodiment and imagining has ramifications for pedagogy. Empathy can be learnt through embodied opportunities and imagining experiences (*creative iteration*, chapter 7) that harness affective, relational, cognitive and meta-cognitive skills (*reflected experience*, chapter 7). Empathy and trust are necessary for collaborative learning, but in a mutually reinforcing way, learning collaboratively and reflecting on the process helps to build empathy (*collaborative inquiry*, chapter 7). Empathy can be mindfully practised in classrooms as everyday actions to foster a learning culture of understanding and acting for others (*deliberate practice*, chapter 7). Empathy can be applied to the conditions of learning and to learning in the curriculum. As a condition of learning, it is to ask: are the learners empathic to each other? Are teachers empathic to students? Are students empathic to teachers? Empathy as curriculum learning is to ask: how does what is being learnt support empathic awareness, understanding of others and action for others?

What are some deeper questions to explore empathy?

It is useful to consider whether the three categories of empathy are features of the learning:

- Cognitive empathy – How can students use their imagination and take different perspectives in the learning?
- Emotional empathy – How can students be aware of their emotions and read the emotions of others in the learning?
- Compassionate empathy – How can students be moved to take action for others in and beyond the learning?

Teamwork – co-constructs and commits to the group

What is teamwork?

Teamwork is to commit to a group that is co-constructing a shared endeavour through collaboration. Collaboration is more than cooperation, sharing ideas and working together; it is an interdependent relationship that leads to the synergy of everyone's ideas, actions and trust. Everyone in a team has a role to play, and in that role must feel equal and agentic to realize a shared and productive vision. Psychology and education scholars Seana Moran and Vera John-Steiner explain collaboration as 'the intricate blending of skills, temperaments, effort and sometimes personalities to realize a shared vision of something new and useful'.[67]

How does teamwork relate to learning?

The benefit of collaboration is the power to generate ideas and actions beyond what the self is capable of. Vygotsky's theory of proximal development explains how collaboration as a social process consolidates and facilitates learning.[68] Proximal development is the dynamic threshold of what the learner is capable of learning through interactions with others, rather than what they can already achieve alone. To achieve the extending of self through collaboration requires the navigation of complex dynamics in communications and relationships. Individuals should feel changed (emotionally, cognitively and relationally) by the experience of collaboration. Understanding and applying the process of teamwork can deepen our capacity and confidence to problem-solve, create, reflect and act in a complex world. John Steiner says of collaboration, 'By joining with others we accept their gift of confidence and through interdependence, we achieve competence and connection.'[69]

How do you learn teamwork?

We use our coherence maker Collaboration Circles (see chapter 1) to explain learning in the dynamics of teamwork. Collaboration Circles begins with 'offering' and the initiating of an idea or action towards the group's goal. An offer is seen not as a solution but as an idea to allow other ideas to emerge. Offering necessitates everyone's active participation and opportunity to communicate in the group. Collaboration requires an emotional climate of empathy and trust to allow risk-taking and being vulnerable when making offers. The response to offering is 'yielding', which is to connect and elaborate on the offer, rather than ignore or dismiss it. Active listening is critical for yielding and is developed through repeating others' ideas, asking questions about them, and elaborating on what has been said or done. The skills of offering and yielding are the mechanism for building ideas and actions as a team.

Collaboration Circles describes how 'challenging, evaluating and extending' are necessary to explore and deepen the group's ideas and actions. Having to challenge, evaluate and extend in the collaborative process encourages rigorous, divergent and diverse thinking (or actions) from the group and as a process provides psychological safety for group members to probe and question ideas in the group. Questioning assumptions and refining and expanding ideas are developed through reflection, debate and understanding using skills in constructive questioning, offering alternatives, perspective taking, counter-arguing, reasoning, persuading and summarizing. The 'genius' in teamwork is the perspective of different people's thinking to enrich and spark a productive tension in the co-construction of a shared vision. Teamwork leads the group to feel joint ownership in an endeavour if all members have a sense of shared purpose in the process of collaboration. 'Advancing co-constructions and connections' in Collaboration Circles indicates that teamwork is more than just achieving an agreed goal or product. Teamwork in learning can be an experience that focuses on continuing co-constructions and connections between people to build their expertise and agency.

How do you teach teamwork?

Group work is most effective when there are connections between explicit modelling, scaffolds, reflection and feedback in the processes of collaboration.[70] Teachers can create opportunities and experiences that demonstrate the benefits to the individual in teamwork (*collaborative inquiry*, chapter 7). Feedback and assessment can be used to reflect on the role of the individual and the group in the process and outcomes of the collaboration (*dynamic feedback*, chapter 7). A schema like Collaboration Circles is useful in making coherent the practice of teamwork. As a schema, it helps to connect with other schemas (in communication and creativity, for instance) and develops a deeper understanding of teamwork processes (*networked schemas*, chapter 7). Teamwork across all curriculum areas can be developed through explicit and mindful pedagogy in practising collaborative processes (*deliberate practice*, chapter 7). Teamwork is particularly necessary and beneficial in bringing different skill sets together in integrated and transdisciplinary curricula.

What are some deeper questions to explore teamwork?

Individual learners may see the value of teamwork if these questions are addressed in the learning design of collaboration:

- Is the group size appropriate for the task and the capacity of the participants?
- Are the groups arranged to encourage productive dynamics for diversity and growth, both socially and cognitively in the learning?
- Are the learning tasks open and complex for different entry points for learners?
- Are there group goals and individual accountabilities in the learning?
- Is there regular feedback and reflection about the progress and process of the teamwork?

We conclude this chapter with a brief discussion of the university Ecole 42[71] in Paris (figure 5.6) to highlight the necessity of all the skills in the Learning Disposition Wheel.

An example of practice: Ecole 42

Ecole 42 is a free, coding school set up by French billionaire Xavier Neal, who founded France's second largest internet service provider, Iliad. In 2013, he decided that the French education system was broken and he set up his own coding school. Ecole 42 is a university where students self-organize without teachers and work out

Figure 5.6 Students at Ecole 42 in Paris, France.

solutions to problems through project-based learning and collaboration. According to the head of Ecole 42, Nicolas Sadirac, 'We don't teach anything. The students create what they need all the time.'[72] Students depend on their own internal resources and their peers to complete digital projects set for them.

The school tries to replicate what real life in the workforce is like. A student says of the self-directed learning approach at the coding school, 'Sometimes I want a teacher so I can get to the solution faster but when I get the answer myself it's more self-gratifying.' Sadirac says Ecole 42 is 'not about learning' because learning and memorizing 'makes you less agile'.[73] Instead the school emphasizes creativity and problem-solving rather than knowledge acquisition. At Ecole 42 it appears creativity, communication, collaboration, critical thinking and agency are recognized as necessary for learning and essential to success in the real world of coding and digital industries. Is Ecole 42 illustrative of schools of the future?

Although free, only the academically able students can access Ecole 42 (they complete a logic exam to qualify for entry and then a month of tests to get a place). To be a student there, you already have to be highly competent in learning disposition skills such as grit, focus, think why and how, teamwork, etc. Ecole 42 does not intend to offer learning for everyone. Education researcher Kyle Peck points out that the peer-to-peer learning system at Ecole 42 is novices helping novices, and this is problematic. He argues that there is a place for expert wisdom in learning when shared at the appropriate time.[74] Ecole 42 is successful in many ways, but it gives opportunities to students who already have strengths in the capacities of the Learning Disposition Wheel.

As educators, we are dedicated to giving all students the opportunity to develop their potential and their interests at whatever capacity. In education, this necessitates opportunities for everyone to learn the Wheel's dispositions.

Concluding reflections

Some years ago, when we shared and discussed the Learning Disposition Wheel with a politician visiting a school, his response was somewhat dismissive. He said, 'Well, it's not rocket science.' Our reaction was that if it wasn't rocket science, why wasn't self-regulated learning and agency everywhere in education? We argue that the Wheel is a simple entry point to understanding and exploring what is actually complex. Facilitating our own learning capacities and the learning capacities of others is as difficult as, or harder than, rocket science. Learning how to facilitate deeper learning is both complicated and complex (see chapter 1). If education does not address and develop the Wheel capacities through deep, experiential and reflective learning, access to schools like Ecole 42 is only ever for those already equipped with learning dispositions. Our mission as teachers is for equity and access to education. We can transform learning by developing learning dispositions in all young people so they can navigate their futures with greater confidence and success.

The next chapter examines the role of pedagogy in transforming learning.

Transforming pedagogy
Curating learning

6

A story of curation: MONA 104	How can the 4Cs support the enabling of transformative pedagogy? 113
Curation of pedagogy and curriculum 105	Creativity and transformative pedagogy 113
What is pedagogy? 106	Critical Reflection and transformative pedagogy 114
What are the challenges for teachers and pedagogy? 108	Communication in transformative pedagogy 115
Is there an explicit pedagogical knowledge base for teachers? 109	Collaboration in transformative pedagogy 116
How does pedagogical knowledge affect learning? 110	Curating transformative pedagogy 117
What is pedagogical content knowledge? 110	An example of practice: LearnLife in Barcelona 118
What is general pedagogical knowledge? 111	Concluding reflections 120
What is transformative pedagogy? 112	

A story of curation: MONA

A visit to the Museum of Old and New Art (MONA) on the sparsely populated island state of Tasmania in Australia often begins with a rather spectacular boat ride up the Derwent River. Once you arrive, you enter a museum that lures you deep underground into a large, dark, subterranean, sandstone cavern. As you descend and explore the museum you realize the gallery spaces are a labyrinthine architectural artwork in themselves (see figure 6.1). In these spaces you encounter intriguing objects from antiquity that are juxtaposed with provocative, contemporary artworks. As you wander in this mysterious world, you begin to realize the objects reflect a preoccupation with sex and death. Whether you appreciate the art or not, your senses are stimulated, your thoughts challenged – it is an unforgettable experience.

MONA is a private gallery open to the public, owned and founded by David Walsh who made his millions from the proceeds of gambling. The artwork and the museum are the idiosyncratic and provocative vision of Walsh and his team of curators, designers and architects. MONA is a curatorial experience of not only the artworks, but also the experience of arriving there and exploring its space and environment. There are no labels or explanations on the art, only a visual and aural personal technology device called 'The O' (see figure 6.2). The O knows where you are in the museum and offers a choice of information about artworks depending on where you are and what you want to know. On The O, you can choose 'Gonzo', for David Walsh's personal take on the artwork; or 'O Minor', family friendly information; or 'Art Wank' for art connoisseurs; or interviews with particular artists. The experience is framed by the museum's curation but also by a sense of playfulness with the visitors' wonderings and wanderings. Although the gallery has to consider pedestrian flow and public safety, there is no authorised way to explore the museum.

Figure 6.1 Tunnels and chambers at MONA (the Museum of Old and New Art) in Tasmania, Australia.

Figure 6.2 The technology device called 'The O' gives visual and aural information about the artworks at MONA.

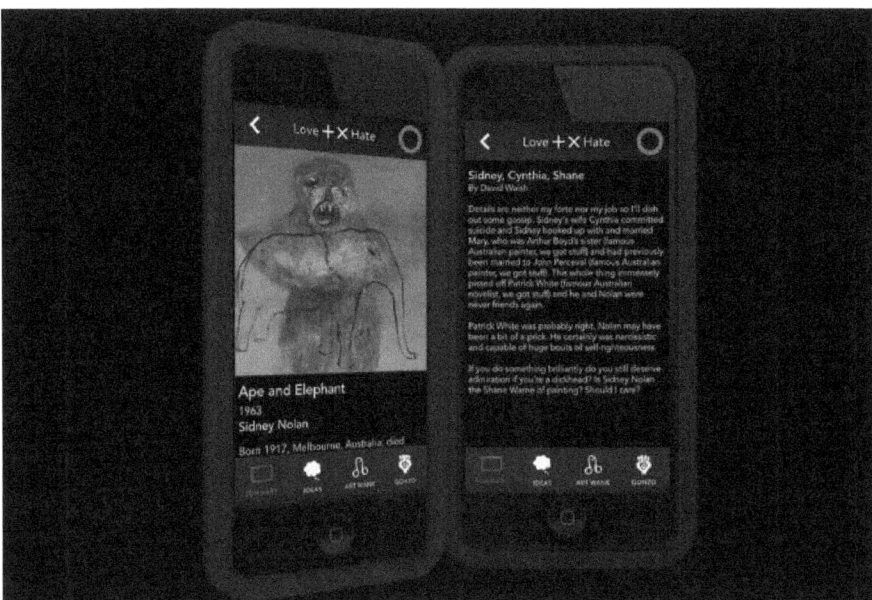

For Jane Clark, the Senior Research Curator, MONA's curatorial approach with The O technology allowed the museum to be nimble, flexible and responsive. The intent of MONA, she says, is to be a museum of ideas: 'Our exhibitions are there for a purpose. And so if you don't use The O, you may miss out on the reason that David's spent his money and made so much effort to share his collection. He doesn't – we don't – want to tell people what to think, but we really do want people to think.'[1]

So, what has the MONA story about curation got to do with transforming pedagogy?

Curation of pedagogy and curriculum

Just like MONA's curatorial experience, the classroom should not be about telling students what to think but should stimulate them to think and feel through a curated learning experience. Through choices in pedagogy and curriculum, expert teachers curate learning experiences for students to think and feel. We have opened this chapter on transforming pedagogy with the MONA gallery experience to illustrate the significance of the act of curation in creating an experience that is purposeful, interactive and offers choice. It is an interactive experience that affords agency to the participants. We liken this gallery experience to the kind of experiences that can develop learner agency described in chapter 4. To allow for and build learner agency, teachers can be curators of learning that is purposeful, interactive and offers choice.

Michael Bhasker, author of *Curation: The Power of Selection in a World of Excess*,[2] examines how with information and data overload, curation has transferred from museums and art galleries to the internet and business. Rather than computer algorithms suggesting to us what we might like or what we might need, he argues that we increasingly need the idiosyncratic selections that humans make – like the owner, David Walsh makes at MONA. Bhasker describes curation in this way:

> Curation can be a clumsy, sometimes maligned word, but with its Latin root *curare* (to take care of), it captures this irreplaceable human touch. We want to be surprised. We want expertise, distinctive aesthetic judgements, clear expenditure of time and effort. We relish the messy reality of another's taste and trusted personal connection. We don't just want correlations – we want a why, a narrative, which machines can't provide.[3]

Educators are expert curators who can provide students with rich opportunities to discover, imagine and be surprised by learning. To curate pedagogical choices, teachers develop a deep and ever-evolving knowledge about learners, learning deeply, and why we learn what we learn. It is expertise that takes time and effort, it can sometimes be messy and there are aesthetic judgements made by teachers to create those experiences. Teachers are the curatorial 'human touch' of learning, but in the end, we believe that through transformative pedagogy for deep and self-directed learning, students can be curators of their own learning.

This chapter highlights the central role that teachers and their pedagogy play in the experience of students' learning. We firstly examine what is pedagogy and what it means in relationship to learners and the curriculum. We explore why pedagogy is a critical capability in education and how a pedagogical knowledge base can support teachers as mounting evidence suggests that the process of *how* we teach is equally if not more significant than *what* we teach. We focus on the concept of *general pedagogical knowledge*, which helps introduce the coherence maker we present for pedagogy in chapter 7 (the Pedagogy Parachute). Pedagogy for transformation is then discussed as both a collaborative and autonomous culture of learning for students and teachers that can be sustained through 4C processes in creativity, critical reflection, communication and collaboration.

Our curatorial choices for pedagogy and curriculum essentially depend on our knowledge of learners and learning, our emergent and developing knowledge of pedagogy and our deep inquiry about the *why* and *how* of the *what* in learning. Teaching is a complex process and we endeavour to bring some coherence to that complexity. We begin by considering what pedagogy is.

What is pedagogy?

The word pedagogy comes from ancient Greek and literally means the 'leading of the child'.[4] Pedagogy has come to refer to the knowledge base that connects teaching to the theories and practice of learning. The education and linguistics sociologist Basil Bernstein describes pedagogy's place in learning this way: 'Curriculum defines what counts as valid knowledge, pedagogy defines what counts as valid transmission of knowledge, and evaluation defines what counts as a valid realization of the knowledge on the part of the taught.'[5] If the curriculum is how knowledge is organized, pedagogy according to Bernstein is the framing and messaging of the learning. Pedagogy is the way learning is 'transmitted' and connected to and experienced by the learner. How learning is experienced through the process of pedagogy fundamentally affects the characteristics of the learning and the learner. Pedagogy defines the *how* of what is taught, and the *how* has a profound effect on *what* is being learnt.

If we return to the MONA curation analogy, an artwork is about the viewer's experience interacting with and interpreting the curated artworks. The art is defined by the interaction of the viewer with the works as a curated experience. Like the gallery experience, curriculum learning is defined by the interaction of the learner with curated experiences. Teachers curate interactive experiences between the learners and the curriculum. This interactive concept of curriculum, teaching and learning is explored in the Didaktik tradition[6] from Europe.

Didaktik is a teaching and learning philosophy that explains how learners make sense and meaning of the curriculum through the relationship between the why, what and how of learning. Essentially a Didaktik approach does not overpower students with knowledge but allows them to develop their own access to knowledge. The Didaktik approach considers how pedagogy can inform and inspire learning by deeply examining the why of the curriculum learning and creating experiences that every learner will make sense and meaning of in different ways. For example, rather than knowing the history of the Second World War, or knowing fractions, or being able to sing a certain song, exploring the *why* of curriculum learning is to ask:

- What can we learn about people and the world today by understanding the course of the Second World War?
- How do fractions of what we count help us to navigate the world?
- How does learning a song affect how we think and feel?

In these examples, the meaning of the curriculum is explored and made sense of by each unique, individual learner in a different way (this is explored in the Learning Disposition Wheel through *focus* as metacognition and *think why and how*, see chapter 5). How a teacher chooses to allow the content of the curriculum to emerge and make meaning for the students depends on teachers' curation of pedagogy. Curating teaching and learning choices in how the curriculum is explored recognizes that teachers and learners have an autonomous role in the way learning is experienced. It is to acknowledge that there is ambiguity and complexity in a pedagogical process that opens up possible, individual pathways for every learner.

How we teach can be linked to the *why* and *what* of the curriculum, and as such, teaching can be a sophisticated 'dance' and exploration of these considerations and relationships. If teaching does not consider these relationships, it is not curation but a procedural delivery of curriculum content. Understanding and responding to learners, learning and the curriculum is what defines expert teaching. Curating learning is, however, a complex process, and it is ever more complex with the increasing demands teachers are dealing with. These challenges, if acknowledged and understood through pedagogy, can strengthen teacher professional knowledge.

What are the challenges for teachers and pedagogy?

In 2017, the Organisation for Economic Co-operation and Development (OECD) released the report *Pedagogical Knowledge and the Changing Nature of the Teaching Profession* to address challenges in the teaching profession. The report suggests developing a pedagogical knowledge base as one of the key strategies to strengthen teaching as a profession. It argues the need to develop pedagogy begins by looking at teachers' knowledge of teaching and learning and working out how teachers can adapt their practice to meet new educational demands in a rapidly changing environment. The report says:

> Evidence of the key role teachers play in the success of school systems is growing, while at the same time expectations regarding teachers are becoming increasingly more complex. Teachers are no longer merely expected to transmit information, rather they need to facilitate that all students acquire the knowledge and skills and adopt the attitudes that enable them to become citizens who live a life they value and who can effectively contribute to the 21st century society. As education needs to adapt to an environment characterised by changes in society, the labour market, technology etc., teachers are required to revisit and update their skills continuously.[7]

Teachers are key to the effectiveness of students' learning[8] yet their context and role are becoming ever more complex, requiring them to be continually flexible and adaptive in their practice and in the learning of professional knowledge. In discussing the dynamics of knowledge in the teaching profession, the report acknowledges that new research and contemporary perspectives on teaching and learning are not making inroads into school cultures across OECD countries.

> We do not know . . . to what extent this new research has penetrated into the educational sphere. Some have suggested that it is not sufficiently integrated, and mention a lack of a coherent and integrated knowledge base for education as a potential reason . . . or that a large part of teachers' knowledge is implicit rather than explicit, making it difficult to be codified and thus transferred or shared within the profession. While there has been much speculation about why teachers' knowledge is thought to be outdated, the dynamics underlying the knowledge base of the teaching profession are still not well understood.[9]

To get a sense of teachers' perception of their pedagogical knowledge base in our professional learning setting with schools, we asked teachers what they thought pedagogy was. Some of the responses were:

- 'the philosophy of teaching',
- 'research and theory',
- 'the teacher's belief system',
- 'the experience of learning',
- 'the big picture',
- 'the why of teaching and learning',
- 'a combination of strategies and programmes',
- 'informing teaching and learning', and
- 'forming the basis of why you do what you do'.

All these descriptions were right to some extent, but the responses indicate that teachers find the concept of pedagogy amorphous, abstract and intangible. Is pedagogy a concept tacitly understood by teachers rather than one that can be explained explicitly? In other words, is it an 'aerosol word?

Is there an explicit pedagogical knowledge base for teachers?

Education academic David H. Hargreaves, in comparing teachers to doctors, argues that doctors' medical competence necessitates drawing on a knowledge base comprising anatomy, physiology, pharmacology, etc. that has become the technical language of the medical profession. Teaching, on the other hand, cannot draw from a knowledge base or technical language largely due to a culture that dichotomizes theory and practice. According to Hargreaves:

> There is no agreed knowledge-base for teachers, so they largely lack a shared technical language. It was once hoped that the so-called foundation disciplines of education – psychology, sociology, philosophy and history – would provide this knowledge-base and so were given great importance in the curriculum of teacher training . . . Unfortunately, very few successful practising teachers themselves had this knowledge-base or thought it important for practice. It remains true that teachers are able to be effective in their work in almost total ignorance of this infrastructure. After qualification teachers largely abandon these academic influences and the use of social scientific terms within their professional discourse declines: the disciplines of education are seen to consist of 'theory' which is strongly separated from practice. Trainee teachers soon spot the yawning gap between theory and practice and the low value of research as a guide to the solution of practical problems.[10]

The 2017 OECD report argues that a pedagogical knowledge base can be developed through collaborative praxis (teacher research and practice) and rigorously engaged with by teachers throughout their careers. The report contends that pedagogy takes time and deliberate practice and 'expert teachers are effective at helping their students learn successfully because of quick decision-making that hinges on a well-developed foundational pedagogical knowledge base'.[11] We also argue that the education community is better served if a teacher's career can involve a rigorous and continual engagement with a dynamic, coherent and integrated knowledge base in pedagogy.

How does pedagogical knowledge affect learning?

In Germany, educational researchers Jürgen Baumert and colleagues[12] investigated the impact of pedagogical knowledge on student achievement in mathematics. They found that teachers' higher level of pedagogical content knowledge has more impact than the content knowledge of the subject matter (mathematics). Their results revealed that teachers with higher levels of content knowledge were better able to align the subject matter with the curriculum; however, higher levels of content knowledge had no direct effect on supporting students when learning difficulties arose. It was pedagogical content knowledge that significantly affected the quality of learning. In another study, educational psychologists Thamar Voss and colleagues[13] investigated the relationship between students' perceptions of the quality of teaching and a teacher's general pedagogical knowledge and knowledge of learning processes. Their study found that students of teachers with higher general pedagogical/psychological knowledge reported higher cognition activation, better engagement, better student-teacher relationships and higher teacher awareness of students' problems with learning. The 2017 OECD report claims that 'research thus far is beginning to show that teachers' general pedagogical knowledge is relevant to understanding quality teaching as understood by its impact on student learning outcomes'.[14]

But what is meant by general pedagogical knowledge? In figure 6.3 we illustrate the relationship between general pedagogical knowledge, pedagogical content knowledge and content knowledge. First, we explain what pedagogical content knowledge is.

What is pedagogical content knowledge?

Educational psychologist Lee Shulman defined pedagogical content knowledge as the knowledge that integrates the content of a specific subject and the pedagogical knowledge of teaching that particular subject. Pedagogical content knowledge, he claimed, 'represents the blending of content and pedagogy into an understanding of how particular topics, problems and issues are organized, represented, and adapted to the diverse interests and abilities of learners, and presented for instruction'.[15] Teaching

Figure 6.3 A diagram illustrating the relationship between general pedagogical knowledge, pedagogical content knowledge and content knowledge.

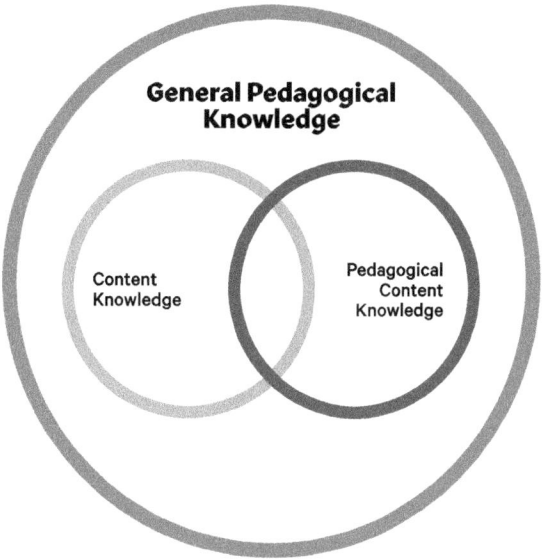

reading, for example, has specific pedagogical content knowledge such as the way teachers introduce sight words and phonics. In science, teaching the process of scientific method is integral to its pedagogical knowledge. In design, the elements of design and the processes of design-based thinking are pedagogical content knowledge, or in music, how aural skills are developed is pedagogical content knowledge.

What is general pedagogical knowledge?

Shulman defined general pedagogical knowledge as the principles and strategies of classroom management and organization that are cross-curricular.[16] General pedagogical knowledge is pedagogies that are common to all learning and can be applied generally across the curricula and classroom practice. For example, the processes of learning to read described above are related specifically to the pedagogical content knowledge of teaching literacy, but more generally the pedagogy of using sight words and phonics is a learning scaffold. The general pedagogical intent of a learning scaffold is to guide and prompt learning. An example of a learning scaffold in another subject is the use of concrete materials for counting in mathematics. The concept of a learning scaffold is applicable to any learning area and is general pedagogical knowledge. Pedagogical content knowledge specific to a learning area, like teaching students how to read, is necessary knowledge for a literacy teacher. Literacy teachers also need general pedagogical knowledge, such as knowing how learning scaffolds work for the learner and learning. General pedagogical knowledge explains how students learn in any context and with any content.

Since Shulman's seminal work, general pedagogical knowledge has become central to developing a common framework for pedagogy across curricula. More recently the definition of general pedagogical knowledge has been re-conceptualized to combine teaching and learning processes. For instance, researchers Voss, Kunter and Baumert's[17] model for general pedagogical knowledge comprises aspects of pedagogical knowledge as well as what they term a teacher's psychological knowledge of learning processes and the knowledge of cognitive, social and affective-motivational characteristics of individual learners (knowledge we explore through our Learning Disposition Wheel, see chapter 5). In their model for 'general pedagogical/psychological knowledge', there are five sub-dimensions:

1 knowledge of managing the learning (awareness, engagement, momentum of the learning),
2 knowledge of what teaching methods (e.g. direct instruction, discovery learning) to use, how to apply them and when to use them for student involvement,
3 knowledge of the purposes and forms of formative and summative assessment and their impact on student motivation,
4 knowledge of learners, learning processes and strategies to support, encourage and foster individual learning progress, and
5 knowledge of individual learner characteristics (e.g. ADHD, dyslexia, cultural background) that affect cognitive, motivational, emotional needs

Voss, Kunter and Baumert's dimensions for general pedagogical knowledge illustrate how teachers are navigating and making decisions in a complex classroom system involving classroom management, teaching methods, knowledge of learners and learning, and assessment. To achieve this, expert teachers require extensive pedagogical knowledge, content knowledge, problem-solving skills, the abilities to adapt and modify for diverse learners. They also need skills in decision-making, improvisation, noticing and perception, challenging learners, and giving timely and motivational feedback, testing assumptions, knowing and respecting students and having a passion for teaching.[18] We argue that the capability of transformative pedagogy and the 4Cs can support teachers to understand and plan for this complexity.

What is transformative pedagogy?

Transformative pedagogy generates the circumstances for deeper, transformative learning. Transformative pedagogy creates the conditions for teachers and learners to develop confidence and agency within a collaborative culture of learning. It is pedagogy that encourages the vitality of human relationships and inter-dependence, as well as nurturing human autonomy and independence. Education theorist Jack Mezirow,[19] describes transformative learning as 'learning that transforms problematic frames of reference – sets of fixed assumptions and expectations (habits of mind, meaning perspectives, mindsets) – to make them more inclusive, discriminating, reflective, open, and emotionally able to change'.[20]

At the core of transformative pedagogy is the wisdom of critical consciousness and awareness informed by moral-ethical values affecting the way we make sense of the world and act in the world.[21] Transformative pedagogy is about creating dynamic and authentic learning experiences that are personally and socially transformative. It is pedagogy informed by:

- creativity that enables possibility,
- critical reflection that fosters metacognition,
- communication that generates agency in learning, and
- collaboration that advances co-construction.

How can the 4Cs support the enabling of transformative pedagogy?

Processes in the 4Cs (creativity, critical reflection, communication and collaboration) enable teachers to engage continually with a general pedagogical/psychological knowledge base with awareness, inquiry and decision-making. In our work with schools, we use processes inherent to our 4C coherence makers to equip and enhance teachers' expertise with the general pedagogical skills of classroom management, teaching methods, knowledge of learners and learning, and assessment. We describe examples of how each of the 4Cs can support teachers to deal with the complexity of classroom learning and how the 4Cs help to generate a dynamic pedagogical knowledge base for teachers.

Creativity and transformative pedagogy

Creativity learnt by teachers through our schema, the Creativity Cascade (see chapter 1), begins with deep noticing of the context, and then questioning and analysing those noticings. Based on this deeper engagement with the context, teachers can then play with the possibility of ideas for future directions. The generating of ideas is where risk-taking and playfulness allow for the releasing of the imagination and for spontaneous, divergent thinking. From the possibilities, ideas are selected and evaluated and from this, emergent ideas are iteratively explored and refined. Creativity for teachers is the inspiring process of dealing with the uncertainty of problem-solving and the possibility of new ideas. In the classroom, creativity can empower teachers to improvise and respond to what arises in the learning. Expert teachers tread the paradoxical line of planned structures for learning while simultaneously responding and improvising spontaneously to what is revealed in the learning (see flexible purposing in chapter 8). A spontaneous improvisation for a teacher may happen, for example, from a student's question, or an interesting anomaly in a group's idea, or a noticing in an experiment, or a relevant world event or incident that occurred in the learning that is worthy of or necessary for exploration.

Creative processes enable teachers to generate new ideas to problem-solve learner difficulties, to co-teach in new, more effective ways, to co-plan learning programmes and to co-reflect on what can be improved or done differently. Creativity and particularly collaborative creativity foster a more dynamic, interesting and engaging learning environment in the school or organization. Creativity allows for the emergence of new ideas in the classroom, and through creativity teachers can generate new pedagogical knowledge.

Critical Reflection and transformative pedagogy

Through opportunities and learnt processes in critical reflection, teachers can make insightful decisions and judgements about their learning context and practice. The coherence maker the Critical Reflection Crucible (see chapter 1) frames, for example, a process we use called 'Deep Noticing and Action' (see the DNA Eye in figure 6.4). This is a process where teachers develop continuous reflections into their own (and others') classroom context. To make informed pedagogical decisions, teachers notice

Figure 6.4 The Deep Noticing and Action Eye.

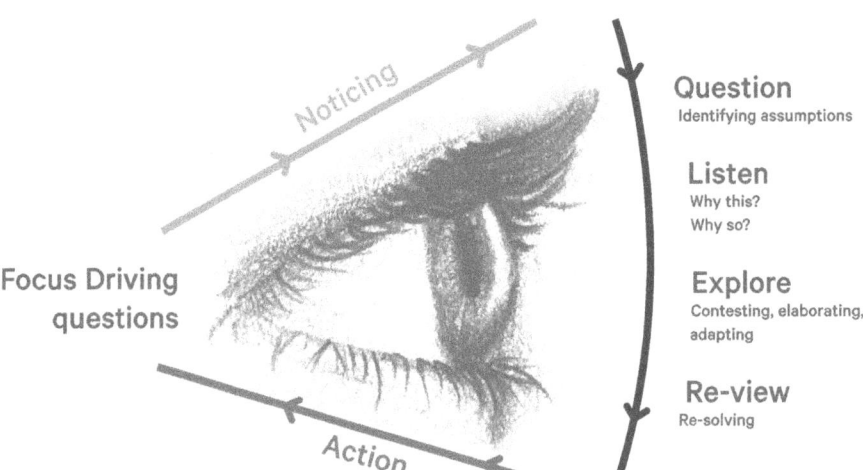

and interpret the situation-specific context of the learning and the learners.[22] 'Noticing' refers to the teacher's ability to bring mindful attention to relevant moments and facets of the learning and the needs of the learners as it occurs in the classroom. The DNA process is a 'post-noticing' or 'about-action' collaborative inquiry prompted and facilitated by questions that allow teachers to reflect critically on their noticings (and others' noticings). By exploring their assumptions, asking why and contesting, elaborating and adapting their noticings, they take action (with collegial support) to re-solve their ongoing inquiry into their practice. Critical reflection is learning how to stand back from our experience to develop insight and to feel empowered to take action to change future experiences.

Critical reflection is fundamental for the ongoing growth of teachers as professionals. The skills of critical reflection can be understood, learnt and sustained as a habitual mindset in individuals and in the collective learning culture of schools. This is our starting point for all of the 4Cs; they are learnt skills that underpin the operating of a teaching and learning culture of a school.

This means learner critical reflection is essential to the culture of the classroom as well. Learner critical reflection and inquiry is feedback for teachers' critical reflection inquiries. The opportunities for teachers to reflect on and research their practice is captured by educational thinker Lawrence Stenhouse, who argues that 'it is not enough that teachers' work should be studied; they need to study it for themselves. What we need is a different view of research which begins with our own work and which is founded in curiosity and a desire to understand; which is stable, not fleeting, systematic in the sense of being sustained by a strategy.'[23] Critical reflection is a strategy vital to *becoming* a teacher and *being* a teacher, and it supports teachers to be learners able to engage with and grow their own pedagogical/psychological knowledge base. We discuss this further in chapter 9.

Communication in transformative pedagogy

The processes described in our coherence maker the Communication Crystal (see chapter 1) enables pedagogical decision-making and critical reflection in and about teacher practice. Being alert to the messaging of others and enabling other voices opens the space for empowering dialogue. If communication processes do not allow for a heightened awareness of our own messaging and the messaging of others, or the opportunity for all voices to be heard, there is no space for empathy, vulnerability and trust. Without empathy, vulnerability and trust, there can be no honest and thoughtful dialogue focused on developing the individual and collective inquiry of teachers into their own pedagogical knowledge base. This is the case with the DNA process referred to above. In this process, the discussion with teachers is formally structured and facilitated so that active listening is developed, and all voices are heard without judgement. The communication strategies develop the trust, honesty and encouragement required for reflective self-awareness and the taking of action for growth.

The type of communication that supports critical reflection and learning is focused and purposeful, conveying clear meaning and an intentional purpose that generates future action and a sense of agency. True and empowering communication skills are learnt through scaffolded processes that teach the metacognition of communication. Mezirow argues the communication conditions for free and full participation in true discourse require:

- full accurate and complete information,
- freedom from coercion and distorting self-deception,
- openness to alternative points of view: empathy and concern about how others think and feel,
- the ability to weigh evidence and assess arguments objectively,
- greater awareness of the context of ideas and, more critically, reflectiveness of assumptions, including their own,
- an equal opportunity to participate in the various roles of discourse, and
- willingness to seek understanding and agreement and to accept a resulting best judgment as a test of validity until new perspectives, evidence, or arguments are encountered and validated through discourse as yielding a better judgement.[24]

Teachers can learn and be empowered by their colleagues and their learners through true communication. Communication that generates agency builds people's sense of identity, empowering them to act in the world. It is communication that gives teachers greater agency to explore transformative pedagogy.

Collaboration in transformative pedagogy

Collective, collaborative capacity, argues Michael Fullan, 'generates the emotional commitment and the technical expertise that no amount of individual capacity working alone can come close to matching'.[25] A school environment that encourages ongoing and dynamic opportunities for collaboration of shared endeavours such as co-teaching, co-planning and group critical reflection enhances and motivates teacher learning and innovation in pedagogical knowledge.

The learning schema and processes of our coherence maker Collaboration Circles (see chapter 1) support teachers to experience the process and benefits of collaboration. The coherence maker begins with all participants (co-constructors) offering and yielding ideas rather than silencing, blocking or coercing ideas. In one of our 4C processes for planning a learning program for instance, we use playing cards to allow all voices in the group to put forward ideas (offering) and to accept and elaborate on those ideas (yielding). Then further cards are used to challenge, evaluate and extend those ideas to avoid groupthink. 'Playing the cards' in the collaboration process diversifies and deepens ideas and allows the best idea to develop and emerge. Like true communication processes generate agency in participants, true collaborative processes (rather than just cooperating and working together) enrich and enhance individual thinking through the connections of co-construction.

Beyond individual schools, the shared endeavour of true collaboration can be expanded to learning and connectivity between schools and beyond, with learning partnerships. The Donaldson report (*Teaching Scotland's Future*) in 2011 was a major review and revision of Scottish teacher education, and it argued:

> Education policy should support the creation of a reinvigorated approach to 21st century teacher professionalism. Teacher education should, as an integral part of that endeavour, address the need to build the capacity of teachers, irrespective of career stage, to have high levels of pedagogical expertise, including deep knowledge of what they are teaching; to be self-evaluative; to be able to work in partnership with other professionals; and to engage directly with well-researched innovation.[26]

The skills of true collaboration in teaching, reflecting, planning and inquiry enable teachers to engage with and evolve pedagogical knowledge, and their knowledge of learners and learning. Collaboration is a commitment to co-constructing ideas through a shared endeavour that can motivate and activate a teacher's passion for teaching.

The 4Cs (creativity, critical reflection, communication and collaboration) are capabilities that can motivate and deeply engage teachers with their pedagogical knowledge base. The 2017 OECD report claims that 'existing evidence suggests that teachers' pedagogical knowledge is relevant to understanding quality teaching as understood by its impact on student learning outcomes. On the other hand, evidence also shows that the quality of instruction requires not only knowledge about teaching and learning, but is also influenced by teachers' affective, motivational and self-regulatory characteristics.'[27] Ongoing teacher learning through 4C processes can develop a pedagogical knowledge base for teachers to revisit, adapt and transform their practice with motivation, commitment and integrity. Through the 4Cs, teachers can meet the diverse needs of their learners and respond to the complex and rapid social, technological and economic changes of the twenty-first century. But what teaching methods can teachers use to curate particular experiences for learners?

Curating transformative pedagogy

No longer can teachers be one-way deliverers of information in a world where information can be delivered through the technology of a click or a swipe or a dab or voice recognition request or the movement of an eyeball. Instead a teacher's 'delivery' of knowledge should evolve as a curation and facilitation of a learning experience. In *Rethinking Teacher Quality in the Age of Smart Machines*, education academic Yong Zhao argues for a new approach where teaching is not to instruct, but to create opportunities and possibilities for individual students' passions and talents. In this paradigm:

> Teachers are curators of opportunities and resources for learning. They critically examine, thoughtfully select, and carefully construct a 'museum' of learning opportunities to expose students to different possibilities and resources. These opportunities and resources are curated in response to each student's needs. They guide students through these opportunities and help them develop individualized pathways of learning. They provide necessary support to help students make use of these opportunities.[28]

We also view teaching and learning in a paradigm that supports the development of self-directed learners. Understanding and manipulating pedagogy is critical for teachers to know *how* to create learning experiences that can develop autonomous learners. But what kind of pedagogy can teachers use to curate these learning experiences?

An example of practice: LearnLife in Barcelona

LearnLife in Barcelona (figure 6.5) is dedicated to innovation in education and creating a learning paradigm that places the learner at its centre. This 'education startup' is structured around the dynamic of personal and adaptive group learning to develop the skills of learner self-direction. The LearnLife model adapts learning to the uniqueness of the individual learner's abilities, prior learning and passions, and focuses on capacities to develop agile, lifelong learners that deeply understand themselves, others and the world. What pedagogy does it use to achieve these goals?

The LearnLife model uses a toolbox of twenty-five diverse methodologies that can best meet the needs of their learners, develop self-direction and create learners as active change agents in the world. They have based their pedagogy on a constantly evolving knowledge base of multiple methodologies, listed in table 6.1.

LearnLife offers a smorgasbord of teaching and learning approaches based on pedagogy that is place-based or process-based. The choice of subject matter and process methodology is open, challenging and authentic for students. But what are the pedagogical *elements* that make up these powerful and compelling approaches to methodology? What are the essential elements of transformative pedagogy that nurture the growth of self-regulated learners in all these LearnLife approaches?

Figure 6.5 Students learning at LearnLife in Barcelona, Spain.

The innovative methodologies at LearnLife indicate different approaches to pedagogical content knowledge; however, what is the general pedagogical knowledge common to them all? How can we understand what is elemental to transformative pedagogy?

We have endeavoured to address this issue in the creation of a schema or coherence maker called the Pedagogy Parachute that we introduce in chapter 7. The Parachute is not a definitive version for transformative pedagogy or pedagogy generally, but it does present a way to access, understand and explore the foundations of pedagogical methodology. It offers teachers a common language and instrument to build their pedagogical knowledge base.

Table 6.1 The diverse methodologies at the school LearnLife in Barcelona, Spain

• Place-based learning	• Social entrepreneurship-based learning
• Experience-based learning	• Learning by tinkering/making
• Peer-to-peer, crowd-sourced and social learning	• Authentic learning – real world activities
	• Passion projects – learning without limits
• Project-based learning	• Deep dive learning and deeper learning
• Challenge-based learning	• Mobile learning
• Play-based learning	• Learning through adventure
• Nature-based learning	• Internship based learning
• Sustainability-based learning	• Boot camp learning
• Phenomenon-based learning	• Agile learning
• Game-based learning	• Research-based learning
	• 'Open space' learning

Concluding reflections

This chapter highlights the critical role teachers and their pedagogy play in learning. Pedagogical choices are a dance of learner needs, how learning can happen and how learners may make meaning of the why and what of the curriculum. For this reason, pedagogy is a complex interaction to curate. Pedagogy is transformative when it is responsive to learners and gives them the skills to generate their own learning and knowledge. The significance, power and complexity of pedagogy in learning means a pedagogical knowledge base is critical for teachers to engage with and to develop throughout their professional career. We explain how the 4Cs – creativity, critical reflection, communication and collaboration – underpin the processes for teachers to expand and challenge their pedagogical knowledge base, whether it is pedagogical content knowledge or general pedagogical knowledge.

As we continue our work in schools, teachers recognize there is a gap in naming and understanding pedagogy to curate learning experiences for deeper and self-directed learning. We have endeavoured to address this gap in the creation of a schema or coherence maker called the Pedagogy Parachute explained in chapter 7. We have developed the Pedagogy Parachute to support teachers and ultimately learners to understand how teaching and learning can work. The Parachute aims to make learning about pedagogy explicit and coherent by describing the 'elements' of pedagogy. It offers a common metalanguage for teachers to learn about, recognize and apply pedagogical processes based on what they know about their learners, learning and the why and what of the curriculum. It works as a schema to identify, codify, critique and assess why and how pedagogy is working and for what purpose. Using specific pedagogies at specific times is to 'fly' the Parachute; the objective is to 'land' on the Learning Disposition Wheel and deeper curriculum learning. The Pedagogy Parachute is part of a suite of knowledge that teachers can use to curate the optimal conditions for students to make sense and meaning of deep learning experiences.

We opened this chapter with MONA's museum experience as a way to explore the concept of curation. At MONA, the gallery experience endeavours to be as interactive for visitors as possible. Although the visitor has the free will to explore the museum in any way they wish, there is a purposeful, curatorial experience that allows choice. How artworks are experienced at MONA exists in the structure and environment of the museum, in the choice and juxtaposition of the artworks presented, the experience of The O device, and the interest and response of the visitors (MONA uses the terms 'reverie/anxiety' on their website). This chapter focuses on how the development of a pedagogical knowledge base can support the curatorial role teachers have in creating learning experiences that foster self-determination and co-determination in their students.

The word 'curation' (like 'bespoke', 'artisan' and 'transformative') has come under attack or been satirized as a fashionable buzz word in recent years. Journalist Alex Williams of *The New York Times* writes that 'the word "curate", lofty and once rarely spoken outside exhibition corridors or British parishes, has become a fashionable code word among the aesthetically minded, who seem to paste it onto any activity that involves culling and selecting'.[29] Curation with its derivation from the Latin root, *curare* (to take care of), from *cure* (care, concern, responsibility), is the appropriate word to describe how teachers can respond to, support and challenge the learning needs of students. Teachers take care of and are responsible for creating purposeful and effective learning opportunities for students. We introduce the Pedagogy Parachute in the next chapter to support teachers to curate learning for all of their students.

The Pedagogy Parachute

A short history of the parachute 124

The Pedagogy Parachute origin story 127

The Pedagogy Parachute as a schema of elements 128

What are the theoretical underpinnings of the Pedagogy Parachute? 130

How do the elements of pedagogy work in the Parachute? 132

The elements of the Pedagogy Parachute 135

Networked Schemas 135
Motivated Instruction 137
Discovery Scaffolds 139
Deliberate Practice 140
Dynamic Feedback 141
Authentic Connections 143
Collaborative Inquiry 145
Creative Iteration 146
Reflected Experience 148

Concluding reflections 149

A short history of the parachute

One of the first known sketches of a parachute is by the great polymath, Leonardo da Vinci in 1514 (see figure 7.1). It is a rigid pyramidal structure designed to use the drag principle to slow the fall of a human being. It was the creation of da Vinci's fervid imagination since there was no real need for a parachute, unless you needed to jump from a burning tower without endangering your life. Another renaissance polymath, Fausto Veranzio, built on da Vinci's parachute by keeping the square frame and replacing the canopy with a bulging, sail-like cloth (see figure 7.2). It wasn't until the eighteenth century when experimentation with hot-air balloons emerged that parachutes had a practical reason to exist. Up until then, parachutes were used by exhibitionists and stuntmen to jump off tall towers and jump out of hot-air balloons, and live to tell the tale. Only after a number of hot-air balloon accidents was it recognized that the parachute could save lives.

In 1797, André Gamerin made the first descent in a frameless, silk parachute from a hot-air balloon (see figure 7.3). The first recorded emergency landing by parachute was in 1808, when Polish aeronaut Jordaki Kuparento descended safely from a burning balloon over Warsaw. Despite a succession of experiments, however, the parachute remained crude, impractical and unreliable throughout most of the nineteenth century. There was the oscillation problem of the parachute swinging wildly back and forth in descent, and there was the problem of the parachute being cumbersome to carry around. It wasn't until late in the nineteenth century that the parachute was folded and packed in a bag, but there were still accidents. Franz Reichelt was testing his wearable parachute and jumped to his death from the Eiffel Tower in 1912. It was at the turn of the century, however, with the advent of

Figure 7.1 Leonardo Da Vinci's sketch of a parachute, 1514.

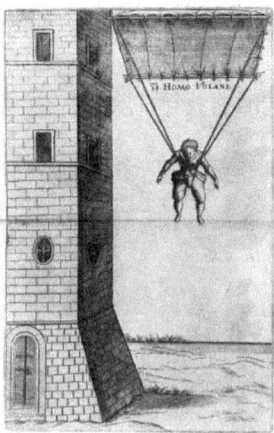

Figure 7.2 Veranzio's Parachute, 1615.

Figure 7.3 Garnerin's use of frameless parachute in 1789.

the aeroplane that the parachute as a successful safety device came to fruition. Through a rigorous scientific approach, pioneering inventors like Charles Broadwick, Georgia Broadwick, Albert Berry, Štefan Banič and Pino experimented with the parachute's many issues such as the release problem, solved by the ripcord and pilot chute. In 1916 during the First World War, an Australian pilot was the first to escape successfully from a disabled plane over the Russian front using a parachute. The invention of the aeroplane led to the parachute as the 'deployable aerodynamic decelerator' of today.

The history of the parachute demonstrates that an idea can be first conceived and imagined, and like da Vinci's sketch sometimes just begins as a thought experiment and possibility. From there the idea of a parachute underwent experimentation through trial and error. The design of the parachute was methodically refined when it was recognized as a safety device for aeroplanes. Without a clear purpose, an invention or idea isn't fully formed or developed. Ideas are evolved and refined when they have a clarity of purpose and use. It is then that the idea can flourish.

Like the aerodynamic parachute, the origin story and development of our coherence maker or schema, the Pedagogy Parachute, is an idea that has been gestating for some time in education. Skills in how to teach have been implicit to successful learning, but as we argued in chapter 6, this professional knowledge hasn't necessarily been explicit or coherent. As demands on teachers grow, the need for a pedagogical knowledge base is ever greater. The US National Academy of Sciences in their 2020 report, *Changing Expectations for the K-12 Teacher Workforce: Policies, Preservice Education, Professional Development and the Workplace*,[1] concluded:

> There are more explicit demands placed upon K–12 teachers today. There continues to be an increase in the level of content and pedagogical knowledge expected of teachers to implement curriculum and instruction aligned to newer content standards and deeper learning goals. Teachers are called on to educate an increasingly diverse student body, to enact culturally responsive pedagogies, and to have a deeper understanding of their students' socioemotional growth. Integrating these various, layered expectations places substantially new demands on teachers.[2]

As with the origin of the aerodynamic parachute, there is now a pressing purpose for cohering knowledge about pedagogy to support teachers with the complex demands of schooling. Understanding and using pedagogy more explicitly can provide clarity and allows pedagogical knowledge to evolve and expand. The development of the Pedagogy Parachute schema is our endeavour to make coherence of pedagogy that develops deep learning and self-directed learners. And like the descending parachute, the Pedagogy Parachute is going through iterations (without harming anybody) in a quest to find the most effective way for educators to understand, explore and use pedagogy. So, how did the Pedagogy Parachute emerge?

The Pedagogy Parachute origin story

As educational researchers and practitioners, we set out to name and synthesize the elements of transformative pedagogy. We began by looking at the theories and research of pedagogical knowledge to generate a list of concepts and terms. Based on our praxis, we distilled the list down to ten elements. We used two words or terms to describe the element most accurately, and within those terms were an entry-level and higher-order pedagogical practice. A metaphorical concept emerged when we were creating a diagram that depicted how the elements were equally interrelated to each other and related to theoretical underpinnings. The diagram looked like a parachute, and as we explored the metaphor it became apparent that it helped explain how the elements (making up the parts of the canopy) have to work together (to 'fly' the parachute).

We introduced our first iteration of the Parachute to a group of sixty teachers and leaders across some schools we partner with, and they explored the Parachute through four full-day workshops over a period of six months. From their responses, our observations and collected data, we refined the Parachute and reduced the elements to nine, and terms were reworked. We developed rubric definitions and a continuum for each element that was then investigated in detail by a working group of experienced educators from a range of educational institutions (primary, secondary and tertiary) and curriculum backgrounds. Over six months, the rubrics, continuum and design for the Parachute were scrutinized and challenged by this group. The more they worked with the Parachute, the more they realized the Parachute's potential as a powerful tool for teachers to deeply understand and develop their pedagogical practice.

As a culmination of these validation phases, a final version of the Pedagogy Parachute and the rubrics were introduced to another diverse group of eighty educators and students over two workshops. We were surprised by the depth of engagement and understanding from this group, given the dense complexity of concepts they were exploring. The pedagogical elements of the Parachute are:

- Networked Schemas
- Motivated Instruction
- Discovery Scaffolds
- Deliberate Practice
- Dynamic Feedback
- Authentic Connections
- Collaborative Inquiry
- Creative Iteration
- Reflected Experience

We have designed rubrics for teachers to apply the Parachute elements in their lesson programming, to codify their learning from collaborative classroom visits (CCVs, see chapter 9) and to identify teachers' ongoing reflective inquiries and research into their own practice (through DNAs, see chapter 6).

In this chapter, we describe each element of the Pedagogy Parachute so educators can begin to develop a common understanding and metalanguage for pedagogy. The implicit and tacit knowledge of pedagogy is made explicit and coherent through the language of the Parachute, and the exploration and action of pedagogy in the classroom. Pedagogy can be applied, integrated and imagined depending on the teacher's curation of the pedagogical elements for the learning experience required.

The Pedagogy Parachute is designed as a tool for educators to discern the pedagogical methodologies that can develop the skills of the Learning Disposition Wheel and deeper engagement with curriculum learning. The Pedagogy Parachute can provide a connection to research into pedagogy and be used as a learning, planning and evaluation tool by teachers to develop, extend and deepen their pedagogical practice. To curate pedagogical choices, teachers develop a deep and ever-evolving knowledge about learners, learning deeply, and why we learn what we learn. How then does the Pedagogy Parachute work as a schema to explain pedagogy?

The Pedagogy Parachute as a schema of elements

As a schema (or coherence maker), the Pedagogy Parachute (see figure 7.4) endeavours to codify and integrate elements of pedagogy that generate self-directed learners and deeper learning as general pedagogical knowledge (see chapter 7). The elements describe the essential teaching methods that transcend curricula and are common to expert teaching in any context. The Pedagogy Parachute is a learning schema that breaks down pedagogy into its constituent parts or elements, although most often these elements work together in powerful combinations. It is in distilling pedagogy down to its elements that we can name them, see them and understand how they work together.

We have used the diagrammatic image of a parachute to represent the elements of pedagogy. Our use of the parachute as a metaphor is both playful and high stakes in its messaging about the role, manipulation and significance of pedagogy. We argue that the identified pedagogical elements in the parachute canopy support the development of self-regulated learning. The elements of pedagogy can be curated by teachers according to the needs of the learners. Teacher professional judgement is knowing which string to pull in the parachute for what purpose and when. If teachers pull on one string or one element in the Pedagogy Parachute for most of the time, the parachute does not fly. If one element is overemphasized such as *motivated instruction*, the parachute does not open, and to use the language of parachuting, will fall 'like a roman candle'. All the connected and equally significant elements of pedagogy in the

Figure 7.4 The Pedagogy Parachute.

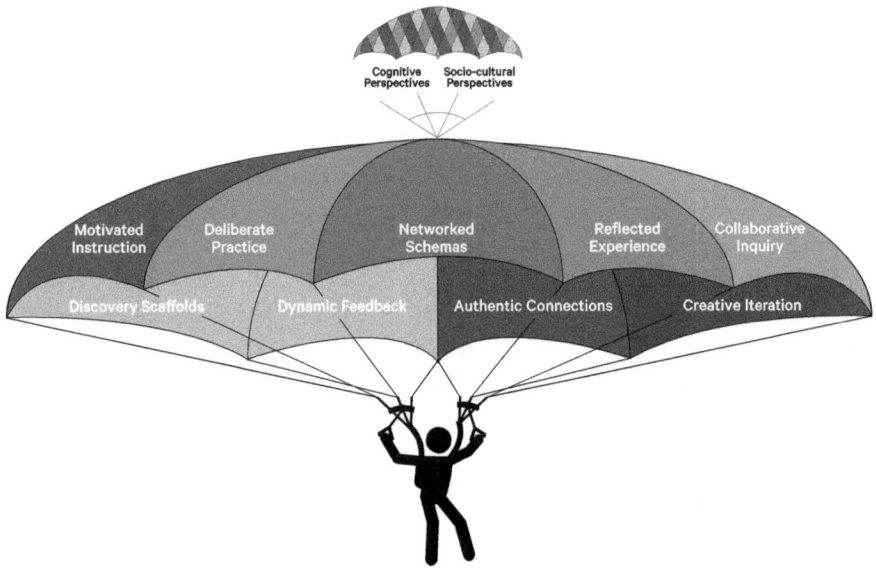

parachute canopy can be used and manipulated at the appropriate time for the appropriate circumstance to guide the learner to self-direction and deeper learning.

The metaphor for the Pedagogy Parachute is not perfect. When flying with a parachute you cannot control each panel of the canopy, but you do manipulate and control the parachute with toggles connected to steering lines. These are used to guide the parachute depending on where you want to go, where the winds take you, how long you want to be in the air, and how fast or slow you wish to descend. This is our metaphor for the decisions that teachers make to guide the experience of the learning. To begin, the parachutist is the teacher making pedagogical choices based on the needs and interests of the learner. Ultimately the learning experiences crafted and curated by teachers can lead to learners being the parachutist making pedagogical choices for their own learning.

In chapter 5, we argued learning is more effective when learners are empowered to know the mechanics of how learning works in their own brain and body (metacognition). We apply the same notion to pedagogy, for not only should teachers have the toolkit of the elements of pedagogy but learners as well. Yong Zhao argues for a paradigm shift where teachers 'need to be able to help students develop the ability to create their own learning ecosystem'.[3] We argue that integral to building the learner's own ecosystem is building essential pedagogical skills in learning how to learn. There are two interrelated aspects critical for the development of the elements in the Pedagogy Parachute. The development of teacher skills and understandings are intertwined with the development of learner autonomy to self-direct their learning.

The essential elements of pedagogy in the Parachute schema emerge from theories and research from both cognitive and sociocultural perspectives represented in the pilot chute. Most Parachutes have three chutes: the main parachute, a reserve parachute and a small pilot chute above the canopy used to open the main parachute. The elements of pedagogy in the main parachute cannot be deployed without the theories and research of the pilot chute. In figure 7.4, the pilot chute has a harlequin pattern, suggesting that these two perspectives (cognitive and sociocultural) are not dichotomous but inform and intermingle with each other.

All the elements in the Parachute are of equal importance and can work together, but where they are organized in the canopy helps to clarify and support their meaning and relationship with the other elements and with the theoretical underpinnings in the pilot chute. The elements of pedagogy are often combined, and a teacher's skill depends upon their knowing why, when and how to use a pedagogical element. Using different elements of the Pedagogy Parachute also depends on the depth and expertise of learning required. We argue that over a period of time, all elements of the Parachute are utilized for the development of self-directed learners. To create the best learning opportunities for students, teachers begin by asking: 'What are the research and theoretical underpinnings for the pedagogies we are using?'

What are the theoretical underpinnings of the Pedagogy Parachute?

In the history of education, scholars have conceptualized knowledge and learning in many ways. Sociologist Basil Bernstein's meta-theoretical analysis of education (see figure 7.5) gives an overview conceptualizing the overarching perspectives influencing knowledge about pedagogy. In Bernstein's pedagogical matrix there is a vertical axis of theories that emphasize learning competencies emerging within the individual (intra-individual) to those theories that emphasize learning emerging from the relations between social groups (inter-group). There are also theories on a horizontal axis that emphasize teacher centred instruction of knowledge (transmission) to those that define the teacher as a facilitator of learning knowledge (acquisition). These two axes intersect to define and explain a typology of pedagogical theories and approaches.

In Bernstein's matrix, our approach to transformative pedagogy combines theories and research of intra-individual and inter-group learning and supports a transition from teacher-centred to student-centred, self-directed learning. In our Pedagogy Parachute diagram (see figure 7.4), we simplified the many pedagogical theories to two larger sets of knowledge: cognitive perspectives and sociocultural perspectives. Cognitive perspectives view knowledge as being individually constructed in the brain's cognitive architecture, underpinning how we think and act. Sociocultural perspectives view knowledge and dispositions as being culturally shaped by the environment. The elements of pedagogy in the Parachute are derived from both these

Figure 7.5 Adaptation of Martin and Rose's[4] (2005) adaptation of Basil Bernstein's matrix of pedagogical theories and approaches (1990).

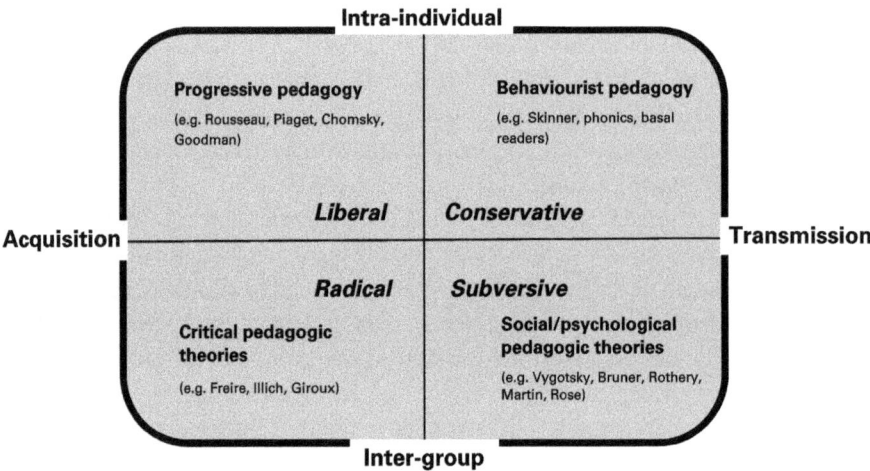

sets of knowledge, some more from a cognitive perspective, and others more from a sociocultural perspective. These two overarching perspectives in education inform each other in a dynamic way. It is in this dynamic we can better understand deeper, authentic learning. Education academic Stephen Billett argues the bridging of the two perspectives is necessary to understand how learning can be situated and transferable across contexts:

> ... situated learning necessitates a bridging of the contributions of socio-cultural and cognitive theories. It is proposed that learning cannot be understood without considering the social contribution to the mutually transforming process of appropriation. Taken together areas of complementarity between the cognitive and socio-cultural constructivist perspectives enrich these two perspectives, thereby providing a basis for understanding thinking and acting which they could not achieve on their own. Together, these combined contributions have the capacity to transform views about learning, the transfer of knowledge and expertise.[5]

Education researcher Knud Illeris also integrates the cognitive and sociocultural perspectives in his approach to learning theory, as 'all learning implies the integration of . . . an external interaction process between the learner and his or her social, cultural or material environment, and internal psychological process of elaboration and acquisition'.[6]

Cognitive and sociocultural perspectives are also interrelated with the growing field of neuroscience and brain plasticity. Plasticity refers to the way the brain changes its neural structure in response to experiences. Connections in the neural structures of the brain can be created, eliminated or strengthened depending on environmental and experiential circumstances. Researchers in epigenetics (the study of changes in organisms that does not involve alterations in the DNA sequence) are investigating how genes and experience interact and affect the expression of genes and shape the development and preferences of individuals. Researchers Daniel Ansari and colleagues argue that 'neuronal plasticity is the result of a complex interplay between experience, biology and individual differences. This is an important point for educators to be aware of because it shows that the knowledge and behaviour of students in their classrooms is not the result of one variable alone, but a complex interaction of experiential and biological factors.'[7] The convergence of cognitive and sociocultural perspectives in education emphasizes the continuous influence that the individual mind and social culture have on each other in teaching and learning.

The elements of the Pedagogy Parachute are a confluence of cognitive and sociocultural perspectives. Education theory and research is complex and evolving, and the Pedagogy Parachute can be a coherent entry point for teachers to engage with and inform their pedagogical knowledge base. The Pedagogy Parachute allows teachers to consider the theories that underpin their developing practice and supports understanding of why they do what they do, to better meet the needs of their learners. To engage with the research and theories of pedagogy, we will explore in more depth the elements of the Pedagogy Parachute and how they work.

How do the elements of pedagogy work in the Parachute?

Pulling pedagogy apart and distilling it to its essential elements is like pulling atoms apart. The natural state of the pedagogical elements is their connections with the other elements, but it is in pulling them apart we can see them, name them and explore their individual characteristics and better understand their relationships with other elements. We can use the periodic table of chemical elements (see figure 7.6) to explain how the creation of a schema can organize the parts and relationships of a connected whole. The periodic table separates the elements into a sequential order, but the structure of the table also organizes connections and patterns across the elements at certain intervals according to their properties. Like the periodic table, the Pedagogy Parachute infers connections and relationships between the elements of pedagogy. All the elements in the Pedagogy Parachute are of equal significance and work together, but where they are organized in the parachute canopy helps to clarify and support their meaning and relationship with the other elements and with the theoretical underpinnings in the pilot chute.

There is no hierarchy in the elements; they are equally significant and all interrelate. No one element of the Pedagogy Parachute works in isolation, but it is

Figure 7.6 The periodic table for chemical elements.

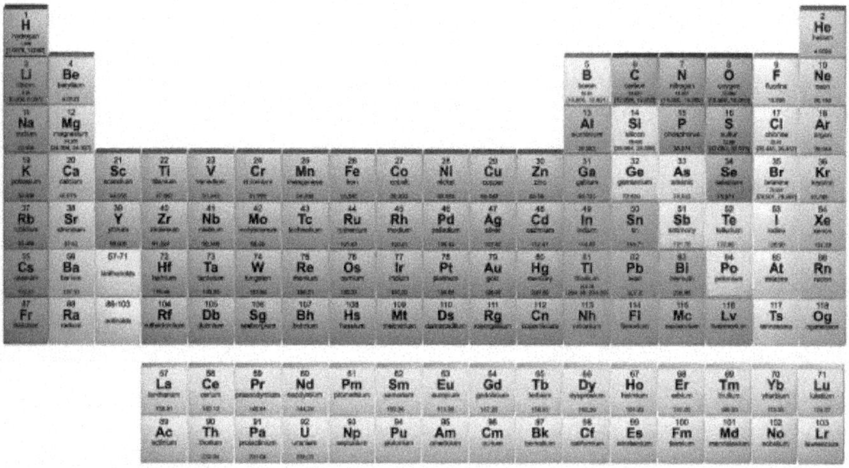

through knowing the parts that we can understand and cohere the whole. For instance, to reflect on an embodied experience can contribute to a scaffolded discovery. Or motivated instruction may be a form of feedback that galvanizes a collaborative inquiry. Or deliberate practice may work hand in hand with creative iteration. Or authentic connections may help network schemas and so on. Some learning may emphasize certain elements in the parachute more than others, depending on the needs of the students and why 'what' is being learnt. Using a range of pedagogical elements in the Parachute can support the development of self-directed learners and deeper learning experiences.

In breaking down each of the elements of pedagogy, there is a progression in the learning of that pedagogy (see figure 7.7). For instance, the element *discovery scaffolds* begins with teachers using *scaffolds* and progresses to teachers facilitating *discovery scaffolds*. Understanding and applying *scaffolds* is an integral step to the higher-order practice of teachers implementing *discovery scaffolds* as pedagogy for deeper and autonomous learning. We recognize that through experience, reflection and inquiry, teachers continue to develop expertise in the depth and breadth of pedagogical practice by integrating and imagining the possibilities of all the pedagogical elements in the parachute.

There are two interrelated aspects integral to the development of using the elements in the Pedagogy Parachute. The development of teacher skills and understandings is intertwined with the development of learner agency and self-direction. The continuum in pedagogical knowledge mirrors a continuum of learners' knowledge in self-regulation. For example, an expert teacher may be able to facilitate *discovery scaffolds*, but if the learners do not yet have the skills to self-regulate, the

Figure 7.7 Developing pedagogic practice.

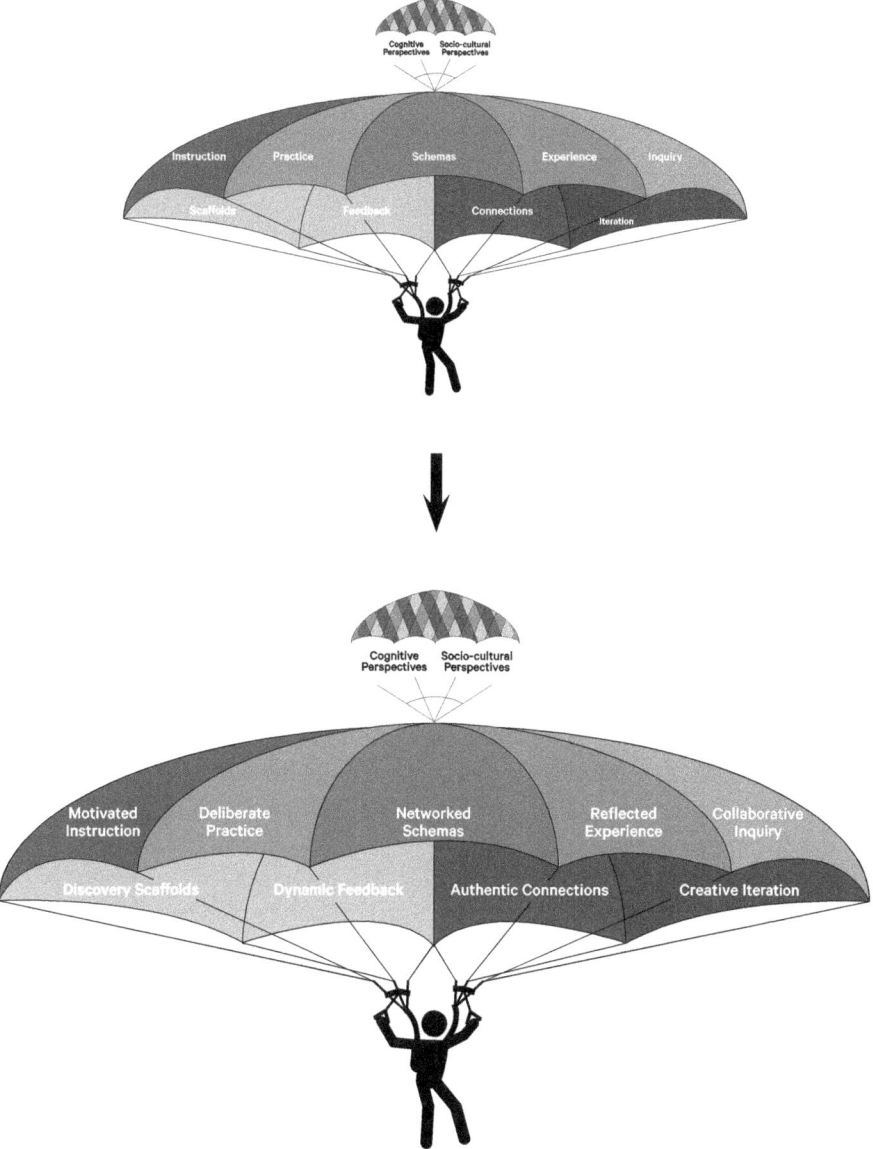

teacher begins with *scaffolds* to guide and prompt their learning. The elements of pedagogy as a continuum are responsive to learner needs but also develop learner skills in self-regulation and deeper learning. The threshold in the development of skills in the pedagogy continuum is dependent on the capacities of both teachers and learners.

The elements of the Pedagogy Parachute

For teachers (and learners) to 'curate' learning experiences using the elements of pedagogy, we need to explore what they are. We provide a brief description of each element of pedagogy, beginning with understanding its entry point practice and then connecting this to the higher-order practice. Connections and relationships between the nine pedagogical elements become apparent the more they are understood as a metalanguage, and used in practice. We begin our descriptions at the centre of the Parachute with the element Networked Schemas, and then move from the right of the canopy to the left with the elements Motivated Instruction, Discovery Scaffolds, Deliberate Practice, Dynamic Feedback, Authentic Connections, Collaborative Inquiry, Creative Iteration and Reflected Experience.

 ## Networked Schemas

What is a schema?

The word schema comes from ancient Greek and means form or shape,[8] and it has come to describe a framework that coheres and organizes knowledge. The periodic table of chemical elements and the Pedagogy Parachute are examples of schemas. Within the Parachute is an element that recognizes the integral role schemas play in learning. We are reflexively acknowledging the pedagogical role of schemas within the Parachute schema. Schemas in education are rarely named as a pedagogy, yet they are used all the time, often without teachers realizing it. It is something the Pedagogy Parachute seeks to remedy.

In psychology, schema theory explains how we organize experiences and knowledge in our memories. Schema theory describes how the memory structures knowledge into organized units that affect how we take on new experiences and retrieve established ones. Schemas are mental templates that assimilate, accommodate and recontextualize new knowledge. The psychologist, Jean Piaget defines schemas as follows:

> Concerning the relationship between the parts and the whole which determine the organization, it is sufficiently well known that every intellectual operation is always related to all others and that its own elements are controlled by the same law. Every schema is thus coordinated with all other schemata and itself constitutes a totality with differentiated parts. Every act of intelligence presupposes a system of mental implications and interconnected meanings.[9]

Schema-based learning in education has evolved from schema theory in psychology. In education, learning *schemas* are generated and used by teachers as organizers and frameworks to help learners comprehend and connect knowledge.

What do schemas look like?

Schemas are a synthesis of core generalizations that condense and crystallize knowledge for learners to make coherence of the complex. For example, in literacy learning, story structure can be learned with many schemas but a simple introductory one is 'orientation, complication and resolution'. Other schemas are: how we organize and learn numbers in units of ten; background knowledge in learning to read; musical notation; scientific method; assessment criteria for learning tasks; rules of grammar; our 4C coherence makers; the Pedagogy Parachute, etc. Schemas work to cohere knowledge as a mental template by clarifying and categorizing essential elements that make up a connected whole. For learners, learning schemas become part of, or compared to, existing schemas that have become part of their mental framework.

Learning schemas are continually expanding mental index cards that lay foundations for and activate further learning, actions and experiences. For instance, understanding and learning everything about the human capacity to learn is extraordinarily complex, dense and confusing. The Learning Disposition Wheel in chapter 5 is a learning schema to make coherence of that complexity so that learners and teachers can comprehend, connect and continue to act on their developing knowledge. A learning schema is a synthesis that provides coherence to explore the complex; it is a learning door that can open up many other learning doors. The periodic table does the same for scientists; it is a coherent and clear schema for understanding the essential design of the chemical elements, and also opens up possibilities to explore and challenge the element's properties, relationships and patterns.

What are networked schemas?

Teachers progress from using *schemas* to facilitating *networked schemas*. *Networked schemas* are when teachers curate learning by combining, extending and challenging existing learning frameworks to generate more complex skills and understandings. Schemas can limit learning if they are fixed, so teachers provide opportunities and encourage learners to interconnect, challenge and create schemas of knowledge for more complex learning. Academics JungMi Lee and Norbert M. Seel explain, 'Schema-based learning allows for incremental development of complex cognitive structures through aggregation from a restricted stock of schemas ... to more complex interactive structures.'[10]

What do networked schemas look like?

There are more nuanced and extended schemas beyond, for example, the basic story structure described earlier, such as 'exposition, problem, rising action, climax, falling action and denouement', or the story schema can be challenged by telling part of the plot backwards such as in the film *Memento*. Newton's law (or schema) for gravity is challenged by Einstein's schema for special relativity, but Newton's law still has its place as a schema for the approximation of the effects of gravity. Schemas are networked in mathematics such as when fractions as a schema are combined with decimal points as a schema. Or in transdisciplinary knowledge when mathematical data is used to explain, for example, the natural world (the population and extinction of species), economics (the growth of the wealth divide) or astronomy (the probability of life beyond earth).

Another example of networked schemas is when teachers combine and extend on schemas or coherence makers we have developed. When teachers understand how the Learning Disposition Wheel and the Pedagogy Parachute work together in creating self-directed learners, they are networking schemas. Teachers and learners also experience networked schemas when they connect and interrelate the 4C coherence makers and make connections between collaboration and creativity, for example. How networked schemas are presented to learners involves other elements in the Pedagogy Parachute; however, one of the ways networked schemas are introduced to learners is through motivated instruction.

 ## Motivated Instruction

What is instruction?

Instruction has generally come to refer to teaching and learning in education. The word 'teach' derives from the Old English *taecon*, which means 'show, present and point out'.[11] Instruction as 'showing, presenting and pointing out' has traditionally and long defined teaching. The impact of American psychologist B.F. Skinner's version of behaviourism (learning as conditioning through external stimuli) shaped teaching instruction and knowledge creation to be a technical process of teacher output for student input. Instruction is a more teacher-centred element in the Parachute, but it has a place in pedagogy towards learner self-regulation.[12] We are using the word instruction to mean directing or imparting knowledge as a clear and purposeful form of communication.

In our definition, *instruction* develops skills and understandings in learners through explanation, demonstration and questioning.

What does instruction look like?

Instruction is not 'chalk and talk' or 'death by PowerPoint'; instead effective instruction is clarified, elaborated and supported by questioning between teachers and learners. If instruction does not connect or interact with learners, it is, according to educational philosopher John Dewey, passive and submissive learning.[13] Subject matter in education, argues Dewey, is not fixed and readymade and outside the learner's experience but must be fluent, embryonic and vital in its connection to the learner's growing experience.[14] For instruction to be engaging and understood, teachers have clear communication skills, strong disciplinary knowledge and deep knowledge about the learners and how learning is constructed. Instruction can be framed through our coherence maker, the Communication Crystal (see chapter 1). Expert teachers through instruction are alert to the messaging of their students and their own messaging. They enable all student voices to question, and they convey clear meaning and purpose in the learning. The last step of the coherence maker, 'generating action and agency', belongs to the higher-order motivated instruction.

What is motivated instruction?

Teachers progress from using *instruction* to facilitating *motivated instruction*. *Motivated instruction* activates and inspires students to engage and explore learning in a more generative way. As well as explain and demonstrate learning, motivated instruction encourages and galvanizes students to learn and share their learning. The teacher motivates by using communication dynamics (positive belief, passion, encouragement, challenge, questioning) and generative processes to energize internal motivation in learners to produce, connect and sustain learning concepts.

What does motivated instruction look like?

The teacher can consider the learner's connection to and interest in the material that is being taught and mediate that connection by identifying key and higher-order questions and analysing student responses.

Using generative learning processes[15] (ways to process learning) such as:

- discussion,
- summarizing,
- mapping,
- drawing,
- teaching,
- imagining,
- enacting,
- self-testing, and
- self-explaining

helps to reinforce, connect and extend the learning. Communication, higher-order questioning and generative processes activated by motivated instruction support deeper learning and self-directed learners, but meeting every learner's needs requires discovery scaffolds.

Discovery Scaffolds

What are scaffolds?

Scaffolds are temporary and adaptive supports provided to learners until they are able to construct the learning task on their own. Educational researchers David Wood, Jerome S. Bruner and Gail Ross define scaffolding as a 'process that enables a child or novice to solve a problem, carry out a task or achieve a goal which would be beyond his [sic] unassisted efforts'.[16] Scaffolds can involve mentoring, guiding or prompting by a more experienced person, or it can be a tool or technology that guides and prompts.

Learning scaffolds are informed by psychologist Lev Vygotsky's zone of proximal development,[17] where an expert or more expert peer supports and continues to challenge the potential threshold of the learner from guided learning to independent learning. Wood, Bruner and Ross explain that 'scaffolding consists essentially of the adult "controlling" those elements of the task that are initially beyond the learner's capacity, thus permitting him (sic) to concentrate upon and complete only those elements that are within his range of competence'.[18] At the same time there must be support in learning, there must also be challenge in scaffolding. Learning scaffolds must be extended, dismantled, made redundant or replaced as learning is understood, practised and developed.

What does a scaffold look like?

A person may guide students to undertake a science experiment, for instance, or the same can be achieved by a written guide as a tool. The scaffold must be appropriate for learner needs and learners need to be cognizant of the scaffold as a temporary support and enabler. Over time the scaffold is unnecessary, since the task has to be achieved independently of the scaffolded support.

Technology such as online programmes and software can be enablers for scaffolding, particularly in supporting teachers to meet the diverse needs of students. We argue, however, that teachers as curators of learning experiences have the human capacity to diagnose, adapt and replace not only cognitive scaffolds but also emotional and relational ones. Scaffolds for cognitive, intra- and interpersonal learning are critical to a holistic and effective approach to pedagogy. For instance, teacher-supported scaffolds are needed for students to learn collaboration, self-control, empathy and taking responsibility with others, which are skills in the Learning Disposition Wheel (see chapter 5).

What are discovery scaffolds?

Teachers progress from using *scaffolds* to facilitating *discovery scaffolds*. *Discovery scaffolds* encourage and develop skills and initiative in learners to seek, explore and build relationships between what learners know and what they don't know. Through discovery scaffolds, learners discover new and emergent thinking and ways of doing things. Educational psychologist Jerome Bruner argues there is power in learners being allowed and able to work things out for themselves and discover their own learning through what he calls 'the development of an attitude toward learning and inquiry, toward guessing and hunches, toward the possibility of solving problems on one's own'.[19] Shalin Hai-Jew, an instructional designer, explains that discovery scaffolding involves 'strategic minimal guidance in order to enhance self-directed learners' opt-in metacognition, decision-making, self-regulation, self-assessments, self-directed learning, and skills acquisition'.[20]

What do discovery scaffolds look like?

In discovery scaffolds, teachers create and shape learning processes that develop students' skills and efficacy to problem-solve, take risks and make mistakes that enable learning. Without these skills, learners cannot initiate learning and navigate the uncertainty, ambiguity and non-linear trajectory of self-directed learning. The aim of discovery scaffolds is to support and build learners to discover learning for themselves. This could be, for example, working out why their experiment did not support their hypothesis, or how their mathematical formulas did not match their physical measurements, or why their video communicated an unintended message. Through discovery scaffolds, learners develop the skills to observe and realize ideas, solutions and questions for themselves. Like all skills, the capacities of self-direction facilitated by discovery scaffolds are developed through deliberate practice.

 ## Deliberate Practice

What is practice?

Author Malcolm Gladwell brought practice to prominence with his best-selling book *Outliers*, in which he argued that 10,000 hours of practice is the key to expertise in any field. Leading researcher in deliberate practice Anders Ericsson explains it is not enough to engage 10,000 hours to gain expertise, but agrees with Gladwell that expertise of any kind requires a 'tremendous amount of effort exerted over many years'.[21] *Practice* in learning reinforces skills or components of skills through an engaging or purposeful process of repetition. Cognitive psychology explains how practising skills and understandings begins by using the working memory and then, through the practising, knowledge is transferred to the long-term memory. In this process the cognitive load is reduced, freeing up the working memory for further learning.[22]

What does practice look like?

The continued rehearsing of skills allows learners to embed and refine those skills, so they become automatic, fluid and routine. The embedding and maintaining of skills through practising allows for that knowledge to be enhanced and added to and gives learners confidence in their ability to learn. Examples of practice are practising to read using phonics, sight words and reading for meaning, or practising counting numbers, or practising communication through writing, singing or dancing, or practising to master technical proficiency in playing sport or an instrument.

What is deliberate practice?

The higher-order *deliberate practice* is purposeful, mindful and systematic with the ultimate goal of the learner becoming more proficient in the skill being developed. For practising to be deliberate, it must have an intent that raises the level of difficulty and or complexity of the skill in a supported learning environment. It requires the learner's focused and mindful attention to the practising and as the practice is deepened, the learner's understanding of the purpose of that practice deepens. To attain proficiency in the skills being learnt, deliberate practising requires a self-determination by the student to explore challenge and complexity. Deliberate practice is more about trying things differently rather than just trying harder, and this means creating high expectations for students to go beyond their comfort zone.

What does deliberate practice look like?

According to Ericsson, motivation, specific and realistic goals, challenge, persistence, feedback and recovery time are key to achieving the benefits of deliberate practice.[23] Teachers can facilitate opportunities for learners to experience and be aware of the benefits of being determined, of using mindful and incremental steps, receiving feedback and finding challenge. Deliberate practice means being mindful of the processes of practice rather than focusing exclusively on the products or goals of the practice. It is the metacognition inherent to deliberate practice that leads to greater expertise. The metacognition, increased confidence, skill refinement and reduction of cognitive load developed through deliberate practice all support the capacity for deeper learning.[24] An impact on the effectiveness of deliberate practice is the nature of the dynamic feedback given.

 Dynamic Feedback

What is feedback?

Feedback is the process of engaging and encouraging learners to recognize the processes of their learning and how they can be developed further. Feedback is more than a result or response to a learning task. Results alone can be detrimental, as Paul Black and colleagues found in a comprehensive review of research studies:

> In general, feedback given as rewards or grades enhances ego involvement rather than task involvement. It can focus students' attention on their 'ability' rather than on the importance of effort, thus damaging the self-esteem of low achievers and leading to problems of 'learned helplessness.' Feedback that focuses on what needs to be done can encourage all to believe that they can improve. Such feedback can enhance learning, both directly through the effort that can ensue and indirectly by supporting the motivation to invest such effort.[25]

Effective feedback is explanatory and meaningful to the learner and considers the context of the learning and the motivational impact of the specific feedback on the learner. The intention of feedback is formative as it gives learners continued opportunities to act on the focused and purposeful feedback.

What does feedback look like?

Feedback occurs between teachers and learners in individual and collaborative interactions and informs teachers and learners where and how the learning can be progressed and challenged. *Why* feedback, *what* feedback, *how to* feedback and *when*, are critical questions for teachers to address. For feedback to be relevant, it must be understood and encouraging for each individual's learning characteristics. Researcher Susanne Narciss explains: '... even the most thoroughly designed feedback strategy can be useless if the feedback components delivered by this strategy are not processed in a mindful way. Each feedback component has to be attended to, understood, and interpreted, and finally transformed into a corrective action by the learner before it can influence subsequent learning.'[26]

It is the nature and quality, timing and precision of the feedback to a task or process that makes it effective in developing self-regulation in learners. Educationalist Dylan Wiliam argues that 'the whole purpose of feedback should be to increase the extent to which students are owners of their own learning'.[27] For instance, asking an open question as a feedback strategy rather than a statement is often more empowering and motivating for students to direct their own learning. Through questions (with wait-time to allow for more thoughtful responses) students can become more aware of and active in addressing the understandings, gaps and misconceptions in their own knowledge.[28]

What is dynamic feedback?

From understanding and using *feedback*, teachers and students progress to implementing *dynamic feedback*. *Dynamic feedback* is an interactive process where learners self-assess and seek responses to their self-assessment from a range of sources. In essence, dynamic feedback promotes a 'public' learning environment where students are active participants and responsible collaborators in the feedback cycle of their learning. Black and colleagues argue feedback as a 'collaboration between teachers and students and between students and their peers can produce a supportive environment in which students can explore their own ideas, have alternative ideas in the language of their peers, and evaluate them'.[29] Strong interpersonal skills (influence, empathy and teamwork in the Learning Disposition Wheel, see chapter 5) in teachers and students are needed for dynamic feedback and enriching a collaborative learning environment.[30]

What does dynamic feedback look like?

Learners can use self-assessment and feedback from teachers, their peers and others to form, shape and refine their skills, understandings and processes of thinking. By questioning, evaluating and generating feedback, learners clarify and select positive directions forward. Focused and purposeful feedback can be communicated in diverse ways and from different directions to inform and motivate future teaching and learning. For example, dynamic feedback can involve interactions that are: one on one, small groups or large groups; face-to-face or virtual; questions that are spoken or written; embodied through a collaborative tableau; a response to a stimulus picture; conceived and drawn as a map or picture, etc. Through these feedback processes, teachers can facilitate opportunities for learners to create individual and shared goals that support them to direct, develop and challenge their own learning. The adjustments students (and teachers) make to guide and optimize their learning through dynamic feedback develop learning expertise and learner metacognition for deeper learning. Dynamic feedback must be informative and able to engage and motivate learners as an authentic connection.

 ## Authentic Connections

What are connections?

A sociocultural perspective in learning focuses on the connected nature of knowledge between the individual and the social world, and the processes that help learners make *connections* with what they already know. Fred M. Newmann and associates[31] used the dimension *connectedness to the world* in their influential research on authentic achievement in 1996. Education researchers Debra Hayes and colleagues extended on Newmann's work in the Productive Pedagogies Research[32] and used *connectedness* to describe 'the extent to which knowledge is built on students' existing knowledge; connections are made between different bodies of knowledge (rather than compartmentalizing the curriculum); connections are made with the world beyond the classroom; and students' knowledge and skills are developed in the context of solving real-life issues or problems'.[33]

What do connections look like?

This means teachers connect the learning with students' background knowledge (their cultural, linguistic and everyday experiences) to enhance the learners' abilities to comprehend and engage with new learning. Connections also occur when learners can assimilate, generalize or transfer their knowledge to new learnings and contexts. This is better achieved if connections are made across the curriculum by integrating knowledge, rather than being in silos or isolated bits.[34] When learning is connected to the real world, it also develops the capacity for students to transfer learning to new contexts. Teachers can frame the why, what and application of the learning so that students understand why they are learning and for what purpose. Through this metacognitive understanding of the intention of learning, students (and teachers) are more able to connect and transfer their learning to new situations.[35]

What are authentic connections?

The higher-order *authentic connections* are facilitated by teachers when learners are encouraged and have the opportunity to identify, explore and act on meaningful and relevant real-world problems and projects that are of interest to them. Learners construct and transform their learning by making it relevant to them and applying it to their lived experience. There are strong social reasons for the things we do that shape how we do them and for what purpose. Learning often only makes sense and is useful when it is contextualized in the social world of the learner.[36] Anthropologist Jean Lave and educational theorist Etienne Wenger argue, 'Activities, tasks, functions, and understandings do not exist in isolation; they are part of broader systems of relations in which they have meaning.'[37] So learning that does not make authentic connections to the learner and the world has little or no meaning.

What do authentic connections look like?

Authentic connections are made through practices such as internships, job-shadowing initiatives, cultural immersion experiences, real-world virtual projects assisting an astronomy experiment, running a school event, writing a letter to a councillor about a local issue, performing at a festival, etc. Students are motivated by their interest, and the relevance and rigour of the task specific to them or to wider concerns of the real world.

Authentic connections are developed when learners use metacognition to question and perceive the why, what and how of their learning. Connectedness in learning develops abstract and critical reasoning in learners to transform their thinking and transfer their learning to new contexts and the wider world. Authentic connections are made when knowledge is problematized by solving issues grounded in reality, and this is developed through collaborative inquiry.

# Collaborative Inquiry

What is inquiry?

Inquiry learning has its antecedents in sociocultural theories and the understanding that learners actively make meaning for themselves through questioning, thinking critically and problem-solving. In *Pedagogy of the Oppressed*, critical theorist Paulo Freire argues, 'For apart from inquiry, apart from the praxis, individuals cannot be truly human. Knowledge emerges only through invention and re-invention, through the restless, impatient, continuing, hopeful inquiry human beings pursue in the world, with the world, and with each other.'[38] Inquiry requires a want or need for questioning or researching, and Freire explains how 'problem-posing education' is the joint responsibility of students and teachers to challenge each other to ask questions, shape problems and seek answers and solutions in learning.

Inquiry is to approach learning as a question to be posed, solved, challenged and re-solved by the learner. It encourages learners to be involved in the learning process by questioning and investigating matters as they search for knowledge. Curiosity motivates the learner to inquire into what they do not know and begins by posing a question, shaping a problem or generating an idea. These are explored by developing skills and strategies in observation, resourcefulness and investigation.

What does inquiry look like?

Students are encouraged to inquire through questioning that asks for inference, interpretation, transfer, hypotheses and reflection. Inquiry requires critical thinking and reasoning skills, and our coherence maker the Critical Reflection Crucible (see chapter 1) explains how the nature of inquiry is to identify the assumptions we make when trying to solve a problem or come up with an idea. The assumptions are then explored through questions of *why this* and *why so*? Investigating is to contest, elaborate and adapt what is discovered through the inquiry, which then leads to a solution that in the cycle of inquiry will always be open to further inquiry and re-solving.

What is collaborative inquiry?

Collaborative inquiry involves learners being extended and enriched by investigating with others. Collaboration enhances and motivates learner capacities to problem-solve through a joint approach in investigation and idea co-construction. Through collaboration, divergent perspectives and diverse capacities extend and deepen skills, understandings and relationships in the learning processes of the inquiry. A collaborative inquiry needs a clear objective in the form of a question that underpins the investigation and connects the developing and possible learning processes and concepts. Teachers can also facilitate processes that develop the social structures and skills that promote participation and agency from all those involved in the collaboration.

What does collaborative inquiry look like?

Researchers Rebecca Wing-yi Cheng and colleagues[39] found the quality of group processes in project-based learning is critical to learner efficacy in collaborative inquiry. Their results indicated that learner efficacy was contributed to by four elements: positive interdependence, individual accountability, equal participation and social skills. These skills can be learnt through our coherence maker Collaboration Circles (see chapter 1). It explores how everyone in the collaboration can co-construct the inquiry by learning to offer, yield, challenge, evaluate and extend questions and ideas. Collaborative inquiry is a shared endeavour that facilitates and consolidates learning and should be shared in a dynamic and engaging way with a developing 'community of practice'. Wenger describes a community of practice as a collective and shared learning endeavour made up of 'groups of people who share a concern or passion for something they do and learn how to do it better as they interact regularly'.[40] Collaborative inquiry has to generate a dynamic learning environment that advances further co-constructions and connections with the wider group or community of learners. Collaborative inquiry enables greater possibilities for solutions and ideas, as does the pedagogy of creative iteration.

 ## Creative Iteration

What is iteration?

Iteration is learning through experimenting, analysing, developing and testing successive versions of a particular idea, task or project to reach a desired or discovered result. In a sequence of iterations, each iteration is a starting point for and informs the next iteration. Iteration is a series of drafts, prototypes or a cycle of inquiry with multiple possible outcomes and further implications. Iteration involves reworking, reshaping, taking risks and making mistakes and sometimes starting over again.

What does iteration look like?

Drafting a letter, communicating a science report, writing a speech, constructing a webpage, building an engineered prototype such as a rocket or a robot, translating a poem, testing the effects of a chemical compound, testing the force of objects acting on each other are all examples that require iteration to arrive at a refined or effective result. Learning develops through the continuous cycle of changing and refining the task or project. Teachers guide learners to observe and consider implications of the changes made through each iteration.

What is creative iteration?

Creative iteration occurs when learners continue a sequence of iterative learning to imagine and create something new (to them). Learning is generated from the process of challenging, combining and transforming concepts, ideas, processes and products into new ideas. Creative iteration is a recursive and active process of generating and expanding ideas that explore meaning, knowledge, the self, and engagement with the world. Creativity is no longer viewed as a mysterious phenomenon inhabited by rare individuals; it is an 'everyday' social, cultural and cognitive construct that is central to human existence and learning. Educator and researcher Alfonso Montuori explains: 'Creativity is not, in the new view, limited to gifted individuals, to a process that leads to a new product, to a revolutionary idea of earth-shaking proportion, or exclusive to specific domains such as the arts and sciences. Creativity is now increasingly seen as a distributed, networked, paradoxical, emergent process that manifests in all aspects of life.'[41] For learners, everyday creativity is the exploration of *what is* thinking to *what if* thinking.[42]

What does creative iteration look like?

For learners, creative iteration is applied to learning they are passionate about.[43] Through the cycle of iteration, learners observe, question, explore and refine multiple possibilities to allow for the emergence of new knowledge. This could be creating, or interpreting or 'cracking' a new code for a computer game, observing a phenomenon and using mathematics to explain it, conceptualizing and constructing an artwork, hypothesizing a historical cause and effect based on new evidence, designing a novel fit-for-purpose tool, generating unpredictable team plays for a sport, interpreting and staging a classical story as an interactive theatre event for children, etc.

In our coherence maker the Creativity Cascade (see chapter 1), we explain creative iteration as a learnable skill and process. It begins with the process of 'noticing' or perceiving something, and then asking *why? really why?* of these noticings. These deeper insights alongside an attitude of 'not-knowing' but also 'what could be', create a space and openness in students that allows novelty to emerge. Playing with possibility encourages an expansive and playful approach that generates many ideas rather than an obvious, established and expected answer or idea. Playing with possibility requires divergent thinking, but then through convergent thinking, ideas are selected and evaluated, and the best idea emerges. Creativity researcher Keith Sawyer describes creative iteration as 'zig zagging': 'Successful creators engage in an ongoing dialogue with their work. They put what's in their head on paper long before it's fully formed, and they watch and listen to what they've recorded, zigging and zagging until the right idea emerges.'[44]

Creative iteration requires teachers and learners as individuals and collaborators to be confident with unpredictability and uncertainty. It uses both the creative 'play' of improvisation with the rigour, focus and structure of iteration to allow new ideas to emerge. Through creativity, learners develop skills and understandings of how knowledge can be imagined, transferred and transformed. Cognitive science demonstrates the correlation between creativity and neural executive function or higher-order thinking.[45] To iterate through the creative process also requires wise action and consideration of ethical consequences of what is being created, and this is developed through learning that is a reflected experience.

 ## Reflected Experience

What is experience?

Experience in learning is active or physical and it is designed to involve the whole person and be conducive to growth. Experiences should have an internalized effect on the psychology of the learner and an externalized effect on the social learning environment. An experience in learning recognizes the critical role the body plays in cognition.[46] John Dewey argues that learning must be experiential, situated and sensory, and that 'education must be conceived as a continuing reconstruction of experience'.[47] Continuing in this tradition, experiential learning theorist David Kolb defines learning as 'the process whereby knowledge is created through the transformation of experience. Knowledge results from the combination of grasping and transforming experience.'[48] Embodied theories of cognition support these ideas by explaining how the body has evolved for perception, action and emotions and contributes to 'higher' cognitive functions.[49] Embodied cognition involves the mind, the body and the environment, and developing research is demonstrating the effectiveness of learning as a physical, lived experience.[50]

What does an experience look like?

An embodied experience in learning could be using concrete manipulatives to solve a mathematics problem, creating tableaus to illustrate a historical inquiry, practising a sports drill, role-playing a character's dilemma in a story, making a podcast about the effects of a built environment or embodying the connections of a group reflection etc. The embodied experience creates a learning dynamic that affects the emotions, senses, cognition and relationships of the learners and their capacity for learning.

What is a reflected experience?

Reflected experience is noticing the perceptions and interpretations of an experience. Reflection facilitated by teachers and learners before, during and after an experience embeds and deepens the meaning, connections and consequence of the embodied learning. Experience alone cannot consolidate, facilitate or contest the learner's capacity for deeper learning. When an experience is reflected upon, the experience affirms, challenges or extends the learner's skills, understandings and assumptions. Dewey suggests, 'When we reflect upon an experience instead of just having it, we inevitably distinguish between our own attitude and the objects toward which we sustain the attitude . . . Such reflection upon experience gives rise to a distinction of what we experience (the experienced) and the experiencing – the how.'[51]

What does reflected experience look like?

Reflection is a conscious act that develops metacognition or self-awareness of the learning experience. Reflective processes can be facilitated through thoughtful questioning and using varied communication modes and stimuli (spoken, written, bodily, visual, dialogue, group, using an object, pictures, etc.). The communication of reflection, whether individually or collectively undertaken, develops awareness and coherence of the learning experience for the self. 'Critical' reflection takes reflection a step further and changes how we perceive ourselves and how we act in and relate to the world.[52] The intent of a reflected experience is to generate or influence further action and experiences. Communication through critical reflection deepens and develops the cognitive, emotional and relational meaning of an experience and influences how we make decisions and take action with our learning.

Concluding reflections

Understanding and curating pedagogy is critical to creating deep learning experiences. To engage with ongoing professional learning, a common language supports a rigorous collaborative inquiry into a pedagogical knowledge base. A full understanding of pedagogy as a capability cannot be realized without a language for it. Pedagogy has sometimes been tacit, vague, or based on intuitive hunches in a teacher's practice without a precise language to make it explicit, coherent and tangible. For teachers to define, discuss and mindfully practise pedagogy we need to understand and investigate the elemental structures that create successful learning experiences. Often, we have strategies ('Socratic questioning', group work, 'think, pair, share', 'jigsaw', etc.) that support learning, but not the understanding or time to discern how and why pedagogy works (or doesn't). Often, we don't know how they are connected and serve larger pedagogical structures, or what their theoretical origins or ethical implications are. Knowledge about pedagogy can support teachers in understanding and exploring what a deep learning experience is, how it is facilitated and how it develops self-directed learners.

In chapter 6, we compared teaching to curation. Gallery and museum curators cannot curate an exhibition if they do not understand what they are curating and for what experience. Teachers can only curate learning experiences if they understand what they are facilitating through pedagogy. To learn deeply about pedagogy requires the elements of pedagogy identified in the Parachute. Pedagogy is something we as teachers have to *scaffold* and *deliberately practise*, and through our practice we *discover* new ideas about pedagogy that can develop through *creative iteration*. This can only happen if the development of our pedagogy is *authentically connected* to the needs of students. We can learn about pedagogy by flying (embodying or experiencing) the Parachute and *reflecting* on the *experience* as a *dynamic feedback* loop to discover more about the use and purpose of the elements of pedagogy. The Pedagogy Parachute aims to provide a common language across a school to deepen and broaden the profession's development of pedagogy. With a common language, pedagogical concepts can be expanded through *motivated discussion* and *collaborative inquiry* among teachers. The Parachute is a schema that, when understood with other schemas, such as the Learning Disposition Wheel and the 4C coherence makers, provides a sophisticated combination of *networked schemas* that can deepen and extend a teacher's practice.

Pedagogy is a powerful capability for knowing, exploring and innovating the craft of teaching for transformative learning. The Pedagogy Parachute is a tool, and like any tool (such as the descending parachute) it is best understood in practice. It is a tool for teachers to explore, discover, predict and refine the purpose and effectiveness of pedagogy.

Just as scientific method and technologies at the end of the nineteenth and early twentieth century aligned with the invention of the aeroplane and need for the descending parachute, the twenty-first century is heightening and converging the need to understand and achieve deeper and self-directed learning through pedagogy. When to 'pull on' what pedagogy in the Parachute is part of the professional, curatorial expertise of a teacher. Teachers are curators of rich learning experiences, but in the end, we believe that through pedagogy for deep and self-directed learning, students can be drivers of their own learning, 'flying their own parachutes'.

The next chapter considers how transforming the curriculum accompanies transformative pedagogy.

Transforming curriculum
Connecting education to students and their contexts

8

Curriculum and the 'real world' 152

The status quo curriculum 153

International pressures reinforcing status-quo curriculum 155

What is curriculum? 156

Curriculum in a complex world 158

Templestowe College: creating a transforming curriculum 160

Beyond the practice/policy divide in curriculum 161

Indigenous knowledge in the curriculum 162

Unlearning false dichotomies 164

Pedagogy versus curriculum 164
Subject depth versus integration 166
Assessment versus curriculum 170

The Transformative Curriculum Framework 172

Consult – alert to messaging 172
Contextualize – enabling voice 173
Co-construct – conveying meaning and purpose 175
Craft – generating action and agency 176

Concluding reflections: transformative curriculum for deeper learning 177

Curriculum and the 'real world'

Around September 2001, I (Michael)[1] began a job as an educational officer within the New South Wales Department of Education in Australia at what was then called the Curriculum Directorate. The Curriculum Directorate was located in an old high school in a residential suburb of Sydney and the place had all the feel of a high school without the joy and the excitement of students. All the colour and movement had been replaced by officer dividers, filing cabinets and education bureaucrats (of whom I was one). Around about the time I began there, the events of 9/11 unfolded (figure 8.1 shows the 9/11 Memorial). The day after 9/11 happened, there was barely a discussion of this event that changed human history at the Curriculum Directorate. The interminable meetings went on as normal, the briefings for the Minister carried on like clockwork – the Curriculum Directorate went on as if nothing of consequence had happened, when in reality the whole world had shifted on its axis and everything we once understood as normal had gone post-normal.[2]

We tell this story to highlight the problem with current and some of our historical notions of curriculum. At the end of my six years working at the Curriculum Directorate, I was still unsure what a curriculum was and who it was for. Notwithstanding some of the outstanding educators that worked in that soulless

Figure 8.1 9/11 Memorial and One World Trade Centre. Photo by Julien DI MAJO on Unsplash.

place, there was never a clear understanding of our values or mission as a Curriculum Directorate (or at least there wasn't to me). This was in contrast to the school I had just been teaching in. The school wasn't perfect but at least we knew why we were there and what we were doing most of the time. To me there was a disconnect between the Curriculum Directorate and reality. The profound and world-changing events of 9/11 affected our world and therefore must have an effect on what and how we teach. Yet in the Curriculum Directorate the production of curriculum went on as if the world was unaffected by these events – the status quo remained.

If curriculum is to be effective, it must engage with learning that responds at least in part to the realities our students face in the world. Curriculum can provide intellectual rigour by allowing our places of learning to respond to the changing circumstances in our world so our students can analyse and respond to these circumstances. A status quo and fixed curriculum seriously limits the potential of schools to create learning relevant to the needs of students.

In this chapter, we will explore the possibilities of a transforming curriculum as a capability for beneficial change. The chapter is not intended to be an exhaustive history of the concept of curriculum but rather an examination of the 'status quo' curriculum and what we might need to unlearn to make curriculum relevant and dynamic as a capability for transformation. We present a framework for transforming curriculum at the conclusion of the chapter to support schools as they consider the process of curriculum transformation. Before we discuss what we mean by a transforming curriculum, let's consider the implications of maintaining the status quo.

The status quo curriculum

The status quo curriculum seeks to maintain education as it is currently. This approach preserves often outmoded teaching practices, views of knowledge, school governance and other elements of education that maintain things as they are. Status quo curriculum is not inherently dynamic and struggles to flexibly respond and reflect on shifting circumstances. Status quo curriculum also has the tendency to entrench and reinforce advantage and disadvantage rather than providing pathways for all learners. Educator Pat Thomson, reflecting on policy in the United Kingdom, argues that status quo curriculum produces privilege and disadvantage:

> Educational researchers, many now derided and dismissed out of hand, have systematically documented how particular curriculum, pedagogies and assessment practices combine with the administrative processes of schooling to produce and reproduce both educational privilege and disadvantage. The same system leads to both success and failure. The direction of policy travel in England has been to consolidate the kinds of conservative educational regimes (e.g. large classes, streaming and setting, textbook driven pedagogies, a steady diet of direct instruction and whole class teaching) which have been shown to consistently (re)produce educational failure for a minority of young people.[3]

A transforming curriculum, by contrast, seeks to reimagine the possibilities of learning for all learners. The relentless rise of the Global Education Reform Movement (GERM), with its focus on restricted curriculum, top-down management and standardized testing,[4] has limited the possibility of schools attending to the needs of learners directly. This generates winners and losers as opposed to learners. As Thomson argues, those in traditionally disadvantaged groups are further disadvantaged by a decontextualized curriculum. A transforming curriculum puts the learner rather than the system at the centre of learning. This allows each student's strengths and yet-to-be strengths to be integrated into the learning.

A transforming curriculum is in a constant state of evolution, and recognizes that everything students learn at school, university, polytechnics, etc. *is* the curriculum. When schools see curriculum in this way, they have the opportunity to reimagine curriculum, learning, design and pedagogy, making them responsive and dynamic. Reimagining curriculum means schools can see everything they do as curriculum. This approach to curriculum includes:

- learning that occurs perhaps unintentionally (e.g. the attitudes of educators to bullying, signs around the school),
- the written curriculum (sometimes called syllabus),
- the role of 'co-curricular' (sport, theatre performances),
- creativity, collaboration, communication and critical reflection evident in the school (whether it is taught explicitly or not),
- learning dispositions (as found in the Learning Disposition Wheel, including grit, teamwork, etc.),
- the school's culture, and
- the school's physical environment.

For instance, a university colleague of mine once commented to me:

> When you come into this university one day just count all the signs that tell student's what they can't do – 'don't park bikes here', 'don't sit on the grass', 'no food in the rooms', 'no access' etc. All of those signs are the curriculum, whether we intend them to be or not. They teach students this is a negative place and we never give that a second thought. Learning is everywhere not just in the classrooms, and that learning shapes the culture of this place – that's as much the curriculum as what we teach in our classes.

While curriculum is shaped by these seemingly unintended messages, educators' attitudes to events unfolding in the world and in the lives of students also shape curriculum. What, for instance, does status quo curriculum have to say about bushfires in Australia, airstrikes on Iran, terrorism in Christchurch, the social or political effects of social media applications, the refugee crisis in Syria or pandemics? A transforming curriculum can begin when we understand learning occurs in intended and unintended ways and must be responsive to the lives of our students.

The drive for relevant and responsive curriculum is not new or original to us. In the OECD's vision for learning, *The Future of Education and Skills 2030*, they call for a transformational view of learning. They argue that a status quo curriculum will not meet the needs of our students in an increasingly complex world and that 'radical' evolution may be required:

> In the face of an increasingly volatile, uncertain, complex and ambiguous world, education can make the difference as to whether people embrace the challenges they are confronted with or whether they are defeated by them. And in an era characterised by a new explosion of scientific knowledge and a growing array of complex societal problems, it is appropriate that curricula should continue to evolve, perhaps in radical ways.[5]

If curriculum is to mean anything for a transforming school, it must reflect and affect the world and communities it is situated in. More than words on a page it needs to be infused with 'real world' implications and move with the ebbs and flows of life, not not a static document or website. Educators need ways to design and curate learning through a curriculum that respects and builds the agency of students and teachers, builds competence and is inherently about how we relate to each other and to what we are learning about. There are also international policy pressures reinforcing the status quo.

International pressures reinforcing status-quo curriculum

The legacy of international testing regimes driven by GERM, such as the Programme for International Student Assessment (PISA), entrenches a culture of international comparison with little or no consideration of learning contexts. These kinds of comparisons rarely support deep learning; rather they drive an international competitiveness on a limited range of learning, based on tests that do not measure or attempt to measure the depth and breadth of learning in schools. In many cases, the rich cultural and social traditions that are situated around schools are ignored in the drive for better performance on test scores. This assumes that better PISA rankings equate to better national economic performance. In the opening chapter of their handbook on curriculum, pedagogy and assessment educational researchers Dominic Wyse, Louise Hayward and Jessica Pandya argue:

> Globalisation has been manifest in political forces of performativity that have resulted in attention to standards, measurement of learning, increased scrutiny of teachers and schools, national curricula and linked assessment, and emphasis on education as a driver of economic prosperity. At the same time, the unique cultural, historical traditions of nation states, and the fight for democracy and self-determination have resulted in different perceptions and counter positions to

those influenced by performativity [results on international league tables based on test scores]. Historical traditions of curriculum in the UK, the other countries of Europe, and in the US reflect these two major geopolitical trends.[6]

Their point is that test scores are not the only thing that curriculum is good for. Curriculum can also help our young people learn democratic values, the relevance of their culture and history, the place of art in their lives etc. Curriculum, if understood as evolving and transformative, can be contextualized nationally and locally with the aims of building a more civil and democratic world. Curriculum has a vital link to the growth and maturity of civil societies where learning is driven not by external and international league tables but by learners' needs. The pressures on curriculum are complex and significant, but the opportunities in a transformative curriculum are substantial. Before we consider an example of transformative curriculum, we would like to discuss what curriculum is.

What is curriculum?

Curriculum is a source of tension in education. For many, curriculum is simply dot points in a syllabus. As we discussed earlier, sociologist Basil Bernstein argued that schools have three 'message' systems: curriculum, pedagogy and evaluation (what we might today call assessment).[7] He argued that through these overlapping message systems, students, parents and the community become aware of what educational systems value and do not value.

The meaning of curriculum has shifted from decade to decade and has often been the plaything of politicians and others who wish to drive partisan agendas through learning and teaching.[8] As educators Jerry Rosiek and Jean Clandinin argue, people are often at cross purposes as they discuss curriculum:

> The word 'curriculum' is a contested term. It is less a word that refers to a single thing, and more a textual Rorschach test[9] upon which teachers, policymakers and scholars project their own values and ideologies. Failure to acknowledge these differences in definition account for the way people seem to talk past one another in conversations about appropriate educational goals and outcomes.[10]

In its most reductive sense, curriculum is often defined as a set of documents produced to prescribe learning and teaching. Many of the teachers we have worked with over the years often see syllabus and curriculum as synonymous. The Curriculum Directorate, which we referred to earlier, reflected this view in the documents they routinely produced. This approach reflects a command and control approach to curriculum as a set of (often state or system authored) documents that are 'implemented obediently' by teachers. Education systems should provide support around curriculum; however, an overly prescriptive approach to curriculum diminishes teacher professionalism and agency. This prescriptive approach also reduces the ability for educators to contextualize learning and to understand deeply why they are teaching what they are teaching.

Curriculum is not experienced in the abstract – it is always explored in the context of learning relationships (student to student, teacher to student, etc.). This means that the intention of the curriculum varies depending on the learners and the learning context. In reality, no two learning experiences based on the same curriculum will ever be the same, because learning varies depending on human relationships and contextual factors. Often policy makers and politicians imagine that curriculum, once written, will be implemented uniformly across all school contexts. This presumption leads to the deterioration of student and teacher agency. One of the critical skills of a teacher is to consider the learning needs of the student first.

We define transformative curriculum as a coherent set of learning experiences that focus on the learners' dispositions, needs, context and vision. A transformative curriculum allows teachers flexibility to meet the needs of students directly. Status-quo curriculum can diminish the potential for contextualized and relevant learning. As Jerry Rosiek and Jean Clandinin point out:

> Curriculum . . . presumes a hierarchical relation in which some external authority (usually the state) establishes the curriculum, teachers transmit it with minimal modification, and students are located as passive recipients at the end of a curricular delivery process. This sense of the term is so pervasive it often functions as common sense, making it difficult for listeners to hear 'curriculum' in other ways. Worse, it can function as part of a hegemonic view of education, in which other conceptions of curriculum are ridiculed, deflected with awkward silence, or actively suppressed as subversive.[11]

As Rosiek and Clandinin argue, the imposition of curriculum from above is often the prevailing model (such as system to school, school leader to teacher, teacher to student). Educational researchers in the United States[12] Erica Nevenglosky, Chris Cale and Sunddip Aguilar relate the familiar story of a phonics curriculum that was centrally mandated for implementation by the state authorities. The researchers looked in depth at the lack of engagement with the phonics curriculum in one particular school. The study suggested that a lack of teacher 'buy in', collaboration and professional learning led to poor outcomes in the teaching of the programme. While a centrally imposed model of curriculum is common, it underestimates the influence of teachers on the learning and teaching process. A transforming curriculum that puts a learner's need for autonomy, competence and relatedness at the centre of the curriculum is more likely to inspire and drive deep learning. As Rosiek and Clandinin argue:

> Curriculum, according to this view, is far more than a set of ideas that we pour into students' empty minds. Curriculum, instead, involves assisting students to acquire new habits of being in the world – not just what we narrowly call knowledge, but also temperament, disposition, aesthetic appreciation, enthusiasm for specific topics, emotional intelligence, ethics, compassion, etc. Because everything happening in students' schooling experience potentially contributes to their habits of being, a school's curriculum is essentially everything that happens at school. The ultimate measure of the value of this curriculum is the quality of the overall transformation it works in the life of each child.[13]

This understanding of curriculum broadens its potential for learning. It makes curriculum agile, multidimensional and multidirectional, not flat or static. It includes intended and the unintended learning. In this sense the terms 'curricular' and 'co-curricular' dissolve as learning happens in multiple sites.

The realization that the curriculum is everything that happens at school and how it happens (or in any other education setting) is simultaneously alarming and energizing. If educators are not mindful, noticing the messages they send through the curriculum, all kinds of dispiriting or even debilitating messages can be communicated to students. In some places anti-democratic, anachronistic and even bigoted views might be conveyed. For instance, if a school selects a student representative council based on teacher nomination rather than student vote, that sends a message that students can't be trusted to select their representatives. These kinds of messages may not appear in the values statements of schools, but they might be conveyed by autocratic behaviour management strategies, bullying, disconnected and irrelevant subjects, the condoning of sexism, racism or misogyny and a culture that permits oppression of various kinds. More constructively, if educators understand that the education experience is everything that a student experiences, a more mindful approach to designing and enacting curriculum is possible. Principal Alison Rourke explains how a transforming curriculum begins with student agency:

> Rethinking the way we do things to provide opportunities for authentic learning to occur is a shift away from mandated syllabus. Changing a static mindset and allowing for the beauty of innovation and inquiry is probably the greatest gift that an educator can be given at a time of change. In a transformative school, we are constantly talking about new possibilities and deeply noticing where the values of our school lie. If we are advocating for contemporary learners what does this look like, sound like and feel like in our school? If we are empowering students, what does this mean for us as educators? Active voice and agency from our students will force us to think more deeply about what we teach, how we teach and when we teach, the necessary skills for them to be global citizens. It is an exciting time in education to build partnerships with our learners and provide them with the necessary skills (4C skills) to be lifelong learners who will participate and contribute to the global world they live in.[14]

As Alison suggests, we need to enable a more agentic, comprehensive and transformative curriculum for our students to engage with their complex world.

Curriculum in a complex world

As we argued in chapter 2, education is a complex endeavour. A static 'status quo' and untransformed view of curriculum is inconsistent with a complex world with complex problems and a necessarily complex view of learning. Not only do we need to renew and reimagine our 'taken for granted' practices relating to curriculum, we can transform our view and enactment of pedagogy to enable a transforming curriculum. A complex view of learning driven by an understanding of schooling as complex opens up the curriculum. Jerry Rosiek and Jean Clandinin argue for a more complex, dynamic and experiential curriculum:

> . . . these more complex ideas of curriculum make clear the inadequacy of a view of curriculum as something fixed, that is, a discrete object to be delivered by teachers and consumed by students. Curriculum, considered through these multiple lenses, is revealed as an experiential process. It is made or co-constructed as teachers, learners, subject matter and milieu interact in schools and classrooms.[15]

The status-quo or fixed curriculum leaves no space for schools to become learner centred in response to the dynamic changes students see around them. When the world shifts, schools have a responsibility to support students to process, understand and respond.

In the Covid-19 pandemic, a group of educators, artists and philanthropists created resources to support young New Zealanders to understand, reflect and create in response to the pandemic. The project, Te Rito Toi (see figure 8.2), engaged students and teachers with the arts so they could create in response to the crisis. Educator and artist Peter O'Connor, who led the initiative, explains:

Figure 8.2 A lino cut from the Te Rito Toi project by Charlotte Prebble

> At the heart of Te Rito Toi is the understanding that schools must not just prepare students for the future but they also need to help them make sense of the present. After disasters and crises, schools must as a first priority help learners safely explore the changed world in which they live. The arts are a bridge to a better future. The stories, concerns and questions they have must be addressed in classrooms. Teachers must lead learners to engage with possibility, to reimagine a better world.[16]

Te Rito Toi is a demonstration of how schools can build curriculum that responds to students' needs. This work is transformative as it encourages students to create in response to the world rather than simply consume content. Te Rito Toi encourages students to dance, sing, sculpt and write poetry to help them develop creative responses to their world. In the first three weeks after launching, Te Rito Toi had nearly 300,000[17] webpage views and had been used by 45,000 teachers in New Zealand. It has inspired similar approaches across the world in Toronto and Hong Kong.

A transformative curriculum wraps around the learner and considers what they need at this moment to help them interpret the world and then make a response rather than remain passive. It not only takes account of students' cognitive needs, it attends to their interpersonal and intrapersonal learning (see chapter 5). If curriculum is fixed, the opportunities to respond to crises large and small, local and international, are limited. For schools to be authentic and relevant, they need to grow dynamically to shape and reshape curriculum. to make knowledge dynamic and relevant.

It should not take a crisis for educators to see the need for a dynamic and responsive curriculum. Conceptualizing curriculum as the equivalent of syllabus or curriculum policy robs schools of the power of greater possibilities for learning. Many teachers and some school leaders we connect with in our work assume that mandated policy or syllabus documents are curriculum. This assumption denies educators a powerful strategy to transform their curriculum. One example of a school that transformed its curriculum in response to learner needs is Templestowe College.

Templestowe College: creating a transforming curriculum

In 2009 Templestowe College (figure 8.3), a government school in Melbourne, Australia had an enrolment of 289 and was effectively marked for closure.[18] In 2018 the school had grown to more than 1,089 students.[19] The College Council and a group of committed staff and students took a decision in 2009, facilitated by incoming principal Peter Hutton, to reform its curriculum and engage students directly in decision-making about their learning. The reform programme, called 'Take Control', engaged the whole school community in the change process. As the school explains, 'Take Control is a collaboration, combining the minds of students, families, staff and volunteers, to create a school that everybody wants.'[20] In practice this means students'

Figure 8.3 Templestowe College has transformed education for their students.

progress through their learning at their own pace and choose subjects that they consider relevant. Students do not progress at Templestowe College based on their age but rather based on their growth in knowledge and understanding in learning.

Templestowe demonstrates the possibility of a curriculum that is driven by students and the school community and not just reliant on a series of dot points in a decontextualized syllabus. This example, and many more like it, are an indication of how curriculum can be enacted to create real change for students, teachers and the broader school community. Co-construction of learning with students and the community allows places of learning to make their curriculum agentic and relevant. Templestowe College demonstrates what is possible when the gap between school practices and system policies are bridged.

Beyond the practice/policy divide in curriculum

We have written and discussed frequently the divide between what policymakers intend and what actually occurs in practice.[21] In *Transforming Schools* we called this the pedagogy/policy gap and in *Transforming Organizations* we discussed the practice/policy gap. Essentially we are describing the same phenomenon: the gap between what often external parties intend (such as curriculum boards or school systems) and what happens in practice. Templestowe is a strong example of a local community acting to transform their curriculum by suiting it to their school context. Templestowe closed the practice/policy divide by contextualizing the learning and meeting the needs of their students first, and then justifying it through the centralized policies in process of curriculum reverse-engineering. This in turn alerted the community to the practice of democratic curriculum through their role in influencing, shaping and being partners in the learning. Educators Jo-Anne Baird and Therese Hopfenbeck explain the potential for democratic curriculum: '. . . it is clear that there is no one group in charge of the future of curricula and assessment. Politicians and policymakers might frequently reform these areas of public life, but . . . teachers have strategic ways of engaging with these policies that affect the extent of their implementation in practice.'

At a system level, curriculum transformation is obviously more difficult but possible. In the province of British Columbia in Canada, the reworked curriculum uses the concept of Big Ideas and competencies (including creativity and communication) to focus on deep learning and relevance:

> British Columbia's curriculum is being modernized to respond to this demanding world . . . What and how we teach our students has been redesigned to provide greater flexibility for teachers, while allowing space and time for students to develop their skills and explore their passions and interests. The deep understanding and application of knowledge is at the centre of the new model, as opposed to the memory and recall of facts that previously shaped education around the globe for many decades.[22]

The approach also recognizes the centrality of Indigenous knowledge.

Indigenous knowledge in the curriculum

In post-colonial Canada and Australia, there is a renewed discussion about the opportunities for Indigenous knowledge in the curriculum. We have focused here on discussions from Canada and Australia to identify what might be possible. At the outset we should qualify any discussion with the acknowledgement that Indigenous cultures around the world continue to face poverty, injustice and intolerable gaps in health, education and other areas.[23] These comments on curriculum are not intended to deny any of these realities. This discussion is intended to support schools' considerations of how Indigenous knowledges might make a contribution to developing a transformative curriculum that is contextually sensitive and contributes to authentic reconciliation.

While many syllabus and curriculum offerings have claimed engagement with Indigenous perspectives, the challenge is to make Indigenous knowledge central to learning. Over more than a decade, British Columbia's curriculum has integrated these understandings throughout student learning: 'The education transformation work builds on what was learned and extends Aboriginal perspectives into the entire learning journey rather than in specific courses or specific grade levels. This means that from Kindergarten to graduation, students will experience Aboriginal perspectives and understandings as an integrated part of what they are learning.'[24] This integration across the curriculum recognizes that rather than just a perspective, Indigenous knowledges can be core to learning.

In Australia, 'Aboriginal and Torres Strait Islander Histories and Cultures' have been present in the national curriculum since 2014, yet there have been concerns from Aboriginal people over the relevance, authenticity and engagement in the Australian curriculum with Indigenous knowledges that are situated in their contexts rather than generalized. Indigenous knowledge is inherently contextual, and as researchers Chloe Parkinson and Tiffany Jones argue:

> No singular 'Indigenous knowledge' exists, as knowledge is 'a product of context' and each First Nations community will have distinct knowledges, values, beliefs, and understandings of the world . . . The [Australian] Curriculum however can allow for the inclusion of local Aboriginal knowledges, histories and cultures, to be then put into practice within the localised enacted curriculum. It is imperative that the intended curriculum provides opportunities for teachers to connect the curriculum to the cultures and backgrounds of students, and that teachers have the resources to enact them.[25]

Indigenous education expert Bob Morgan is a Gumilaroi man from Walgett, western NSW, Australia. He explains the link in Australian Indigenous cultures between culture and identity:

> Aboriginal culture and identity is a complex framework of component parts, the core of which is country (not geography, but a living, relational ecology of place) and the symbiotic kinship structures and relationships that define our identity. Cultural knowledge, traditional values, language, and the interrelatedness of all living things are embedded in the cultural grouping to which we belong.[26]

The need for a context-driven authentic partnership is found, in Bob Morgan's view, in the transformation occurring at Templestowe College. In the midst of systemic failure to incorporate Indigenous knowledge, he argues, hope is emerging: 'This hope and inspiration can be found in the actions of non-Aboriginal people who are also disenchanted and frustrated with conventional methods of education . . . Many of the principles and education philosophies of Templestowe College resonate because they resemble and are aligned to many of those espoused by Aboriginal people over many years.'

Indigenous knowledge should not be tacked on as has been the case in curriculum over so many years. In a transforming school such as Templestowe, the opportunity to engage deeply and authentically with local Indigenous knowledge should not be a last thought but embedded within schools' design and enactment of education.

Both Templestowe College as a school and British Columbia as a schooling system recognize that schools, leaders, teachers and the community are critical in what actually occurs in learning. The implementation of policy and syllabus depends on human capabilities and capacities for success. In both cases they have developed curriculum that is driven by sensitivity to context, autonomy and trust in their educators to contextualize learning with their students and communities. Curriculum does not occur in the abstract but in the concrete interactions of students, teachers and others in the school community.

One of the first steps in transforming curriculum is rethinking and unlearning the false dichotomies that limit our imagination for curriculum. In education our choices are not usually either/or, but are more complex. For instance, in a transforming curriculum the question should not be: 'Should we prioritize learning or assessment?' This kind of false dichotomy ignores the power of both learning and assessment to reinforce and support each other when they are reimagined in a transforming curriculum. In the next section we have outlined some of the most damaging, false dichotomies that limit the development of a transformative curriculum.

Unlearning false dichotomies

We have discussed in this book and in other books[27] the role of unlearning in transformation. Unlearning allows a critical reflection on 'taken for granted' assumptions. Unlearning helps educators to 'make strange' the taken for granted structures, approaches and policies that have become unquestioned as 'normal' in curriculum. To transform deeply, curriculum can first identify and then move beyond unhelpful and unproductive dichotomies. Why, for instance, do some educators:

- focus on individual cognitive performance (largely measured by test scores) versus collaborative achievement?
- separate cognitive and embodied learning (e.g. most examinations and assessments are written not embodied)?
- divide experiences in education as curricular and co-curricular when both are critical and essential for the development of students?

Before discussing the components of a transformative curriculum, we will identify and examine three of the most entrenched and damaging dichotomies in curriculum:

- pedagogy versus curriculum,
- subject depth versus integration, and
- assessment versus curriculum.

Pedagogy versus curriculum

There is a long and largely unproductive discussion about what matters most: the teaching (pedagogy) or what's taught (curriculum).[28] Some of the everyday conversations of educators rehash the dichotomy between what is set to be taught and the practicalities of teaching it. The staffroom discussion goes something like, 'How does the curriculum board expect us teach advanced algebra/*King Lear*/quantum mechanics/the water cycle under these conditions – don't they understand what we have to face every day in our classrooms?' The pressure for teachers to 'get through the content' is real, but rethinking how the content is taught can make curriculum and pedagogy interact more productively. If curriculum is the 'what' of teaching and pedagogy is the 'how', they must interact dynamically to ensure learning is effective.

As educator Bill Green argues,[29] '... curriculum and pedagogy go together as it were organically, as two sides of the one coin, each of them mobilised whenever appropriate or strategic: curriculum *and* pedagogy [not curriculum *or* pedagogy]'. He argues that seeing curriculum in this way multiplies the possible rather than creating unhealthy and unproductive dichotomies. Conceptualizing curriculum and pedagogy as interconnected processes enables teachers and students to reimagine learning beyond content delivery to collaborative discovery.

For example, when teaching a language like Spanish, an educator will not just read the syllabus and understand the scope and sequence of the learning ('the what'). They will also consider how Spanish can be experienced, learned and understood by their students. The Spanish syllabus may be the starting point, but the design of the pedagogy, which might include several elements, such as motivated instruction, deliberate practice and collaborative inquiry (see chapter 7), will make Spanish real for their students. Additionally pedagogy has the critical role of contextualizing the curriculum. For instance, if you are teaching Spanish near a Spanish-speaking community, developing an experience where students go into that community and buy groceries in Spanish and ask for directions supports students' understanding of how language and community are in dynamic relationship. Dynamism in curriculum can be supported through flexible approaches in teaching.

Educator John Dewey argues[30] that learners can continuously reconstruct their experiences. He asserts that knowledge is not static, it reshapes based on new learning and new experiences. In essence, Dewey is arguing for surprise as a potent curriculum tool. For instance if in a drama class studying Hamlet's characterisation a question arose from students around existential philosophy a teacher should have the freedom to follow this inquiry. Teachers often feel hamstrung by narrow learning intentions and outcomes when they should be enabled to make learning rigorous, dynamic and engaging.

The potential for dynamism and flexibility in learning calls for curriculum that is a map rather than a script. In other words, educators require resources that facilitate pedagogical flexibility and allow them to curate learning for their contexts and students.

One approach that supports the integration of curriculum and pedagogy is John Dewey's concept of flexible purposing.[31] Flexible purposing creates a dynamic interaction between pedagogy and curriculum to generate agile, creative and relevant learning through flexible curriculum. Eliot Eisner[32] explains the process as driven not by outcomes but by discovery:

> Flexible purposing is opportunistic; it capitalizes on the emergent features appearing within a field of relationships. It is not rigidly attached to predefined

aims when the possibility of better ones emerge. The kind of thinking that flexible purposing requires thrives best in an environment in which the rigid adherence to a plan is not a necessity. As experienced teachers well know, the surest road to hell in a classroom is to stick to the lesson plan no matter what.

A flexible view of curriculum facilitates a dynamic relationship with pedagogy always seeking to support learners' interpretation of experience. This contrasts with the rigidity of status-quo curriculum, which can create uninspired and disconnected learning. A dynamic and flexible curriculum propels teachers beyond 'teaching to the dot points'. It opens up possibilities in learning to allow for the mindful curation of learning experiences (see chapter 6) that are more relevant to students' needs and contexts, and not simply a static and decontextualized set of documents.

Subject depth versus integration

We have argued throughout this chapter that our education system should reflect the circumstances of our world as it is now and not as it may have been or that we would like it to be. Curriculum is often developed at a point in time but knowledge is dynamic, and shifts by making and seeking new connections. For instance, the study of economics has changed dramatically in the last twenty to thirty years as perspectives from psychology and sociology have been integrated. Behavioural economics now has significant influence in the discussions around how our economy works. This evolution of human knowledge was enabled by making the boundaries between psychology and economics porous so that new understandings could be generated. De-siloing knowledge was also a concern of philosopher Pierre Bourdieu. When he was asked by the French government in 1988 to consider the future of education, he argued: 'Concern to reinforce the coherence of teaching should lead to the enhancement of team teaching, that brings together teachers from different disciplines. It should lead to a rethinking of the divisions within disciplines and a re-examination of certain historical regroupings. It might succeed, although always gradually, in bringing closer together the different areas . . .'[33]

An impediment to this approach is the way knowledge is organized in education. Historically and routinely, educators have packaged learning in subject-based 'containers' such as English, physics, dance and so on. However, the world our students will face is not neatly divided across subject boundaries. The issues that led to 9/11 do not fit and never have fitted neatly into one area of the curriculum. This human and geopolitical catastrophe spans history, theology, politics, physics, media and communication. Understanding complex issues such as geopolitical acts of war or terror or climate change, pandemics or the global refugee crisis requires deep understanding of specific disciplines (such as history and science). It equally requires a willingness to connect that specific deep understanding with other areas (mathematics, religion, psychology) to understand how areas of knowledge interact and interconnect in complex problems.

The OECD also argues that integrated and collaborative understanding will be an essential component of a transforming education system: 'To be prepared for the future, individuals have to learn to think and act in a more integrated way, taking into account the interconnections and inter-relations between contradictory or incompatible ideas, logics and positions, from both short- and long-term perspectives.'[34] For educators this challenges us to de-silo disciplines to create learning that seeks connections and integration. As we discussed in *Transforming Schools*, the 4Cs provide educators with the enabling capacities to connect disciplines in interdisciplinary or transdisciplinary learning. The Association of American Colleges and Universities acknowledges the need for a balance between integrative and disciplinary approaches. They argue that integrated approaches such as interdisciplinarity learning allow students to:

> . . . solve problems that draw on multiple disciplines and [are] able to seamlessly integrate information, data techniques, tools, perspectives, concepts, and/or theories from two or more disciplines or bodies of specialized knowledge to advance fundamental understanding to solve problems whose solutions are beyond the fundamental scope of a single discipline or research practice.[35]

We argued in *Transforming Schools* that the 4Cs – creativity, critical reflection, collaboration and communication – are the enabling capabilities to support the development of expertise within and between disciplines. In education, this kind of discussion is often characterized by a dichotomy between understanding a discipline deeply and the ability to collaborate across disciplines to solve applied or theoretical problems. Educators have many choices when they are considering integrated approaches. Problem-based learning is perhaps the most familiar and longstanding, but there are several other ways of thinking about integrated approaches that can support learning. These terms are often used loosely, so we have provided some definitions to clarify these approaches. Music researcher Alexander Refsum Jensenius provides a useful set of explanations[36] that we have adapted to include terms that may be more familiar to school educators.

- Project-based learning: students collaborate, drawing on their disciplinary knowledge to respond to a project that has been designed for them which may include elements of or be 'real world problems'. For instance, students are given a place in the world (e.g. sub-Saharan Africa) and collaborate to design a human civilization that can be environmentally, economically and socially sustainable.
- Problem-based learning: students work together to respond to a 'real world problem'. For instance, they work on a project on redesigning energy supply in a school or a university from fossil fuels to renewable energy.
- Cross-disciplinary: this involves the engagement of multiple perspectives from multiple disciplines without the integration of discipline knowledge.[37] Genetics, for instance, crosses biology, chemistry and environmental sciences.

- Multidisciplinary: people from different disciplines work together, each drawing on their disciplinary knowledge. For instance, when working to restore a wetland, ecologists, biologists and meteorologists might all draw upon their different backgrounds to devise a strategy.
- Interdisciplinary: students integrate knowledge and methods from different disciplines, using a synthesis of approaches. For instance, to understand how a hospital might provide easier access for linguistically diverse patients, students might integrate linguistics, languages, film making and communication studies.
- Transdisciplinary: 'An approach to curriculum integration which dissolves the boundaries between the conventional disciplines and organizes teaching and learning around the construction of meaning in the context of real-world problems or themes.'[38] For example, students blend concepts from psychology and economics to understand human behaviour.

A transformative curriculum will feature both deep understanding of disciplines and the integration of the disciplines through approaches such as interdisciplinary or transdisciplinary learning. Science educators Kathryn Paige and colleagues argue that in an integrated approach, it is essential that:

> ... teachers and students be introduced to the various disciplines and their uniqueness, but also how they can complement each other when addressing complex issues. Each discipline contributes important concepts, ways of thinking and working, skills and values that students need to explore to satisfy their curiosity and become informed citizens.[39]

A balance between disciplinary depth and interdisciplinary connections is a constant challenge for teachers. To strike this balance educators need a curriculum that enables curriculum depth and agility complemented by flexible pedagogy. The ability to integrate and apply learning in a specific subject area (English or mathematics) is a clear sign of depth of understanding. This is not a revelation to most educators – depth of understanding in disciplines will lead to the ability to apply, synthesize and create with that deep understanding. For instance, the ability to apply concepts from music (e.g. rhythm and tempo) to understanding of literature (e.g. iambic pentameter in Shakespeare) demonstrates a deep understanding of the application of concepts across disciplines.

Bloom's taxonomy[40] identifies application, synthesis and evaluation (and in the revised version, creativity[41]) as higher-order cognitive skills. In other words, the ability to integrate knowledge within and outside discipline boundaries demonstrates depth of understanding within that subject. The ability to apply these higher-order skills relies on a student's ability to collaborate to connect, communicate, create and critically reflect on knowledge.

The 4Cs (creativity, critical reflection, collaboration and communication) are the foundational and enabling capabilities for connecting learning. Often they are assumed knowledge rather than explicitly taught in preparation for integrated approaches to learning. For instance, tertiary educator and expert on interdisciplinary learning Veronica Boix Mansilla[42] argues that integrated approaches allow students 'to tackle complex problems and [find] joy in collaborating with people whom they could learn from'. We have no argument with her here; on the contrary, we heartily agree, but where do these enabling capabilities emerge from? The assumption in many of these discussions is that the 4Cs are learnt osmotically. In other words, students come to learning experiences with creativity, critical reflection, collaboration and communication. Sadly this is rarely true.

This represents a massive blind spot in curriculum as it leaves out critical foundational capabilities (such as the 4Cs) that support deep understanding in subjects or disciplines and the means to integrate them. For instance, if students:

- do not have an understanding of group processes for *creativity*, how can teams *collaborate* to generate innovative solutions to real world problems?
- have no framework or shared understanding of *collaboration*, how is it possible to celebrate, integrate and reconcile differing or potentially conflicting perspectives in different subject areas?
- do not understand *communication* deeply, how can they explain their disciplinary expertise as they seek to integrate it with other ways of knowing?
- are unable to *critically reflect,* how is it possible to understand where their attempts to understand a complex problem went wrong?

We see the centrality of the 4Cs for learning consistently and especially in project-based learning (PBL) work. We were recently in a high school that trialled PBL. They had seen it work in other places and they had been persuaded by the claims (some of which we have made here) that PBL can cross subject boundaries and provide a more integrated and relevant learning experience for students. The trial lasted a year and the school decided, based on student, parent and teacher feedback, that it didn't work. Students did not enjoy the collaboration aspects of PBL, teachers found the design of the tasks difficult and did not see the point of working across subject areas, and parents complained that it was taking the place of 'proper learning'.

There are obvious problems here. Too little time was given to the trial, parents and the community were not supported in their understanding of the change, and teachers were not sufficiently supported in the design of the projects. Beyond all of these issues, there was no coherent common framework to support integrated learning (see chapter 5). The enabling capabilities – creativity, critical reflection, collaboration and communication – while essential to the success of PBL were not explicitly taught at any point. Notwithstanding the other issues, it is not surprising that without these enabling capabilities, this PBL programme faltered.

We have great respect for PBL as a learning method; however, like all learning PBL requires foundational understanding and skills in how to collaborate, create, communicate and critically reflect. In our work with educators, the 4Cs are foundational for all learning. More often than not, when we see PBL and integrated learning more generally falter, these foundations have not been established effectively. The next and perhaps most damaging dichotomy is assessment versus curriculum.

Assessment versus curriculum

In many countries, the surest way to generate a moral panic in the media or among politicians is to report a slide down the PISA rankings. The nuances and contributing factors are often ignored in these discussions to make way for teacher blaming and a call for 'return the basics', as if it is that simple. For a few days the media is full of commentary[43] on what these results mean for each country. The curriculum and/or teaching is often blamed for the 'slump in standards'. Often the panacea suggested and sometimes implemented is more testing and a narrowing of the curriculum. As if doing the same thing we have done in response to poor PISA results for a decade or more will somehow magically arrest the decline. Educators Jo-Anne Baird and Therese Hopfenbeck argue that we can grasp the opportunity to rethink the curriculum assessment dichotomy:

> Unless the relationship between curricula assessment and learning is given more attention, the future will be a world of busy fools, striving for targets that divert attention and energy from deep learning. Amidst this future is the prospect of increased surveillance of our behaviour, in the name of assessment. The extent to which this will bring about educational good needs careful consideration.[44]

We believe assessment (summative and formative) plays a crucial role in a transforming curriculum. Formative assessment is the cornerstone of feedback that is critical to creating deep learning. Our concern, and the concern of many others, is that assessment has been disconnected from learning. This creates an unhealthy set of comparisons locally, nationally and internationally that de-emphasizes and discounts context. Baird and Hopfenbeck explain the impact of globalized assessment:

> In the field of assessment, the development of international large-scale assessment studies such as TIMSS (Trends in International Mathematics and Science Study), PIRLS (Progress in International Reading Literacy Study) and PISA (Programme for International Student Assessment) have signalled the increase in competitive global education systems. Policymakers around the world now respond to a nation's results on international tests, in comparison with others. In particular, PISA has had a major influence . . .[45]

The problem becomes that learning takes second place to testing. The whole mission, values and potential of education become distorted as resources and priorities are driven by the need to 'improve rankings'. There is, for instance, currently little or no recognition in these international tests of the climate of the school, the autonomy that teachers and students have over learning, how prominent the 4Cs are in learning, etc. These tests are restricted to critical but limited aspects of schooling that can be economically captured through a multiple choice or written test for the most part. Decontextualized testing (as these are examples of) de-emphasizes the influence that the school's environment, teaching staff and student demographics have on learning. This approach can disconnect teachers and students from learning, and corrodes teacher professionalism. As Baird argues: 'Professionals within these systems, in this case teachers, become disengaged and alienated because the systems do not reflect their local priorities, needs and values.'[46] Perhaps more alarmingly, these tests can lead to a narrow and limited curriculum that disinherits our students from the context, breadth and depth of learning they require to survive and thrive in a world that is growing more complex. This complex world is beyond the capability of standardized tests to assess. How can learning and assessment become reconnected?

In a transforming curriculum, the first question we should ask is: how do we facilitate deep learning? In short, we think assessment should be a process of:

a) supporting the learners' progression and understanding through formative and summative strategies, and

b) generating feedback for educators and students on the success or otherwise of all aspects of their learning (not just those measured in standardized tests) and creating a pathway for growth in that learning.

Educator Wynne Harlen argues:

> . . . schools have to be held accountable for the learning of their students, but this needs to be conducted in a manner that provides a fair and more complete picture of the curriculum and also takes into account the varied circumstances and nature of the school intake. To serve the evaluative purpose well, the assessment data should include a broad range of outcomes that reflect the aims of twenty-first-century education. Several of these outcomes, such as communication skills, problem solving and critical thinking are not easily measured and require qualitative as well as quantitative data.[47]

Critical here is the role of assessment in generating a complete picture of student learning and not just focusing on those areas that have been considered 'easy to capture' through pen and paper testing. The 4Cs are often categorized as 'difficult to assess' and yet when schools can agree on a common framework to define and enact learning in each of them, assessment is not only possible – it is necessary for students to understand their progress. Often this means rethinking how assessment works to ensure alignment with learning. For instance, many of our partnership schools are providing feedback to students on elements of the Learning Disposition Wheel such as 'grit' and 'build new ideas' to support their growth in these areas.

False dichotomies in curriculum have the effect of limiting the imagination of educators. If we are to design effective curriculum that is dynamic, contextualized and relevant, we need to consider a new more flexible way to understand and reimagine curriculum rejecting false dichotomies. Let's turn now to the 'how' of transforming curriculum.

The Transformative Curriculum Framework

The four phases of this framework are not necessarily sequential. They are overlapping processes in an effective curriculum transformation process. The first phase requires consultation to understand the possibilities of curriculum from multiple perspectives including students, teachers, leaders, community and people with expertise in practice and research. We have used the Communication Crystal (see chapter 1) to guide the process of reimagining curriculum. The curriculum framework has four features:

- Consult – alert to messaging
- Contextualize – enabling voice
- Co-construct – conveying meaning and purpose
- Craft – generating action and agency

Consult – alert to messaging

Consultation as a process has become somewhat degraded. Often we see preordained decisions in education and other areas going to a process of consultation as a way of 'performing' community engagement when in reality it is no better than window dressing. At Templestowe College the principal led a process of discussing 'what students wanted and needed in their education'. He formed a small working group to shape the curriculum around some shared values that prioritized the needs of students based on what he heard from students, parents, educators and the school community. As we discussed in chapter 3, values create a framework that shapes curriculum. Templestowe College's values (they call them philosophies) reflect the evolution of that process. The following is a selection from their values that are most relevant to curriculum at Templestowe College:[48]

- Learning is an exciting, lifelong journey, where the challenge is to discover and pursue our passions, which contribute to the greater good.
- We each have our own strengths and talents and work best when we are happy and able to follow and explore our passions and interests.
- People achieve more when they are empowered. If any student, staff member or parent has a suggestion, the answer has to be 'YES', unless it takes too much time, too much money or negatively impacts on someone else. This is called the 'yes is the default' policy.

- Ensuring a positive learning environment is essential for students to reach their potential.
- Community is important and we all have an individual and collective responsibility to make it work.
- Innovative education should be developed collaboratively around evidence-based research and high-quality student learning data.
- An entrepreneurial mindset and entrepreneurial skills are valuable and transferable through all aspects of life. This mindset is vital to be able to participate in the rapidly changing world that we live in, now and in the future.
- Every student benefits from having a detailed individual learning plan.
- Young people have brilliant ideas and can do amazing things. We will not let age be a restricting factor in giving young people the opportunity to display this. Young people have far more capacity than the traditional educational system gives them credit for.
- Students should contribute significantly to the decision-making process and operation of their school, as well as making a genuine contribution to their community.
- It is important to measure growth and individual well-being, as well as achievement. This growth should be across a range of areas and measures, not just literacy and numeracy.

A discussion around a set of values such as these can help everyone involved move beyond the details and engage with a bigger picture. This process opens up space for diverse voices to be heard. While participants in consultation may not always use terms such as 'agency' or 'democratic learning', they may express values that are aligned to these terms. For instance, when students say, 'I want a bigger say in what I learn', they are messaging agency matters to them.

In the first stages of curriculum, being alert to messaging from the students, teachers, leaders and the community lays the foundation for an effective consultation process. In this phase it is critical to be alert to the messages that are difficult to hear. For instance, some parents may feel that their views have not been welcome in the past and may be reluctant to contribute. Creating a consultation process that welcomes these views may bring difficult but critical perspectives into the discussion. When leading a curriculum transformation process, the next phase is to situate the curriculum in context by enabling voice.

Contextualize – enabling voice

A common mistake made by those generating curriculum centrally in departments and systems is that context is of little or marginal consequence. The voices of students, parents, teachers and leaders are not sufficiently enabled to understand the breadth and the depth of the context. By enabling voice, students, teachers and others in the school community can support a deep understanding of their experience (their needs, local resources, local environment, etc.), providing context for the design of curriculum. In a review of the role of context in educational reform, researchers Alma Harris and Michelle Jones argue that context has been discounted, leading to policy failures. They argue: '... policy-makers around the world still seem over preoccupied with identifying the "right" policies to secure change and improvement, rather than considering the conditions and contextual factors that are most likely to make any chosen policy effective in practice'.[49]

In other words, no two education settings are the same so why would we expect any two curricula to look the same? The effect of equating syllabus with curriculum and ignoring context deprives schools of the opportunity to apply and adapt learning to suit their needs. Developing curriculum that meets the needs of students means their community, culture and history of the school can be acknowledged and integrated in a co-creation process. If this process is successful the co-creation process itself will acknowledge and integrate these contextual factors and features. According to educational researcher Javier Fernández-Río, context can be understood in the following ways:[50]

- school location (e.g. urban, rural),
- student demographics (e.g. number, cultural diversity, absentee rate),
- administration (e.g. budget, policies),
- staff (e.g. teaching experience, expertise, motivation), and
- resources (e.g. equipment, facilities).

At Templestowe College the redesign of the curriculum considered all of these contextual factors to drive an authentic and effective transforming curriculum. In practice the community, students, parents and teachers were enabled to contribute in discussions about what skills and capabilities they identified as critical to their learning. The result of this process is their curriculum now includes 'student led electives' where 'students are able to negotiate the content and the activities undertaken with the teacher'.[51] This approach is a legacy of a curriculum designed to be inherently flexible that draws on student and community interests rather than system mandated policy prescription. At Templestowe College, students can choose, depending on their interests, to undertake studies in conjunction with more than thirty-eight electives including the following:[52]

- Architecture
- Backyard Studies
- Computer 3D Modelling
- Entrepreneurship
- Feathers and Fur
- FISH
- Geek Studies

- Media – Writing and Creating Content
- Personal Fitness
- Reptiles
- Robotics
- Sport Management and Coaching
- Visual Communication and Design (VCD).

These electives do not take the place of subjects such as literacy, numeracy, English and Mathematics; rather they are integrated with them. At Templestowe College, the context influenced the development of learning that celebrated the passions and interests of students.

Alma Harris and Michelle Jones argue that context has been undervalued in recent times and 'it is high time that context and culture were brought 'out of the shadows'. They argue, based on extensive research, that if context is not sufficiently understood and integrated, 'education reform will continue to be partial and potentially misleading, thus making our attempts at education change fragile'.

After the context has been integrated in the curriculum, the next critical step is to provide agency to students, teachers, leadership and the community through authentic co-construction.

Co-construct – conveying meaning and purpose

Authentic curriculum transformation will not spring only from an individual or a committee. An approach that puts the agency of teachers and students at the centre of the process will see genuine co-construction of learning. In this phase of the framework, we move beyond the 'imagined' and begin to co-construct with teachers, students and the community a curriculum that will convey meaning and purpose for everyone who has a stake in the learning and teaching at the school. Co-constructing curriculum is a process of creating flexible structures to facilitate the values established earlier. For instance, if one of the values is 'agency', making this meaningful will mean putting structures in place to allow students to make choices based on their own strengths and interests.

At Templestowe College this is managed by encouraging students to progress not in year groups but when it works for them academically and developmentally through different focus pathways, including:

- English
- Civics, Citizenship, Humanities, Economics and Business
- Mathematics
- Science
- Farm and Animals

- Health and Physical Education
- Performing and Visual Arts
- Technologies.

This structure, co-constructed with the school community, puts an emphasis on student choice and agency by creating a flexible structure that encourages progression based on student growth in understanding, not by age.

In a transforming curriculum, structures must be meaningful and purposeful rather than 'taken for granted'. The final stage in the framework is the crafting of a holistic curriculum by generating action and agency.

Craft – generating action and agency

As we have discussed throughout this chapter, curriculum should not be static or reflect a status quo. A transformative curriculum reflects the needs of learners as they navigate the world by responding to their cognitive, interpersonal and intrapersonal needs. The crafting of a curriculum is a continuous and iterative process. By crafting we mean the constant co-construction process that works to align learning programmes with values, context, meaning and purpose. This is not a 'set and forget' model of curriculum, but a participatory and evolving process. In our work with schools we often see curriculum structures and approaches that have not changed for decades. The underlying assumption in these situations is that curriculum is something fixed and static. A transformative curriculum is constantly evolving with the ultimate aim of creating action and agency for students primarily and then others within the school community.

At Templestowe College the curriculum is under constant review. One of the needs that emerged there was for their young people to gain experience in part-time work. Templestowe College crafted a strategy to meet that need by employing students within the school. They explain this approach in their most recent strategic plan:

> To develop business acumen and expand their understanding of the workforce, students are formally employed in a range of roles across the school including: reception, as tutors for other students, maintenance, administration support, IT helpdesk, photography, graphic arts, café and canteen assistants and social media monitors. Students are encouraged to develop entrepreneurial skills by running their own for profit businesses in partnership with the school in areas such as catering, management of the performing arts centre, running the canteen etc.[53]

This is an example of ongoing crafting of the curriculum – in this case, students' needs to build understanding of working in a real job with real pay generated a curriculum response.

A transforming curriculum can reshape to meet student needs through flexible enabling structures. The crafting process is a constant iterative process of shaping the curriculum around student needs. In this example and many others of a transforming curriculum, action and agency make curriculum an ongoing process.

The Transformative Curriculum Framework presents a model for dynamic, active and agentic student learning. It is not intended to be a prescription but rather a guide for a set of approaches that generates engagement and agency from learners, teachers and communities. Critically, it conceives of curriculum as action and not just as a static document. The potential in this process is reimagining curriculum to make it meaningful and dynamic for learners and their constantly evolving worlds.

Concluding reflections: transformative curriculum for deeper learning

Status-quo curriculum is a problem in education because it limits the potential for learning to be deep, connected, authentic and engaging. It does that by assuming knowledge is static and the needs of learners are static. Transforming curriculum means focusing on deep learning that is dynamic, agentic and relevant. As curriculum researchers Jung-Hoon Jung and William Pinar claim, status-quo curriculum places decisions about learners beyond schools:

> Working within the status quo confines conceptions of curriculum to stipulations others (politicians, profiteers, and ideologues but rarely professional educators) make. The focus shifts from the canonical curriculum question – *what knowledge is of most worth?* – to the assessment question – *have students learned what others have demanded?* Assessment (standardized testing in our time) sidelines concerns over the intellectual quality and vitality of the curriculum.[54]

Jung and Pinar's argument is about who should be at the centre of the curriculum design and implementation. We think those best placed to move from the status quo and imagine curriculum anew are educational communities (focused on students and including teachers, school leaders and the community as reflected in the Transformative Curriculum Framework) rather than those far removed from the needs of learners. The status quo will not deliver the kinds of capabilities we need for our young people to survive and thrive in an uncertain future. A transformative curriculum is an activity rather than a document.

We believe understanding curriculum as an active and dynamic process can help deliver transformation by fundamentally reimagining what curriculum is, who owns it and how it can be assessed. This is not optional for education. Our ability to make curriculum focus on deeper learning that prepares our young people for an uncertain future in an uncertain present can be this generation's legacy.

In the next chapter we discuss how teacher education can be a capability for transformation.

Transforming teacher education
Experience, reflection and inquiry

9

John Dewey's legacy: transformative education 181

A continuum for teacher education 182

Building democratic education through teacher education 182

The 4Cs and transformative teacher education 183

Foundational teacher education 184

Foundational processes: experience, reflection and inquiry 185

Experience 185
Reflection 187
Inquiry 187

Lifelong teacher education 188

Building on the foundations: experience, reflection and inquiry 190

Transforming Lifelong Teacher Education at Hurstville Public School 190

Partnerships for transformation 190
Reimagining successful learning 191
From training to lifelong learning 192
Community of Praxis 193
Praxis 194
Experience 195
Reflection 196
Inquiry 197

Next steps for lifelong teacher education at Hurstville Public School 199

Concluding reflections 200

If you were on the shores of Lake Champlain near the border between the United States and Canada around the summer of 1875, you might have spied a boat packed with four teenage boys including 15-year-old John.[1] He would grow up to become one of the key thinkers of the twentieth century. The intrepid band of natural explorers had a tent, blankets and some cooking gear to sustain them on their epic journey across the lake which at some places is 12 miles wide (19.3 kilometres) with more than seventy islands. This adventure in the natural wilderness, reminiscent of Mark Twain's *Adventures of Huckleberry Finn* (written around the same time) deeply influenced John's views about learning later in life and stood in contrast to his experience of school. School was boredom, recitation and irrelevance broken only by experiences in the natural world in the Adirondack Mountains and the waterways of nearby French Canada.

John's father was a grocer in Burlington but young John enjoyed nothing more than working his grandfather's farm and sometimes hanging around the local sawmill where he gained experience in work, commerce and human interactions. His views as an adult on the centrality of democracy in education and society were formed in a family where politics was frequently discussed and where democratic participation in the community was pursued by his parents.

After John left school, he went to university and then became a teacher at a small school in South Oil City, Pennsylvania where he taught Latin, algebra and natural science. He left teaching after two years and studied philosophy at Johns Hopkins

Figure 9.1 Lake Champlain near the United States/Canadian border.

University, and became one of the most influential philosophers and educators of the last 100 years.

John Dewey's legacy: transformative education

John Dewey's work creates a foundation for transformative learning. In the 1900s, making learning democratic by placing the student's experience and reflections at the centre of education was radical. His work today represents the unfulfilled promise and potential of education. Dewey contributed to our understandings of student-centredness, inquiry, problem-based learning, experiential and aesthetic learning. Reflecting on Dewey's views on democracy and education, philosopher David Hilderbrand argues that for Dewey, democracy was made possible through education enabled by creativity, critical reflection, collaboration and communication:[2]

> The success or failure of democracy rests on education. Education is most determinative of whether citizens develop the habits needed to investigate problematic beliefs and situations, to communicate openly, throughout. While every culture aims to convey values and beliefs to the coming generation, it is critical, Dewey thought, to distinguish between education which inculcates collaborative and creative hypothesizing and education which foments obeisance [obedience] to parochialism and dogma.

The 4Cs are evident and active in Dewey's work and legacy. Dewey's view of education, driven by the student's needs and experiences, establishes the foundation for a vibrant and critical democracy. He argues we can create spaces for students to make their own choices and decisions: '. . . the application of democratic methods, methods of consultation, persuasion, negotiation, communication, cooperative intelligence, in the task of making our own politics, industry, education, our culture generally, a servant and an evolving manifestation of democratic ideas'.[3] In Dewey's view, our schools can facilitate growth in democratic citizenship by supporting students to develop independent and critical thinking and action through the processes of experience, reflection and inquiry. To make democratic learning possible, we first need to ensure that it is embedded and active in teacher education.

This chapter considers how teacher education might be reimagined to make it a capability for transformation. We explore how Dewey's call for experience, reflection and inquiry enabled by the 4Cs might form the foundations of a continuum of learning throughout the career of educators to drive democratic and transformative learning for students. We first consider how experience, reflection and inquiry might be embedded in foundational teacher education (preservice). We then explore how one school, Hurstville Public School in New South Wales, Australia has developed a transformative lifelong learning approach in their school, founded in a deep understanding of the 4Cs.

We see the first step in reimagining teacher education as bringing coherence and continuity to the professional growth of teachers by establishing a continuum of education throughout an educator's career.

A continuum for teacher education

The transformative teacher education continuum begins in *foundational* teacher education (also known as initial or preservice). The continuum then articulates throughout the career as *lifelong* teacher education[4] (also known as in service or professional development). The foundational processes of experience, reflection and inquiry enable teachers to understand and respond to the needs of learners and build a professional knowledge base. Teacher education provides the capacity to engage foundational processes to harness teacher creativity, critical reflection, communication and collaboration to enable school transformation.

Dewey's focus on experience, reflection and inquiry, born in the rapid change of the nineteenth and early twentieth centuries, provides the underpinnings for transformative teacher education. The curiosity that began in his experiences – discussing democracy, paddling on Lake Champlain and hiking through the Adirondacks grew into a view of education that recognized experience, reflection, and inquiry as foundational for democratic citizenship. As Dewey argued: 'we are doubtless far from realizing the potential efficacy of education as a constructive agency of improving society, from realizing that it represents not only a development of children and youth but also of the future society of which they will be the constituents'. Dewey's approaches are perhaps even more relevant for today's schools as we strive to design learning that is student-centred, relevant and reinforces democratic values.

Building democratic education through teacher education

Dewey's call for democratic schooling driven by experience, reflection and inquiry directly challenges the status quo of the Global Educational Reform Movement (GERM).[5] As educators Kay Fuller and Howard Stevenson explain, GERM is characterized by 'increased standardisation, a narrowing of the curriculum to focus on core subjects/knowledge, the growth of high stakes accountability and the use of corporate management practices as the key features of the new orthodoxy'. Schools built on this kind of managerialism (rather than leadership), decontextualized testing (rather than assessment for learning) and prescriptive syllabus (rather than a context-driven 4C curriculum) will not equip our young people sufficiently to be active democratic citizens. As we have argued throughout this book, GERM processes have a tendency to strip agency from learning for teachers and students. If we are to encourage democratic citizenship and prepare our young people for the challenges of complexity, chaos and contradiction, we should begin with transforming teacher education.

Research consistently demonstrates that teachers are the most decisive factor in successful student learning.[6] Yet the career continuum of teacher education is often disconnected, incoherent and piecemeal with little or no recognition of teacher agency. If we believe that experience, reflection and inquiry are vital qualities in building democratic citizens, surely those features must be foundational and fundamental to teacher education. As Dewey argues: 'Democracy has to be born anew every generation, and education is its midwife.'[7] If that is the case, we need to reimagine teacher education to nurture creative professionals ready to birth and grow democratic citizenship through the enabling capabilities of the 4Cs.

The 4Cs and transformative teacher education

Transformative teacher education has at least two purposes. Beginning teachers need to become reflectively meta-aware of how they learn. Simultaneously they need to develop the capabilities and processes to conceptualize learning as intrinsically creative, critically reflective, collaborative and communicative for their students. In the foundational stage, beginning educators move beyond status quo conceptions of learning to build agency in themselves and their learners. Experience, reflection and inquiry are the foundational processes that develop innovative, exploratory and expansive teaching. These processes, when enabled by the 4Cs, make authentic learner-focused curriculum and pedagogy possible throughout the teaching career, facilitating a reconceptualization of teacher education.

Reimagining the shape of teacher education, Director for Education and Skills at the OECD Andreas Schleicher argues for a collaborative and creative profession where the 4Cs are critical (our emphasis in italics):

> The past was hierarchical; the future is *collaborative*, recognizing both teachers and students as resources and co-*creators* . . . The past was about prescription; the future is about an informed profession, where professional and *collaborative* working norms replace the industrial work organization, with its administrative control and accountability. Professionalism means emphasizing the internal motivation of members and their ownership of professional practice . . . With all of that, tomorrow's teachers will enjoy deep professional knowledge, a high degree of professional autonomy and a *collaborative* culture.[8]

Schleicher's vision for teacher education answers much of the 'why' of transforming teacher education. To develop the professionalism he is arguing for means teacher education must change.

A collaborative and creative profession requires a reimagining of:

- pedagogy (chapter 6),
- curriculum (chapter 8),
- the teacher's own professional learning (foundational and lifelong), and
- leadership (chapter 10).

To achieve this, educators can collaborate, unlearn and redesign the current disconnect between the phases of teacher education. This disconnect is evident, for example, in the lack of collaboration or communication between universities and schools as beginning teachers begin their teaching careers. A transformation in teacher education will produce a coherent, articulate and developmental continuum that embeds experience, reflection and inquiry throughout the teaching career. That continuum begins by establishing the tools to build transformative learning in the foundational phase of teacher education.

Foundational teacher education

Foundational (preservice) teacher education stands at a crossroads. The changes in schools and schooling largely driven by the changes in society and the world of work that Schleicher refers to (collaborative and co-creative rather than individualistic and hierarchical) are presenting multiple exponential challenges to the way we 'do' school. In the face of this challenge, preservice teacher education has not sufficiently kept pace with change sometimes reflecting irrelevant notions of learning, pedagogy and curriculum.[9]

We use the term 'foundational' to signify that preservice teacher education creates the foundations for lifelong teacher education. Experience, reflection and inquiry are the cornerstones of agentic and transformative learning and teaching for all learners (students and teachers). In a transformative approach to teacher education, educators develop as designers, researchers, innovators and leaders in all aspects of schooling including pedagogy, curriculum, assessment leadership and school organization. The continuum of teacher learning stands in contrast to a 'teacher training' approach where learning stops after preservice education apart perhaps from a few disconnected one-off in-service courses.

The building blocks of high-quality teacher education arise in foundational education, where developing a deep and explicit understanding of learning processes makes possible a creative and collaborative future for the profession. While experience, reflection and inquiry have been evident in teacher education for some time, they are rarely linked explicitly and coherently with the 4Cs. This missing link could potentially leave beginning educators with an inadequate conceptual understanding of learning and teaching. Experience, reflection and inquiry are only possible when the 4Cs are operating effectively to enable educators to design and teach with these approaches. Critically, teachers (at all phases of their education) should have the opportunity to understand and deepen their learning in the 4Cs before they can be facilitated by the teacher in the classroom.

Educators need to experience teaching and learning processes (such as experience, reflection and inquiry) before they can enact them in their own classrooms and schools. Students and teachers need to have the capacity to learn by doing (experience), reflect deeply on those experiences (critical reflection) and then build inquiry to drive further learning through action. As we discuss throughout this chapter, these processes become transformative when educators can create, critically reflect, collaborate and communicate effectively. In our view, you cannot:

- interpret and share *experience* without being able to *communicate* with others,
- *reflect* deeply without understanding *critical reflection*, or
- *inquire* effectively without skills in *collaboration* and *creativity*.

Developing these processes does not mean that teachers (especially in foundational teacher education) should not build deep disciplinary and interdisciplinary understandings. D. Hansen and colleagues argue, 'Dewey emphasizes that learning is impossible—or better, inconceivable—without there being something to learn. He underscores that this something in schools must be rich expressions of humanity's evolving accomplishments in the arts, humanities, mathematics, and sciences.'[10] Dewey's approach to learning rejects false dichotomies such as practical experience versus disciplinary knowledge. We now outline how foundational teacher education might be reimagined around experience, reflection and inquiry enabled by the 4Cs.

Foundational processes: experience, reflection and inquiry

We focus here on three key processes that are enabled by the 4Cs. Figure 9.2 demonstrates the interdependent and overlapping relationship of experience, reflection and inquiry that are enabled and driven by the 4Cs. These are the necessary foundational processes and enablers to generate innovative and agentic teachers and students. These processes take seriously the sometimes trite aphorism 'all teachers are learners'. As Dewey argues, learning begins with experience.

Experience

The saying 'experience is a great teacher' is only half right. John Dewey asserted in the 1930s that 'all genuine education comes through experience'. However, he also argued that experiences that do not lead to reflection are not beneficial for deeper

Figure 9.2 Experience, reflection and inquiry are interdependent processes enabled by the 4Cs.

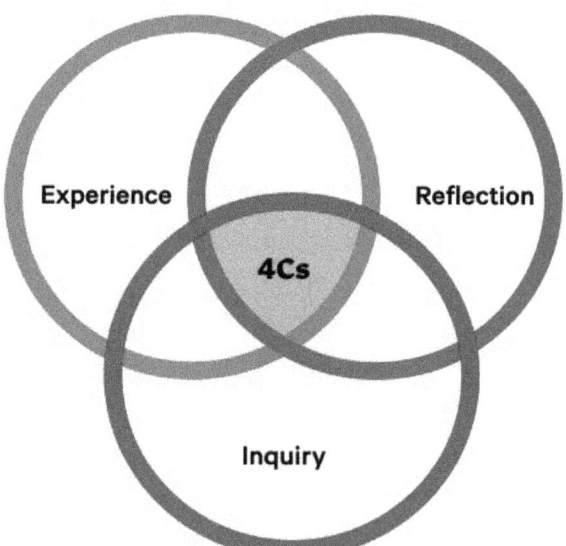

learning.[11] Experience creates knowledge through doing[12] and then reflecting on it. For instance, you can know how a computer works, but the experience of building a computer and the reflecting on the experience provides a much deeper learning experience. Educational researchers Gerald Burch and colleagues found that 'experiential activities work; they generate better learning outcomes than control groups who do not receive experiential activities'.[13] In teacher education, experiential learning includes processes such as practicum, internships, mentoring, collaborative teaching, simulations, etc.

In foundational teacher education, experiential learning is evident in practicum or what is sometimes called professional experience. Often, however, practicum experiences are not coherent, connected to theory, related to school realities or supported by partnerships with more experienced educators (often inspectorial rather than collegial).[14] Rethinking practicums and internships has the potential to reconfigure relationships shifting from supervisor and supervised to collaborative partnerships. These collaborative internships/practicums could be in schools, social welfare settings, museums, etc. to broaden the perspective of teachers in the foundational phases, inspiring a reimagining of what a teaching career could be. If the experiences of practicum focused primarily on collaboration (e.g. team teaching with teacher-mentors) and critical reflection (reflection on school experience with other foundation education students), a more productive understanding of the foundations would be achievable. This can occur through participation, modelling and co-creation of learning experiences with more experienced teachers. These experiences are transformed into learning through reflection that drives action.

Reflection

Reflection is the (often collaborative) process of considering, interpreting, evaluating and acting on experience. As we mentioned earlier, reflection is critical to making sense (and learning) from experience and inquiry. Yet the evidence suggests a lack of reflection in foundational teacher education is impeding the growth of agentic and independent professionals. Educators Mary Dyer and Susan Taylor argue: 'Where reflection should lead to the development of creative and free-thinking experts in the professional field, it has instead led students to believe that there are external and universal rules for good practice.'[15] In other words, preservice teachers may be left with the impression that there is a 'one size fits all' approach that suits any context. While critical reflection encourages the development of agentic and contextually aware professionals, it must also lead to critical action. As social worker Tonya Salomons argues, reflection without critical action is essentially meaningless.

> I am a critical thinker. At least that's what I like to think about myself. I like to think I move beyond implicit assumptions to get to the heart of the matter. While I like to think I am a critical thinker, I have learned that my critical thinking very rarely turns into critical action . . . what I had previously considered critical thinking was really what my professor aptly named, 'navel gazing': reflecting for the sake of reflecting but not actually doing anything with any conclusions.[16]

For reflection to be effective in foundational teacher education and education generally, it builds on experience and research (praxis). It builds agency in teachers and learners and the learning community and leads to transformed action, not just 'navel gazing'. Critical reflection on experience develops some of the necessary skills for the development of inquiry.

Inquiry

Inquiry is a democratic learning process of problem shaping, investigation and making findings. Inquiry in learning emerges from the dialogue and questioning methods pioneered by the ancient Greek philosopher Socrates, who lived from 470 to 399 BC.[17] For Socrates and later Dewey, inquiry was a scaffolded and disciplined exploration and not an 'anything goes free for all'. Dewey argued for structure and autonomy in inquiry learning, suggesting the process could be constructed as 'sensing perplexing situations, clarifying the problem, formulating a tentative hypothesis, testing the hypothesis, revising with rigorous tests, and acting on the solution'.[18] We use the Critical Reflection Crucible coherence maker here (as we do in chapter 7) to structure inquiry in learning. Dewey's process of inquiry is evident in the Critical Reflection Crucible that provides a structure for inquiry as illustrated in table 9.1.

In teacher education, inquiry allows educators to consider theory and research in their own context. For instance, an inquiry relating to languages education in a

Table 9.1 Dewey's approach to inquiry reflected through the Critical Reflection Crucible

Dewey's approach to inquiry	Stages of the Critical Reflection Crucible
Sensing perplexing situations	Identifying assumptions
Clarifying the problem	Why this? Why so?
Formulating a tentative hypothesis, testing the hypothesis	Contesting, elaborating and adapting
Revising with rigorous tests, and acting on the solution	Re-solving

distance education school or a small primary school will draw on research in languages education and distance education or primary education (depending on the context) to shape the inquiry. This empowers teachers to develop and evaluate new practices and drives contextualized responses to achieve deeper learning for students. We discuss inquiry processes later in this chapter.

When structured and supported,[19] inquiry is more effective than transmissive[20] (chalk and talk) approaches to learning. Education and creativity researcher Keith Sawyer explains how creativity and collaboration structure, support and progress inquiry processes. He argues that foundational teacher education students 'learn to participate in creative activities based on their developing knowledge – how to identify good problems, how to ask good questions, how to gather relevant information, how to propose new solutions and hypotheses, and how to use domain-specific skills to express those ideas and make them a reality'.[21] In teacher education, the community of praxis approach (discussed later in this chapter) facilitates shared collegial inquiry on experience and creates a process to co-design and enact new practices. The foundations are, however, only the beginning of the continuum. If we are to grow dynamic, agentic and innovative schools, our teachers need the opportunity to build on those foundations to make lifelong learning a cultural feature of our schools.

Lifelong teacher education

Lifelong teacher education is crucial to students' experience of learning, but many of the old models of professional learning have been unfocused, decontextualized and wasteful. As for foundational teacher education, we need to reimagine in-service teacher education as active, context-driven, continuous and agentic. Educational researchers Christopher Day and Christine Grice report: 'Professional learning is likely to be more effective when it is perceived by teachers to be close to practice, focused on the work place, supported by the principal, and over time.'[22] Unfortunately, by contrast, teacher education (in foundational and lifelong phases) has become somewhat fragmented, disconnected from practice and not integrated with the direction and values of the school. Teachers are often left with no understanding of how their foundational education informs or connects with the rest of their career through lifelong learning.

Educational researcher Helen Timperley argues, 'The need for ongoing learning arises because teaching challenges do not remain static. Changing student demographics and an ever-changing knowledge base mean that teachers need to be kept, and to keep, abreast of current evidence about how best to meet the learning needs of their students.'[23] Yet these old models have not allowed for context or relevance by providing 'one size fits all' training that is often pedagogically suspect, not embedded in deep learning and not based in continuous growth for the teacher or the school. These approaches do not support lifelong professional growth, as researchers Margaret Riel and colleagues argue:

> . . . continuous learning as an essential part of teaching has been at best marginalized. Within many institutional settings, professional development is often delivered by corporate educational entertainers with overly simplistic approaches, often bolstered by claims of research-proven strategies. These approaches lack significant teacher participation in the 'shows' that are in the form of sit and get, spray and pray, and drive by trainings.[24]

Expertise and evidence are key themes in the development of a praxis approach to teacher education. However the balance in some education systems has tipped too far to the 'sage on the stage' rather than the 'guide at the side'[25] that empowers teachers to take control of their learning. The ineffective 'quick fix' training model often leaves teachers to apply learning themselves without supportive structures to embed, sustain and grow the learning in a collaborative community. Education researcher Linda Darling-Hammond argues that many forms of teacher professional development are not effective. She reports that research *does not* support teacher education that:[26]

- relies on the one-shot workshop model,
- focuses only on training teachers in new techniques and behaviours,
- is not related to teachers' specific contexts and curriculums,
- is episodic and fragmented,
- expects teachers to make changes in isolation and without support, and
- does not provide sustained teacher learning opportunities over multiple days and weeks.

Darling-Hammond is calling for approaches to teacher education that build on prior learning, are contextualized in the school, are based on supportive communities and school leadership. The same models of deep learning we are developing for our students (described in chapters 4 and 5) should be our expectation for teacher education.

Building on the foundations: experience, reflection and inquiry

Effective lifelong teacher education goes far beyond the 'one off training' and equips and enables teachers to become leaders of learning throughout their careers by building on the foundations of experience, reflection and inquiry. We use the term *lifelong* teacher education to stress that learning about teaching does not stop when teachers leave the foundational stage and begin teaching. Alarmingly, some experienced teachers tell us, 'We haven't really thought about pedagogy or curriculum deeply since we left uni.'

Dewey's approach to democratic education relies on students and teachers agentically engaging with each other and the world around them in a process of constant and dynamic growth. To enable democratic lifelong learning and teaching, our students and teachers need tools to investigate, analyse, understand and respond to the world. The foundations of democratic learning (experience, reflection and inquiry) are in some ways a literacy for lifelong learning. In the next section of this chapter, we will examine how lifelong teacher education works in practice through the experience of Hurstville Public School.

Transforming Lifelong Teacher Education at Hurstville Public School

For many parents, teachers and others observing Hurstville Public School there was no obvious need for change. The suburban Sydney school has more than 1,200 students and 127 staff, and a tradition that stretches back to its founding in 1876. When we first visited the school in 2017, it was achieving excellent external test results, students seemed happy in the playground and the staff focused on learning in their classrooms. There was, however, a restless concern in the leadership that the school was not sufficiently focused on transformation and that it may have become a little complacent.

Partnerships for transformation

Hurstville Public School began teacher education (professional learning) with our organization, 4C Transformative Learning (4CTL) as regular, ongoing workshops with leadership (focused on leading school transformation) and the 'ground-breakers' group (focused on pedagogy and work practices). The workshops were undertaken in school and after school hours with time between workshops to experiment, explore and embed new strategies and ideas. The partnership with 4CTL explored deeper learning in specific classroom contexts and introduced strategies to develop students' learning dispositions. Processes in the 4Cs were introduced for classroom learning

Figure 9.3 Hurstville Public School, established 1876.

and teachers' professional practice. For instance, teachers used the coherence maker Collaboration Circles as a pedagogical tool in the classroom, and it was used to deepen teachers' collaborative planning processes across classes. The workshops also included Collaborative Classroom Visits (CCVs) and Deep Noticing and Action (DNA) critical reflection (see chapter 6).

The teacher education 4CTL develops with every school is bespoke to the school setting and classroom context based on the values of our organization (see chapter 3). The 4C learning develops and emerges in each educational context responding to the needs of students, staff and their community. 4C processes allow schools to lead their own inquiries and innovations in the transformation of their schools. Our partnerships with schools like Hurstville Public continue to inform our research and practice, and the greater network of schools we work with. One of the key processes in these partnerships is reimaging successful learning through a focus on student and teacher agency, building learning dispositions and creating a relevant curriculum.

Reimagining successful learning

Hurstville began to focus on what 'success' means for their students. They started asking themselves, what learning did Hurstville offer beyond those measured by standardized tests? They began reimagining success as beyond 'results' and started reflecting on what learning for success in life might look like. They were concerned that their curriculum and pedagogy could do more to build learning dispositions and therefore better prepare students for the challenges that they face in their present and in their future. The key question for the leaders at Hurstville PS went to the heart of their reason for existing: do we provide learning that equips our students with the capabilities to survive in a post-normal world of complexity, chaos and contradiction? They outlined their aspiration for learning in their school plan for 2018–20:[27]

> The purpose of contemporary learning is to respond to a rapidly changing society by enhancing deeper collaborative, transformational practices across the whole school and wider community. Successful learners will be able to demonstrate adaptability, effective communication and a growth mindset that supports creativity, critical reflection and lifelong learning.

From training to lifelong learning

This aspiration required a transformation in their approach to teacher education. Assistant Principal Jayne Muir[28] explains the difference between old paradigm training and lifelong teacher education:

> Typically, you would go to head office and there would be a room full of people and it would be 'Death by PowerPoint'. Or we would bring people into the school and they would run professional learning. But it would be one person delivering the professional learning to the group. And it didn't matter if it was something that was of interest to you or not. Learning at Hurstville does not look like that now.
>
> Lifelong learning is continuous growth and reflection for the sake of better learning for our kids. And we now don't expect perfection. We don't have an expectation with kids to get it right the first time. So why would we expect that of teachers? Learning is about trial and error, because we are lifelong learning and playing with possibilities.
>
> We now ask what can we do differently? How can I collaborate with the kids to change up the learning? When I reflect back to my early days of teaching to now, things have really changed. We would sit down with our programme and you'd have this little tick a box at the end. Your supervisor would ask 'how did it go? What went wrong?' It wasn't deep reflection about your practice. We're learning for ourselves now.

For Jayne, the 4Cs have been the matter and the method of lifelong learning. She explains how it permeates her professional and personal life through coherence makers such as the Learning Disposition Wheel and the Pedagogy Parachute: 'If I look at the coherence makers, that's how I am lifelong learning. I use the 4Cs in the classroom, in meetings, and for myself personally. It's continually evolving.' For Jayne, the 4Cs are not just bolted on to her teaching; they have permeated her approach to leadership, her learning and the learning of her students.

The lifelong teacher education approach began and continues as a partnership with 4CTL. Principal, Mark Steed explains the impetus for the shift in teacher education:

> The honest truth of it is that unfortunately for some people, they walked in the school gate in 1984 and it wasn't until 2019 that they have actually asked themselves the question, 'how do I teach and should I change it?' And what should I be doing to promote or create opportunities for students to learn? They have never asked this because reflection is not part of the system that we've worked in unless we create that opportunity. It's not there.
>
> Now we focus on the learner becoming the teacher and the teacher becoming the learner. The teachers are continually refining aspects of practice that cascades into their teaching in the classroom because they are doing it as learners themselves. They are now asking themselves; 'What am I doing, what decisions am I making to drive my learning and what will that mean for the learners in the class that I work with?'

Collaborative practice is evident in Jayne's reflections. One way that Hurstville formalized and extended this approach was through establishing a community of praxis.

Community of Praxis

At Hurstville a community of praxis was a critical step in establishing trust and an openness to new ideas. The community of praxis[29] is a collaboration of educators driven by reflection on theory, research and practice to drive transformation. Individuals alone, whether they are teachers or principals cannot transform without a community who are reflecting and acting collaboratively.

This approach challenges schools to move from individualistic teaching (one teacher, one classroom). This allows a reimagining of collaborative inquiry and teaching (team teaching) to meet the needs of the students and their learning. A community of praxis enables educators to explore the potential for transformation by inquiring together with evidence, theory and practice in their context to generate action. The term community of praxis is derived from two concepts: community of practice and praxis.

Community of practice approaches have been an effective[30] feature of education for many years but their potential has never been fully realized to support school transformation. As we discussed in chapter 3, a community of practice approach is defined as[31] . . . groups of people who share a common interest (e.g. teachers, nurses, psychologists), a concern (e.g transforming pedagogy) or passion (e.g. democratic learning) for something they do and want to learn together (often through inquiry) how to do it more effectively.

For Hurstville PS and many other schools, this involves a group of teachers inquiring, reflecting and enhancing their pedagogy by reflecting on theory and practice. The next critical concept in Communities of Praxis is praxis.

Praxis

In ancient Greece, praxis referred to 'the process of using a theory or something that you have learned in a practical way'.[32] Praxis bridges the divide between the concepts of practice and experience, and theory and research. Practice and theory are often falsely dichotomized but in reality, they are interdependent. John Dewey argued that theory is pointless without understanding its relationship to practice:[33]

> An ounce of experience is better than a ton of theory simply because it is only in experience that any theory has vital and verifiable significance. An experience, a very humble experience, is capable of generating and carrying any amount of theory (or intellectual content), but a theory apart from an experience cannot be definitely grasped even as theory. It tends to become a mere verbal formula, a set of catchwords used to render thinking, or genuine theorizing, unnecessary and impossible.

Praxis relies on each educator's ability to evaluate experience and practice in relation to research, theory and evidence. This, for some, will mark a considerable shift; however, transformation requires an ability to analyse experience alongside theory and practice rather than just 'going with your gut'. For learning communities, the collected wisdom of research and theory can be applied to experience and practice in each school's context.

Hurstville began their community of praxis by putting together a diverse group of their teachers who were 'lateral thinkers' (called the Ground-breakers), including but broader than the leadership team at the school. We refer to this group as the 'Innovation' or 'I' team in our discussion of leadership (in chapter 9). Their responsibility was to reimagine learning or, as Mark Steed puts it:

> . . . we had to throw in some real disruption. And the way to do that is to bring in the people who are the most lateral in their thinking and challenge them. The Groundbreakers included beginning teachers, a whole range of different people. We said, let's try and forget titles and bring in thinking. We needed people who could say things like let's forget the rules, we make the rules, we write the rules. You have to genuinely collaborate with people who you believe will shake things up and give them the agency to let loose.

Alison Duff, who leads teacher education at Hurstville, argues, 'I think that was a very powerful move. It wasn't a hierarchical model of the leadership, it included leaders but also beginning teachers and a range of different people. I think that really gave it power in terms of its communication to the whole staff.'

The Ground-breakers then set about embedding reflection on experience and inquiry into their approach to lifelong teacher education. The Ground-breakers were followed by the development of several communities of praxis who joined when they were ready. This approach builds agency by placing decisions about teacher learning back in teachers' hands, as Mark Steed explains:

> By bringing people in and saying we can only learn from this person, it almost removes our agency. We've got highly skilled people here who are framing and learning from one another. That's the maelstrom that we want. We want that tension between what we know and what we don't know. And it's how much we can learn from each other. We don't need some jumped-up person coming in and telling us in two hours how to change. No, we have to do it, we need to change the world. You just have to enact it.

One of the strategies Hurstville used to enact transformative teacher education is through deeply and collaboratively considering the experience of learning and teaching in the school.

Experience

As we mentioned earlier, John Dewey's observation that not all experiences are equally useful for education is perhaps doubly true for lifelong and foundational teacher education.[34] In teacher education, experiences should be reflected and focused upon with the needs of student learning. For Hurstville and many of our partner schools, there are a multitude of possible experiences to consider, *but* if we are focused on deeper learning for our students, their experience of learning should be foremost.

To understand experience, Hurstville used two interrelated processes: Collaborative Classroom Visits (CCVs) and Deep Noticing and Action (DNA).

Collaborative Classroom Visits engage a group of teachers (and often students) visiting another classroom to observe and reflect on moments of learning. Often 'visitors' are provided with a coherence maker (such as the Learning Disposition Wheel) to frame the experience of learning. At the end of the short visit (five to ten minutes), the host teacher and guests leave the class to reflect on the learning and generate action, known as a Deep Noticing and Action.

Deep Noticing and Action is a process of structured reflection on learning experiences. The DNA (Deep Noticing and Action) Eye (discussed and illustrated in chapter 6 in figure 6.4) is a framework for noticing the experience of learning, critical reflection and action. DNA is not focused on judging or problem-solving for the teacher. Rather it allows participants (the host teacher included) to consider a slice of learning as a stimulus to reflect on student learning in their own classroom and across the school. The group is guided in the reflection by an experienced facilitator who co-constructs a shared reflection of the experience of learners in that classroom.

Jayne Muir describes the process of reflecting on experience through the DNA Eye that led to change in teaching practices:

> In the DNA we watched the lesson where the learning was coming from the students. It wasn't teacher driven. It was the most beautiful learning. When we walked in the teacher barely spoke. When we reflected with her later she said; 'all I do all day is talk and I feel like I am hindering the development of the students in my class because I over talk.' Her whole reflection was about herself and her practice. She wasn't doing anything wrong. She had never even thought about how much she talked until she reflected on it. She then designed a lesson with another teacher to focus on how she could take teacher talk out to provide agency for her students. It was all about looking at the experience from the learner's perspective.

The intent of the reflection is always to unearth assumptions, reflect on practice and drive transformative action towards deeper learning. Jayne explains why reflection on the learning experience through the CCV/DNA Eye process drives action:

> One of my big noticings was when you look at a lesson for five minutes everyone notices something different. And when you notice something different, you're reflecting on something different. So people realise reflection is different for everybody. What you bring to the table makes it different, for instance what your students' needs are. And that's actually encouraging because there was this element of, 'oh, did you notice that? I didn't notice that. Why didn't I notice that?' I realised through the DNAs, personal reflection becomes about you and your students as opposed to we all must reflect the same, we all must go the same way.

Reflection such as we see in these DNAs begins the process of making the familiar strange. Novelist Marcel Proust once observed: 'The journey of discovery consists not in seeking new landscapes, but in seeing them with new eyes.'[35] The familiar landscape of the classroom can be reimagined when we focus on the learner and the learning rather than solely on the teacher and the teaching. One of the key structures that Hurstville employs to build understanding from experience is reflection.

Reflection

Critical reflection enables communities of praxis to ask hard questions about status quo practices and generate collaboration to drive transformative action. In *Transforming Schools,* we argued that critical reflection allows educators '... to stand one step back'[36] and analyse knowledge in terms of power and agency. The ability for educators to 'take one step back' and reflect is the first step, but it is only the first step. Social work researcher Jan Fook explains why analysis of experience uncovers assumptions blocking transformation:[37] '... critical reflection involves learning from and making deeper meaning of experience through a process of unsettling and examining deeply hidden assumptions in order to create better guidelines *for action* and so improve *professional practice* and develop a more ethical and compassionate stance'.[38] Action is critical and that is only achieved through unsettling assumptions about pedagogy, curriculum and leadership in schools.

For Hurstville and many other schools, establishing a culture of reflection enables collaborative rather than individual action. The change of focus from an individual teacher's classroom to a whole-school approach required the embedding of reflective practice across the school. Embedding reflective processes into the culture at Hurstville was critical in ushering in transformative approaches to learning. While reflection is discussed frequently, Mark Steed argues it is not embedded across the school system to shape transformation:

> Our education system has no capacity to encourage educators to continually reflect. So people come out thinking I am qualified now, why do I need to keep growing? There is no capacity and no system driven mechanism for reflection. Reflection certainly was not in the culture here at Hurstville.
>
> So reflection needed to be embedded as part of what happened to be successful as learners and teachers. Reflection should follow a system where we are continually putting ourselves as professionals in that space to reflect on our practice. In the past our reflection was incidental and individual. We actually used a scaffold [the DNA Eye] last year that was based on the principle. To be a buoyant education system reflection should be regular for everyone.

For teachers, this embedding of reflection has allowed them to work more collaboratively and collegially, as Alison Duff explains:

> I feel like reflection has definitely changed. It's not now reflecting on your programme or your practice because your supervisor is looking. It's now a more collaborative process. It's definitely more that we're reflecting together to improve our practice collectively and also to improve learning for students. So I definitely think the mindset around reflection has changed. It's not judgemental.

An ongoing challenge for Hurstville is to facilitate an inquiry mindset for their educators so they might apply praxis to the exploration of familiar and novel challenges 'with new eyes'.

Inquiry

Inquiry in lifelong teacher education is often called collaborative inquiry and focuses on an area of need with the aim of enhancing learning for students[39]. In lifelong education there is evidence that collaborative inquiry is effective in promoting and sustaining teacher learning. Helen Timperley and colleagues claim that inquiry can bring about transformation:

> We propose that it is through a disciplined approach to collaborative inquiry, resulting in new learning and new action, that educators, learners, their families and involved community members will gain the confidence, the insights, and the mindsets required to design new and powerful learning systems. This process will indeed transform their schools into more innovative learning environments . . . Their schools have become collectively energised by the potential to transform learning environments.[40]

At Hurstville, inquiry is still gaining traction but there are some examples that demonstrate its effectiveness in changing teacher practice when developed in unison with reflection on experience. Alison Duff argues that earlier inquiry occurred individually rather than collaboratively: '. . . in terms of inquiry, in the sense of trying out new things, teachers were more individually focused at first. Now, through our systematic collaborative planning and reflection practices and our regular opportunities for co-teaching, inquiry is becoming a shared endeavour.' One area of emerging inquiry for Hurstville is the EAL/D team (English as an additional language or dialect). As Jayne Muir argues the EAL/D team have shifted from a status quo approach to an inquiry mindset: 'the EAL/D team is trying to reframe that narrative and frame their learning and teaching around students and their real needs and how to make that work with collaborative approaches to teaching'. The team have used reflection on classroom experience through DNA Eye processes to drive inquiry.

Schools and learning teams within schools who adopt an inquiry approach have the opportunity to suit the learning to their needs by integrating theory, context and practice to explore challenges collaboratively and creatively. Timperley and colleagues argue that inquiry has the potential to shift mindsets, practices and cultures to develop schools as places of knowledge production and exchange. They claim, 'These re-designed schools have become learning labs for new practices. Their new energy attracts others. Their drive and passion creates a change force that is positively influencing the lives of thousands of learners. This is the kind of sea change that is required.'[41] While Hurstville is just beginning its journey towards deeper inquiry, the foundations have been created. This will enable their teachers through reflection on experience to now generate focused inquiry to support the learning of their students through the 4Cs.

For Principal Mark Steed, education for teachers and students is necessarily founded and enabled by the 4Cs: 'Everything in professional learning is framed around 4Cs. Teachers are consolidating those skills within themselves as learners that they then use with their students. Teachers are continually refining aspects of contemporary practice that will then cascade into what they are doing in the classroom because they are doing it as a learner themselves.' The continued development of reflection, experience and inquiry is made possible through the relentless focus on the 4Cs:

- Creativity allows teachers to develop, design and teach with innovation.
- Critical reflection enables teachers to examine experience and drive transformative action.

- Collaboration supports educators' ability to reflect and act collegially.
- Communication supports the dissemination of inquiries and innovations within and beyond the school.

Next steps for lifelong teacher education at Hurstville Public School

Hurstville has transformed its model and approach to teacher education. It has focused on its context to support the growth of its educators rather than relying on old models of teacher education. Alison explains how more effective teacher education impacts on student and teacher learning:

> Students are now more aware that teachers are continually learning, that we go to professional learning and we learn new things. You hear teachers telling the students, this is something I learnt with my colleagues and I'm going to try it out in class today. So I think the kids are now more aware that we are learning too, and that we're on a journey of teaching and trying out new things. We are modelling lifelong learning and I think that's empowering the kids as well. I also think there's a deeper connection now between teacher professional learning and what happens in classrooms. Before, we used to go to professional learning and we would close the book after it finished; that was it. Whereas now we are putting it into practice, reflecting and refining collaboratively.

In early 2019, the leadership team at Hurstville worked with 4CTL to establish a networked community of praxis across five schools in their area. Mark Steed sees this collaboration as how transformative teacher education can grow beyond the work begun at Hurstville:

> Our DNA Eyes are going to unpack across four of the five schools. We start bringing practitioners together to make it slightly uncomfortable. So, people from the different schools work with each other. But again, that's a leap. We've got to have an opinion about learning and be ready to express it. We have to be clear about what the theory says, what that means to the practical realities of what we do.

Transformation at Hurstville P.S means constantly challenging their teachers and students to seek deeper learning through reflection, experience and growing an inquiry mindset. This restless quest to build a renewed and reimagined school has been enabled by their immersion in creativity, critical reflection communication and collaboration which fundamentally enable their teachers to continue growing on the continuum of teacher education.

Concluding reflections

John Dewey's philosophy of democratic education born of an adolescence saturated in the experiences of the natural world more than 160 years ago is testament to the power of curiosity and imagination to transform education. His provocation to 'cease conceiving of education as mere preparation for later life, and make it the full meaning of the present life'[42] is a reminder of education's potential to build and sustain a democratic and civil society. That potential is only realized when we develop a teaching profession that is supported by foundational learning in experience, reflection and inquiry enabled by creativity, critical reflection, communication and collaboration. Foundational education (at universities and other places) can embed these processes to enable preservice teachers to critically evaluate knowledge and make democratic education a reality. They will also prepare our teachers to drive transformation collaboratively and autonomously at a classroom, school and system level. As teachers move into schools to begin lifelong teacher education, we can develop their capacity to build on those foundations so they can lead and innovate in their own contexts. Teacher education can become a capability for real, sustainable and beneficial change for schools.

In our partnerships, this approach to a continuum of teacher education creates innovative, dynamic, vibrant and engaged communities of learning leaders who, enabled by the 4Cs, are meeting the potential for transformation that Dewey argued for more than a century ago. His achievable aspiration is that educators might build a community of learning with the agency and the capabilities to transform their world collaboratively. We know it is attainable because the schools we partner with are making Dewey's dream a reality through transformative teacher education.

In the next chapter, we consider how leadership can be a capability for transformation.

Transforming leadership
Shared action and agency

10

What is leadership? 205

Why is leadership a capability for building agency? 207

Why should leadership be shared and how? 208

Leadership as self-action 209
Leadership as inter-action 210
Leadership as trans-action 210

What are the components for leading change? 213

Who leads transformation and how? 214

What is the innovation team? 214
What is the guiding coalition? 215
How does the existing operating system become networked team structures? 216

How can leadership teams use the 4Cs to lead? 217

Communicating the vision, values and strategies as emergent 219
Creating networks of collaboration 219
Evaluating assumptions and practices through critical reflection 220
Generating and encouraging creativity 221

What is it to be a transformative leader? 223

Transforming leadership 224

Concluding reflections 225

In 2019, New Zealand suffered a horrendous and tragic mass shooting at two mosques in Christchurch where fifty-one worshippers were killed. The public grief that followed the attack was led by the New Zealand Prime Minister, Jacinda Ardern, who showed compassion and love for the community (figure 10.1). Her response was noted around the world as poised, sensitive and deeply empathic. *The Guardian* commented that Jacinda Ardern:

> . . . has communicated and immediately, giving New Zealanders as much information as she could. She has given them a language in which to talk about the unspeakable, to vocalise the shock and sadness. 'They are us,' she said simply of the dead and wounded. The 'othering' of Muslims as separate, as somehow different, as not quite belonging, was felled in one swoop. 'They are us.' New Zealand had been chosen because it was safe, because it was no place for hatred or racism. 'Because we represent diversity, kindness, compassion, home for those who share our values. Refuge for those who need it.'[1]

Ardern's reaction was recognized by many as a strong stance in compassion and love, but it was considered by some as unusual in a national leader. Her wearing of a headscarf embodied a sense of 'us' and grieving together as a community. Author and journalist Madeleine Chapman says in *Jacinda Ardern: A New Kind of Leader*,

Figure 10.1 Hagen Hopkins. Embracing a mourner via Getty Images.

Figure 10.2 The Leadership Wheel.

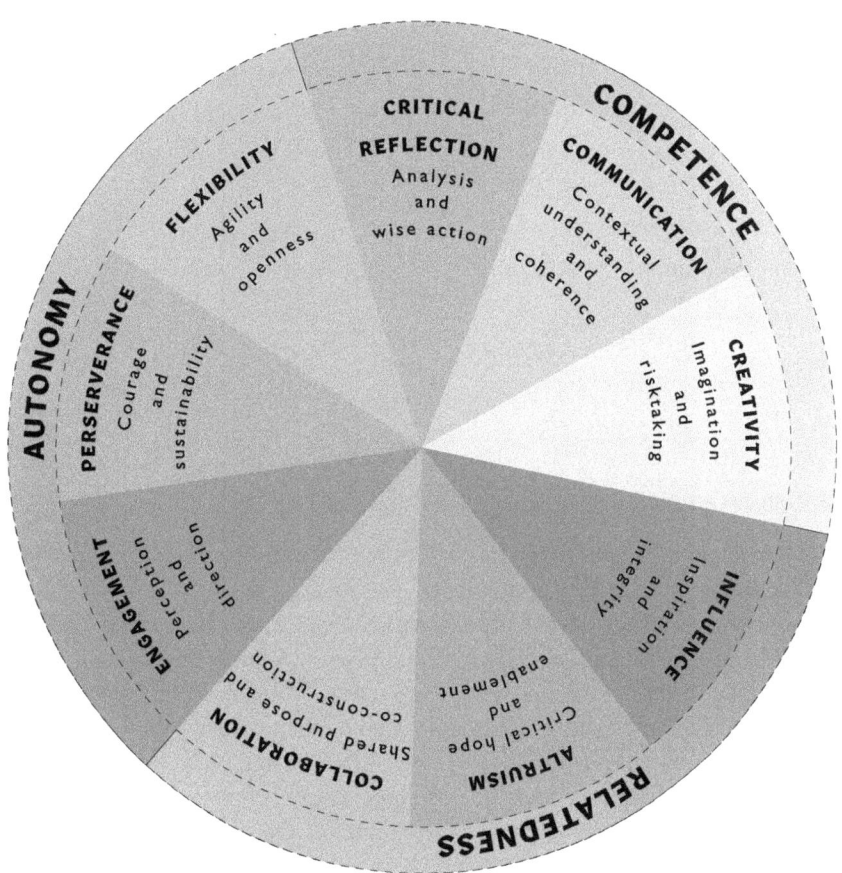

'Politicians acting in the best interest of others, rather than themselves, should be the norm, but unfortunately it's not. By doing so, Ardern has become a global icon of empathetic leadership, both a credit to her and an indictment of her international peers.'[2] Strong leadership is often perceived to be singular, heroic and masculine, and about ego, power, hierarchy, authority, competition and the rejection of emotion.[3] Jacinda Ardern's integrity and decisiveness, empathy and warmth challenge these traditional notions of leadership.

This chapter explores concepts that go beyond the conventional notions of leadership. We argue that leadership is a shared practice central to transformation in schools. Schools can develop the influence needed to change into adaptive and innovative communities of learning through collaboration and the shared practice of leadership. We treat leadership as a capability defined by the capacities we describe in our coherence maker, the Leadership Wheel (see figure 10.2). In the Wheel are nine capacities critical to leading transformation and creating the environment for the shared practice of leadership. The domains for agentic leadership are defined by the three interrelated psychological needs of Self-Determination Theory (see chapter 4).

Autonomy

- engagement
- perseverance
- flexibility

Competence

- critical reflection
- communication
- creativity

Relatedness

- influence
- altruism
- collaboration

While we cannot evaluate Ardern's capacities in all aspects of the Leadership Wheel, we can identify that after the Christchurch massacre, she demonstrated strong skills in communication (contextual understanding and coherence) and altruism (critical hope and enablement). Chapman describes her as 'being a mirror. Embodying empathy, Ardern invited those she encountered to project their worries and struggles onto her, and in return projected understanding and support.'[4] Ardern was also decisive about gun reform after the massacre and set up the Christchurch Call to Action Summit to examine social media as a tool for spreading hate and violence. These actions demonstrate capacities in the Leadership Wheel of engagement (perception and direction) and critical reflection (analysis and wise action). Although Ardern is a national leader, and her context is different to leadership in a school, we can use aspects of her leadership to consider what is fundamental to the capability of leadership.

Leadership is not, however, wholly defined by an individual's capacity. Leadership is also a capability that can be shared. To explore shared leadership in the chapter, we will use another New Zealand reference; the national rugby union team, the All Blacks (see figure 10.3). We argue that effective leadership is a 'team sport' that goes beyond an individual's capacity to lead. Over their more than 116-year history, the All Blacks have a 77 per cent win rate, making it 'possibly the most successful sports team, in any code, ever'.[5] This success cannot be explained by a succession of individual coaches or players. The All Blacks' success can only be explained by a sense of shared leadership and belief deeply woven into the fabric of the team's culture. Shared leadership moves beyond an individual's ego, actions and behaviours. It is the joint and connected positive influences we can have on each other and can be envisioned as a relational and dynamic pattern across a team or school's organization and culture.

Leadership is integral to human agency and vital to transforming education. We examine how transforming leadership is to understand leadership amongst staff, students and the community as a dynamic of different expressions of agency and

Figure 10.3 Going for the ball at a line out; the All Blacks national rugby team in Wellington, New Zealand.

empowerment. 4C transformation is a comprehensively huge and challenging task, and we examine how leadership teams navigate the course of cultural shifts and innovation in their schools. To begin, what exactly is leadership?

What is leadership?

Leadership as a capability challenges the historical and still pervasive cultural construct of leadership as a position of authority and title. Education researcher John MacBeath argues that positional leadership is an embedded tradition and long-held assumption in education.[6] This is evident, he says, in the language we use in English-speaking schools where a leader is the main or principal actor, and widely referred to as the *Principal*. Hierarchal structures are strong default cultures in schools, he argues, because we are generally, as a society, culturally tied to the tradition of leadership as authority, compounded by the growth of an audit and compliance culture in education since the 1990s. MacBeath says that 'the democratic, free and alternative schools of the 1970s enjoyed a relatively brief life, perhaps because we are so culturally wedded to hierarchy, or more persuasively perhaps, because they were overtaken by accountability, performance management and "league tables"'.

We use organizational change and leadership researcher John P. Kotter's definition to establish what we mean by leadership in schools in whatever capacity or role. 'Leadership is a set of processes that creates organizations in the first place or adapts them to significantly changing circumstances. Leadership defines what the future should look like, aligns people with that vision, and inspires them to make it happen despite the obstacles.'[7] Kotter argues that leadership is very different to *management* which is a set of processes (such as planning, budgeting, organizing, staffing, etc.) to keep complicated systems running in an organization. Managing produces predictability and order. *Leadership*, on the other hand, is a set of processes that produces purposeful, useful change in a complex, emergent system.[8]

Leadership is the practice of mobilizing others to tackle tough challenges and create a vision for a better future. Leadership is to diagnose what is needed in a classroom, school and community and establish a clear and structured purpose to achieve that vision. It is to create an environment of collaboration and experimentation, leading by inspiring, motivating and learning in a shared endeavour with others. Leading is to develop and extend your human potential and the potential of others as a 'learning lab' of action and reflection. The Leadership Wheel, based on the U.S. National Research Council's report, *Education for Life and Work: Developing Transferable Knowledge and Skills in the 21st Century*,[9] describes how skills and processes in autonomy (intrapersonal behavioural regulation), competence (cognitive mastery) and relatedness (interpersonal social relationships) are essential for building human potential in leadership.

The Leadership Wheel is based on Self-Determination Theory and the same research as the Learning Disposition Wheel, but the intent and language of the tool are designed for leading. Effective leadership is constantly learning wisdom[10] and inspiring others in learning new ways for an organization to grow and change into the future. 4C leadership is leading by guiding others to transform by realizing their human potential through learning, hence the interrelatedness of the Leadership Wheel to the Learning Disposition Wheel. According to Self-Determination Theory (which also informs the Learning Disposition Wheel), the fulfilment of the psychological needs of *autonomy*, *competence* and *relatedness* is essential for personal growth and optimal performance of people in any organization.

In the Leadership Wheel, *autonomy* involves self-organizing our intrapersonal behaviours in *engagement*, *perseverance* and *flexibility*. Autonomy is developing a sense of choice and not feeling controlled by others. *Competence* describes our cognitive abilities to extend our mastery and effectiveness in the capacities of *critical reflection*, *communication* and *creativity*. *Relatedness* refers to connecting with and being significant to others through the interpersonal capacities of *influence*, *altruism* and *collaboration*. Transformative leaders are social influencers who collaboratively grow capacities in autonomy, competence and relatedness. This is achieved by developing an environment and opportunities that develop these same basic psychological needs in others.[11] The Leadership Wheel describes capacities that are learnt skills and processes that develop our sense of self-concept and the self-concept of the people we lead.

Discussion of Self-Determination Theory in chapter 4 and the skills in the Learning Disposition Wheel in chapter 5 will support and deepen understanding of the capacities in the Leadership Wheel. In schools we support the development of leadership skills using the Leadership Wheel as a diagnostic and reflective tool to ascertain strengths and yet-to-be strengths in leading. We have introduced reflective practice in schools to develop leaders, teacher and student agency in leadership.

Why is leadership a capability for building agency?

In conventional views of leadership, the 'power of agency' (the power to initiate action) is essentially in the hands of the leader. The agentic potential of 'followers' is not fully realized. Leadership as a capability is about developing the agentic potential of everyone in a school culture. As we discussed in chapter 4, agency is not given to people, it is enabled, generated and shared through experiences that develop co-agency between people in the right conditions. Richard Elmore, an educational leadership researcher, explains what shared agency and leadership look like in a school with a culture of trust and collective endeavour:

> When teachers exercise their agency beyond the classroom, with colleagues, with parents and other agencies or with policy, they exercise leadership. When they do so as part of a collective endeavour, leadership becomes a shared activity. Despite a body of writing on teacher leadership, much of it fails to grasp or explore the connections between individual agency and the collective. Teacher leadership is construed as a role or status within the institutional hierarchy rather than captured in the flow of activities.[12]

Understanding agency and leadership as emerging in the flow of practice is also explored by the Carpe Vitam International Leadership for Learning research project.[13] Leadership for Learning argues agency is central to the relationship between leadership and learning in schools.[14] It examines how agency is key to effective school communities' abilities to influence themselves and others. In their view, the concept of shared leadership 'assumes that all members of a learning community have the capacity to influence because being an agent is what being a human being is all about. Being an agent or having agency involves having a sense of self encompassing particular values and a cultural identify, and being able to pursue self-determined purposes and goals through self-conscious strategic action.'[15] The social capital and effective flourishing of a school, according to Leadership for Learning, are built from the collective enterprise of shared leadership between leaders, teachers, students and their communities.[16]

This concept of shared leadership or shared agency is integral to the 4Cs approach to transformation. Critical to embedding the 4Cs as everyday practice and empowering others with agency is understanding shared leadership as 'coactive power'. Mary Parker Follett, a pioneer of organizational theory and behaviour, argues, 'Our task is not to learn where to place power; it is how to develop power . . . Genuine power can only be grown, it will slip from every arbitrary hand that grasps it; for genuine power is not coercive control, but coactive control. Coercive power is the curse of the universe; coactive power, the enrichment and advancement of every human soul.'[17] We treat leadership as a capability of genuine coactive power challenging other conventional views of hierarchical and positional leadership. Leadership as a capability enabled by the 4Cs is essentially a dynamic, emerging and complex 'team sport', where agency is developed and shared in the collective enterprise of the school community.

Why should leadership be shared and how?

Status quo structures can be rigid, hierarchical and resistant to emergent change and can prevent schools being dynamic, flexible and innovative. A shared leadership approach allows for emergence and meets the complex needs and challenges that schools face. In our experience working with schools we recognize the enormous commitment, energy and drive required of leaders to build shared agency as a collective endeavour across a school. Positional leadership can be strong in schools and feelings of powerlessness and a lack of agency can be entrenched legacies. Agentic leadership, however, can be developed in the learning and embedding of 4C processes. Shared leadership recognizes that leadership can reside everywhere in a transforming school. Leadership researcher Barbara Simpson describes how 'it resides in those emergent turning points, or leadership moments, that re-orient the flow of practice towards new, or least different, directions'.[18]

Everyone can learn the capability of leadership, but there are different types of agency that define different and dynamically changing roles of leadership in schools. Exploring the differences and understanding how they weave together can allow school leaders to develop and set up clear, flexible team structures and 4C processes to build shared leadership and agency across the school. We explain how the capability of leadership involves three types of agency that can complement each other in equal and harmonic tension. Barbara Simpson[19] contends that there are different expressions of leadership and agency, and these can be explained as follows:

– leadership as self-action,
– leadership as inter-action, and
– leadership as trans-action

Simpson uses the All Blacks rugby team to examine the different expressions of agentic leadership. As an example, it helps us to understand what it means for schools.

Leadership as self-action

Leadership as self-action is the individual as leader taking agency to make decisions and direct action. In the All Blacks this may be the coach or captain, or it may include a 'star player'. The post-match press conferences often draw attention to these 'leaders' as integral to the success of the team, but as we discussed earlier, this cannot be the only reason for the All Blacks' success. Simpson argues that the concept of leadership as self-action dominates Western consciousness and influences a celebrity culture that both glorifies and vilifies the 'star leaders' it creates. This happened to Jacinda Ardern with the profile she has received from the international press. The expectations are high and often unrealistic about what an individual leader can achieve alone. Leadership as self-action has become a defining perception of what leadership is. It is often assumed that it is the agency and capacity of individual leaders that leads to the success of a team, organization or school.

Leadership as self-action is integral however to shared leadership. In the dynamic flow of shared leadership, there are times the agency or 'power' is in the hands of the self to make decisions and take action. In schools, there are key moments when the principal and other leaders take agency to lead the strategic and transformative direction of the school. Understanding leadership as a capability is to recognize that all of us can lead others by directing, initiating and taking responsibility. Sometimes it is others, however, who make decisions and take actions that affect us, like the coaches and captains for the All Blacks do. Leadership as self-action, however, can still be focused on the growth of agency in others. We see this in the example of Graham Henry, coach for the All Blacks from 2003 to 2011, and a cultural change that moved the emphasis of the organization from 'you and them' to 'us'. James Kerr, author of *Legacy: 15 Lessons in Leadership*, recounts:

> The management always felt', says Graham Henry, 'that they had to transfer the leadership from senior management members to the players . . . they play the game and they have to do the leading on the field. The traditional 'you and them' became 'us'. Leadership groups were formed, giving key senior players a distinct portfolio of responsibilities from on-field leadership to social organization, new-player mentoring to community relations. The players 'induct those [young] players, tell them what the expectations are,' says Henry. 'It's better coming from their peers.
>
> Leaders create leaders by passing on responsibility, creating ownership, accountability and trust.[20]

Leadership as self-action works as a fluid dynamic with inter-actional and trans-actional leadership.

Leadership as inter-action

Leadership as inter-action is when the power to act is distributed among people. With the All Blacks, this occurs when a team member steps up at any time in the game and takes responsibility for finding a way to win. The metaphor of 'passing the ball' among players explains how people leading through inter-action are empowered to take responsibility for the direction of the team. Simpson describes how in passing the metaphorical ball, agency as inter-action still sits with individuals or entities, but the power of influence moves between people in an organized and coordinated way.

> . . . the players are all potential leaders who are expected to actively contribute to each other's leadership . . . In this manner, leadership is continuously passed among the players and their managers, directly challenging more conventional notions of centralized, top-down management. The ball-in-motion is the connection, or the interplay, between players, but it is the players themselves who are the developmental focus of the 'pass the ball' metaphor as they each step into leadership.[21]

In schools, inter-actional or distributive leadership takes place when individuals or entities all work together towards a clear, collective vision. For instance, it is when learning teams (who are responsible for learners for certain year levels) coordinate with faculties (who have responsibility for their subjects across the school) and cooperate with student representative bodies (who have defined responsibilities) towards a common goal. In distributive leadership there is autonomy but still a common purpose and interdependency that binds them. It can be likened to cooperation and coordination in comparison to collaboration. As an expression of leadership and agency, it has a role to play in shared leadership and the organizational structure of a school. Distributive leadership alone, however, does not allow for transformative leadership.

When a team or organization collaborates and becomes one mind working together in blended synchronization, they create something new together, and this is leadership as trans-action.

Leadership as trans-action

We can observe in the cultural change Graham Henry developed as coach of the All Blacks leadership as self-action (the coaches), moving to leadership as inter-action (between the players), to leadership as trans-action (when the players 'take over the asylum'). Kerr describes:

> It didn't happen overnight, and by their reckoning, they didn't get it right straightaway, but slowly the culture change began to take effect.
> The structure of the working week epitomizes this management model: the Sunday evening review meetings are facilitated by the coaches, though

significant input comes from the on-field leadership. Then over the course of the week, you see a gradual handing over of responsibility and decision-making. By Thursday, the priorities, intensity levels and other aspects are all 'owned' by the players. By the time they play on Saturday the players have taken over the asylum.[22]

Leadership as trans-action conceives leadership as an overarching and emergent concept that directs an organization or team in new and different directions with a sense of purpose. The emergent V-shape phenomenon[23] of migratory birds in nature metaphorically illustrates the emergent leadership in trans-actional leadership. Birds such as magpie geese fly in a V-shape (see figure 10.4), where one bird leads, and then another, in an ongoing synchronized fashion.[24] Each bird is only aware of its neighbouring birds and flies according to the changing dynamic of the flock. Flying this way is 70 per cent more efficient than flying solo, and if a bird falls out of the formation it feels the wind resistance and rejoins the flock. If one falls behind, the others wait for it to join again. This phenomenon of the V formation is an emergent system,[25] and schools transforming through the 4Cs can develop leadership to operate in this same way.

Considering the All Blacks again, this occurs when the team play as one organism sensing the turning points in the flow of the game. It is similar to how we describe collaboration as a 'shared affair of the mind'.[26] Each player owns the leadership of the team. According to Simpson, 'Agency is no longer dependent on individual agents to carry the action; rather it is manifest in the movements and changing

Figure 10.4 Migratory birds such as magpie geese fly in an emergent V formation, illustrating the natural phenomenon of emergence in a complex system.

directions that emerge as trans-actors seek to coordinate their work together.'[27] The All Blacks have a culture and tradition rooted in the Maori idea of *whakapapa* (the genealogy of identity through ancestors, stories, myths and symbols). This tradition continues to weave a narrative of purpose, responsibility and legacy in every player. The culture strongly underpins and continues a trans-actional form of deeply collaborative leadership in the All Blacks.

Coach Graham Henry argues the relationships between people are also vital. 'You talk about handling expectation and handling pressure,' says Graham Henry. 'You talk about leaders leading, players leading. You talk about the legacy and what that means . . . But I think the other thing that was really important was the connection between people – and the greater those connections, the more resilient and the stronger we were, the better we were.'[28] In schools the process of trans-actional, collaborative leadership relies on the strength of the connection between people. It takes time to develop agency and leadership across large school organizations, but it is possible and we see it happening in the schools we partner with in 4C transformation.

The All Blacks demonstrate how the leadership concepts of self-action, inter-action and trans-action are integral to their ongoing and constantly emerging success. Leadership is embedded as a capability throughout the team, but it is manifest in varying but complementary ways at different times. The agency of leadership is a metaphorical relay baton passed back and forth from coach to captain, across individual players in the team, and to the team emergently working together as a whole. These three perspectives of leadership (summarized in table 10.1) can be understood and developed by leaders to share leadership effectively across a school.

Table 10.1 Comparison of three different perspectives of shared and active leadership, adapted from Barbara Simpson (2016)

Type of practice perspective of leadership	Leader as a practitioner	Leadership as a set of practices	Leadership as a process in the flow of practice (or praxis)
Type of action	Self-action	Inter-action	Trans-action
Type of leadership	Individual	Distributed	Collaborative and emergent
Type of agency	Individual power to influence, take initiative and responsibility	Individuals or entities influencing each other, by 'passing the ball' in taking initiative and responsibility	Influence, initiative and responsibility emerging in a whole context of mutual engagement
Type of power	Power to . . .	Power over . . .	Power with . . .

Through shared leadership they can achieve the vision or super-objective of the school's transforming endeavour. The shifting of power and agency through these different expressions of shared leadership are in a dynamic and equal tension with each other. 4C processes and new leadership structures accommodate the effective emergence of these approaches to leadership in schools.

To develop the capability of leadership in schools is a transformative, challenging and complex undertaking. A group of leaders and a group of innovators lead the transformation by gradually 'seeding, germinating and growing' the processes, strategies and organizational structures that support the development of the capabilities (values, learning, pedagogy, curriculum, teacher education, leadership) that we argue are central to transformation. A collaborative and strategic leadership group is critical to maintaining the focused energy and sense of urgency needed to drive the moral imperative of transformation. This leadership group has to consider the 'big picture' components that affect the leading of change.

What are the components for leading change?

In *Transforming Schools*, we described a leadership framework for school transformation through and in the 4Cs. This framework is depicted in figure 10.5 and we refer to the diagram as 'eggs in a basket'. In the diagram, the 4Cs is the 'basket' that holds the key components (the 'eggs') of transformation – vision and values, culture, structure, strategy and integration, partnerships, and research and evaluation. The 4Cs inform the processes by which leadership realizes these components, by deepening or reimagining learning and work practices in the school (see chapter 2). For a more extensive discussion of the components for leading transformation in figure 10.5, see *Transforming Schools* and *Transforming Organizations*.

The eggs in a basket diagram suggests the 4Cs are integrated in all facets of vision and values, culture, structure, strategies, partnerships, research and evaluation. These facets are interdependent and influence each other. For instance, structural shifts in timetabling may allow co-teaching that then can affect culture. Alternatively, the growth of collaborative practice in culture may affect structural changes in the timetable. The vision for the school may for example affect the strategy of integrating aspects of the schools professional learning, and the strategy and integration of the professional learning can also inform the developing vision for the school. Partnerships with organizations or communities can influence research and evaluation and vice versa. Part of our work supporting schools is facilitating processes for leadership to consider these big picture concepts in 4C transformation. But who in leadership considers these big picture components for change and who in schools generates and influences change on the ground?

Figure 10.5 A framework for leading 4C transformation that we refer to as 'eggs in a basket'.

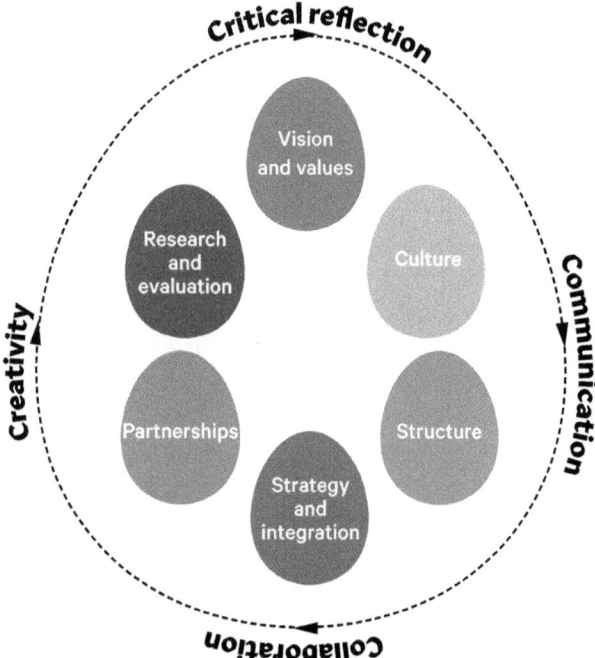

Who leads transformation and how?

Agency is central to 4C transformation and it is this underpinning purpose that supports the collective strategic direction of the school. Through 4C processes, ideas are encouraged to be diverse, challenged and contested in 4C transformation. All stakeholders are integral to co-constructing and advancing the collective vision, but this can only be achieved through the practices and culture of co-agency. The building of a culture of co-agency through people joining the co-constructed and collective vision of the school takes time, however. Transformation can begin with a critical mass of committed, willing and competent leaders and teachers that begin the 4C cultural shift. We refer to this group as the 'innovation team' (or I team, 'I' for innovation) in the Transforming School Structures diagram (see figure 10.6).

What is the innovation team?

The innovation team comprises leaders and teachers who are keen to learn about, experiment with and embed 4C processes in classroom and work practices. The 'I team' are key change agents that can influence the school climate and affect cultural change over time. In chapter 9, the pedagogical innovation group from Hurstville Public School was referred to as the Ground-breakers.

Figure 10.6 Transforming School Structures diagram.

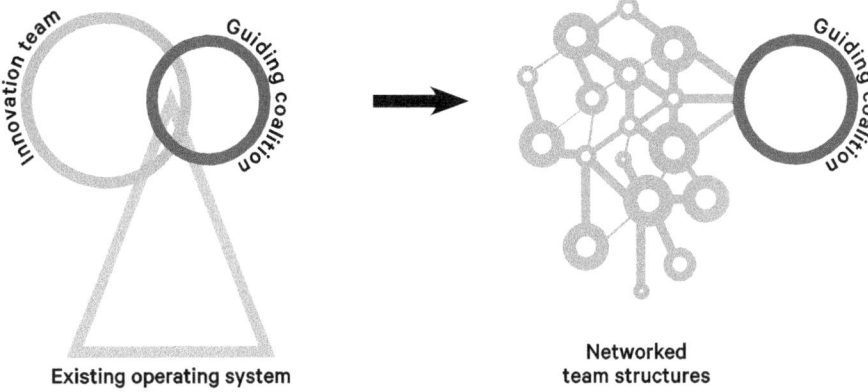

The I team experiments and learns from what can be achieved and learnt from innovative approaches to teaching and learning. The enthusiasm and energy of this team creates a tension of curiosity and interest from others in the school community. Over time, other staff join the learning catalytically begun by the I team and try new approaches and inquire into their own practice. Gradually new but differentiated approaches to teaching and learning permeate the whole school culture through processes of experience, reflection and inquiry (chapter 9). What began as one innovation 'I team' becomes a networked structure of evolving and adaptive innovation teams (see figure 10.5) working together to drive school transformation. This complex and strategic metamorphosis towards networked innovation teams and shared leadership in a school or organization is supported by a coalition of leadership to guide and drive the transformation.

From the start, a key, strategic leadership team can support the ground-breaking innovation team in instigating, leading, driving and sustaining 4C transformation. This leadership team are the 'champions of change'[29] or 'guiding coalition'. We refer to this group of leaders as the guiding coalition (or G team, 'G' for guiding).

What is the guiding coalition?

The guiding coalition are involved in the learning and work of the innovation team (otherwise they cannot know what they are leading) indicated by the intersecting circles diagram (figure 10.5). The guiding coalition or 'G team' is an imagineering and action team that does the 'heavy lifting' in strategic thinking of the change vision. The group requires an unerring focus, energy and enthusiasm for the school's collective enterprise in 4C transformation.

Through 4C processes, the G team diagnose and reflect on the needs of the school and determine the initial steps toward transformative action. The G team have a distanced perspective or 'big picture' view of the school. The metaphor of being on the balcony looking down on the dance floor explains their points of view. The

G team as 'adaptive leadership'[30] move back and forth between balcony and dance floor continually assessing what is happening around them (on the dance floor) and with the larger patterns and dynamics across the school (from the balcony). The G team as a committed, collaborative and strategic team bring a richness of ideas and opinions to advance the momentum of 4C transformation. The G team are not only observers of the dance floor; they use their overview and leadership capacity to influence and effect the 'choreography' on the dance floor.

John P. Kotter argues that there are eight fundamental steps to the guiding coalition or G team leading transformation. He says they must:[31]

1. establish a sense of urgency,
2. create a guiding coalition,
3. develop a vision and strategy,
4. communicate the change vision,
5. empower a broad base of people to take action,
6. generate short-term wins,
7. consolidate gains and produce even more change, and
8. institutionalize new approaches in the culture.

In our experience, all these steps are critical to sustained and effective 4C transformation. We argue that 4C processes can help support and shape how these steps happen.

The guiding coalition or G team is not necessarily the established executive leadership team, but usually include leaders that are 'authorizers of actions', such as the principal and the team leader(s) of the initial innovation team. Often large executive leadership structures in schools are based on the management and administrative organization of siloed structures focused on maintaining the running of the school. This established operating system is crucial in supporting and collaborating with the guiding coalition (the G team), and the ground-breaking pedagogical and curriculum innovation team (the I team).

How does the existing operating system become networked team structures?

In the Transforming School Structures diagram (see figure 10.5), the existing operating system is indicated by the triangle connected with the guiding coalition and innovation team. Transforming begins with two operating systems: one that sustains the existing management structures and processes, and one that is developing, implementing, accelerating and designing new structures and innovation.

The Transforming School Structures illustrates how the established operating system gradually becomes a network of adaptive innovation teams connected to each other and the guiding coalition. This evolution of structural transformation is guided strategically and emergently by the guiding coalition G team. Kotter describes innovation networks as mobilization teams that are creative risk-takers, agile and active agents who turbo-charge ongoing transformation. 'They become permanent accelerators, creating and maintaining a culture of agility and speed within an organization.'[32] The modus operandi of these innovation teams and networks is active experiential and experimental learning using evidence-driven feedback (praxis) as they imagine, create and innovate approaches in transformative teaching, learning and working. The innovation teams' approaches to teaching and learning are accelerated by 4C processes that encourage them to 'try, learn, iterate, adapt'.[33]

Established leadership management systems in organizations are not structures for transformation and innovation, as Kotter explains:

> Hierarchies with great management processes and good leaders on top are not built for leaping into a creative future. Innovation requires risks, people who are willing to think outside their boxes, perspectives from multiple silos and more. Management-driven hierarchies are built to minimize risk and keep people in their boxes and silos. To change this more than incrementally is to fight a losing battle.[34]

The guiding coalition G team leads transformation by maintaining a sense of urgency for change. There are different focuses of change depending on the evolving and emerging diagnoses of need, and there are different speeds of change across the school. The G team considers how to differentiate professional learning, changing structures and work practices according to people's needs, fears, understandings and capacities. The aspiration for the G team is to achieve shared leadership across the school, so the school can constantly adapt with flexibility and agility to change. 4C transformation is an exciting and rewarding endeavour and there are early wins generated in building teacher, student and community agency. There are, however, challenges and tensions in leading school transformation. These challenges can be overcome by leadership teams using and embedding 4C processes.

How can leadership teams use the 4Cs to lead?

Leadership teams can encounter tensions in transformation as described in figure 10.7. As they forge ahead with their moral imperative, clear about the *why* for transformation, they meet opposing forces that stall their acceleration. The challenges may be a limited number of change leaders, or silo parochialism from places such as subject faculties, or perceived and real pressures of compliance from within the school, systems and educational authorities, or complacency, misunderstanding or insufficient buy-in

Figure 10.7 The tension of transformation in schools, adapted from John P. Kotter's[35] diagram of acceleration stalled.

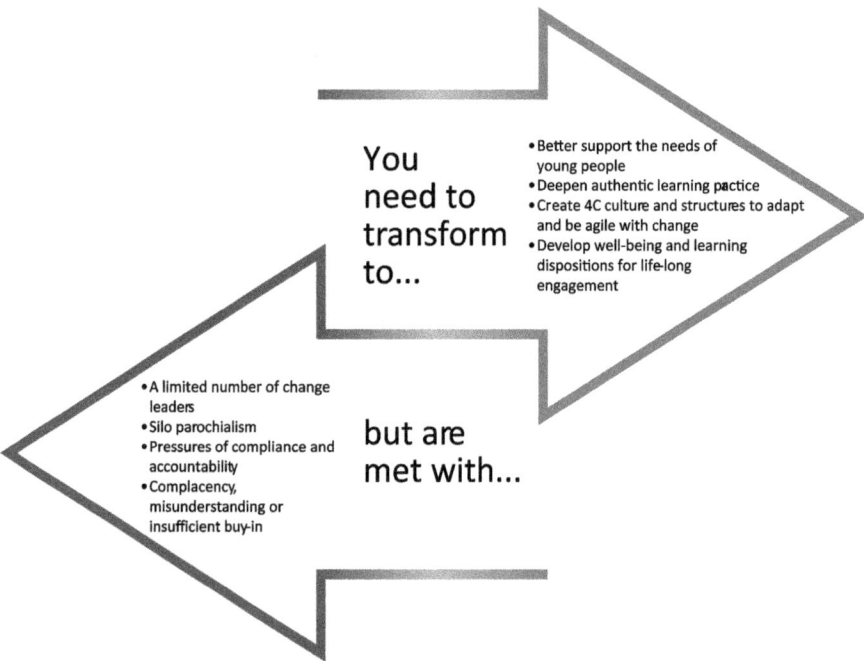

because some staff do not agree with the direction the school is taking. These forces that resist the momentum of transformation are not inevitable, but in our experience, they exist. This is despite the goodwill of a willing and able coalition of leaders and teachers committed to the ideas such as developing agency, well-being and learning dispositions described in the tension of transformation diagram.

The 4Cs approach empowers all stakeholders in the process of transformation and creates a culture of co-agency and leadership across the school community. The objective is buy-in from the whole staff and community. This does not happen overnight, but the role of leaders is to shift mindsets and culture over time using 4C processes to enable the capabilities we describe in this book. To do this, leadership teams can consider how to:

- communicate and integrate the emergent vision, values and strategies,
- empower capabilities in others through networks of collaboration (such as a community of praxis),
- notice and evaluate assumptions and practices through their own and others' critical reflection, and
- generate and encourage creative and innovative practices and structures towards a unified and cohering vision and purpose.

We discuss next what each of these means for leaders and leadership teams.

Communicating the vision, values and strategies as emergent

Communication can build ongoing confidence and trust in the challenging and gradual process of transformation (see chapter 3). The rationale for change must be explored and communicated at all times. Communication as conceptualized in the 4Cs approach is more than a one-way transmission. Communication can make sense of human experiences through empathy and then sharing, constructing and synthesizing those stories. This is what Jacinda Ardern did so eloquently after the Christchurch massacre. Leadership can interact with, explore and co-construct the narrative of the school's transformation with all stakeholders as the vision emerges and evolves. It is however difficult to communicate a vision that is not fully known. There needs to be a clear *why* the need for transformation, but *what* it looks like, and exactly *how* it will be achieved is evolving and emergent.

A metaphorical distinction between gardeners and carpenters, used by psychology researcher Alison Gopnick[36] explains how a school's vision can have a sense of direction but is also open and responsive to the unpredictable, the uncertain and the complex as it emerges. Carpenters have a blueprint as a pre-defined plan for a product and their aim is for the finished product to be as close as possible to the design blueprint. By contrast, gardeners have a clear intention for the garden and create the right conditions for growth, but they adapt and respond to the environment in a dynamic way. 4C leadership resembles 'gardeners' who have a determined vision and direction but modify, critically reflect upon and generate ideas responding to and collaborating with the school environment.

This concept of a purposeful but emergent vision is often difficult to communicate to teachers whose experience of schools and professional learning is procedural and technical implementation. Like the 4C learning philosophy, 4C leadership communicates more by asking searching questions rather than providing 'blueprint' answers. This is all part of a cultural shift towards a transforming, networked and responsive organization rather than a fixed, hierarchical and managed organization. The guiding coalition and leadership teams could ask themselves: 'How do we continue to communicate the vision for transformation as clear but emergent?' Communication of these ideas makes more sense to staff and the community when they are collaborating through new processes and structures.

Creating networks of collaboration

School transformation in the 4Cs approach is charged both emotionally and mentally as it entails a complete change in a school's 'frame of reference'. People do not transform by being told to transform. We have to experience and embody new processes and practices to change habitual behaviours and perspectives. Collaboration is an experience that allows people to learn, unlearn, take creative risks and to innovate with others as a mutually beneficial process. Collaboration is an experience that disassembles and co-mingles our identity as we bravely risk our ideas and actions with others.[37, 38] It is through collaboration that we open up to possibilities, gain confidence and achieve competence to attempt new practices and to innovate.[39] Leadership teams can develop collaborative practices and structures that strategically expand the influence of the innovation teams that begin the transformation process in the school.

Learning how to collaborate is integral to deeper and transformational learning experiences (see community of praxis in chapter 9). Networked structures are also necessary to enable collaboration and influence. We discussed complexity theory in chapter 2 and explained how change does not happen in a linear fashion. Connected and networked collaborative teams in schools allow the sharing of ideas, feedback and the emergence of innovation. These networked interactions between people in a shared endeavour are called 'complex adaptive systems'. They are characterized by:

- connectivity (interconnectedness and inter-relationships between people),
- co-evolution (interactions that provide feedback loops of influence),
- emergent order (where unpredictable ideas and patterns arise), and
- cascading effects (small changes that have a fast ripple effect).[40]

To encourage innovation, leadership can strategically co-construct the development of networked collaborative teams to influence and transform teachers' professional practice. Networked team structures and flexibility and self-organization in these teams can be key to continuous evaluation and emergence of learning growth in schools. A question for leadership to consider is: how can the school be structured as a complex adaptive system with collaborative teams and networks? Leadership can evaluate the progress of these teams and networks through constant critical reflection.

Evaluating assumptions and practices through critical reflection

Reflective practice is to stand back and deeply explore and reassess our thinking and actions. For leadership teams, processes in critical reflection uncover tensions, contradictions and illogical features in schools. They also reveal the successes and wins to be celebrated in the journey of transformation. Critical reflection brings to the surface 'the emotions and politics that are part of the underlying assumptions and expectations that inform everyday practice'.[41] When this thinking is 'surfaced', it is then possible to consider ideas to navigate and evolve the transformation of the school. Critical reflection treats knowledge and what we know as inherently dynamic, contested and contestable. This allows schools to be engaging and dynamic places of knowledge creation and innovation.

If reflective practice is a part of leadership's 'working DNA', leaders are 'awake' to how things work, how things can change, how their agency and power affects others, and how the agency of others affect theirs. Too often leaders in schools are consumed by the 'busy work' of their day-to-day running. To develop wisdom in leadership teams is to make space for and develop critical reflection as an internalized, ongoing, mindful practice.

Critical reflection focuses leadership teams to be open to ideas and stretched beyond their comfort zones. It provides a space for informed learning to ask questions and seek solutions by questioning assumptions, considering possibilities and evaluating actions. Through critical reflection, leadership can acknowledge and learn from mistakes and failure and consider the development of well-being of everyone in a school community. Critical reflection is recognizing and developing our own strengths and yet-to-be strengths as leaders, and those of others. Reflective practice is a basis for leaders to make wise, strategic and consultative decisions. It is to ask: how deeply are we as leaders using critical practice to develop our growth and the flourishing of others? Critical reflection is also the basis of generating and energizing the action of new ideas.

Generating and encouraging creativity

Leaders and leadership teams are bold and courageous in exploring and discovering unfamiliar and unknown territory as they lead transformative and innovative practice. Generating and encouraging creativity is to take risks but requires discipline and grit to withstand the iterations and reiterations as transformation progresses or when things do not work as planned. Creative leadership keeps experimenting and learning through ongoing and iterative 'playing with possibility' that unleashes excitement and hope but sometimes draws discomfort and conflict. Creativity is the engine room of transformation and innovation, but with the novelty and excitement of creativity there can be challenges, setbacks and negative feedback. Leaders are lifelong learners who take risks and are resilient to short-term pain for long-term gain. According to Kotter, leaders who are lifelong learners:

> . . . overcome a natural tendency to shy away from or abandon habits that produce short-term pain. By surviving difficult experiences, they build up a certain immunity to hardship. With clarity of thought, they come to realise the importance of both these habits and lifelong learning. But most of all, their goals and aspirations facilitate the development of humility, openness, willingness to take risks, and the capacity to listen.[42]

For creativity to flourish, leaders can ask themselves: 'How can we generate and encourage processes and networked structures for innovative practice?' As well as modelling and supporting creativity and innovation, leaders of transformation are lifelong learners in the capacities described in the Leadership Wheel (figure 10.2).

In the breakout box, there is an example of practice from school leaders, Peter Howes and Luke Bristow at Murwillumbah High School in regional NSW, Australia. Peter discusses the role of the Leadership Wheel and the 4Cs, and Luke describes the development of agency through the transformation processes of their school.

Peter Howes (Principal)

I've found the Leadership Wheel really useful as a scaffold to develop school leaders. It enables us to drill down into areas individual leaders are strong at, and what their yet to be strengths are. It's an explicit conversation that is far less subjective because it's not my opinion or gut feeling, it's about the capacities in the wheel. These are the elements that make up effective leadership or great leadership. And the conversation is always about leadership growth. 'How can we grow and continue to grow with these capacities?' The Leadership Wheel has been incredibly powerful.

Reflective dialogue about leadership is another disruptor to tradition. The tradition is not to talk about leadership and not to know how to reflect on your leadership. Critical reflection is yet another arrow in the quiver for challenging what we used to do. It just makes things richer.

The 4Cs is a culture of what a school should be. It makes all of the old structures of timetable and concerns around examinations etc. just fade when your real work is the 4Cs. It's exactly what I've been trying to do before I knew it. I believe that collaboration and communication, critical reflection, are absolutely fundamental to setting a culture that enables creativity.

I think the most effective leadership is when you have a whole set of people enabled and have the agency to go about making the brave decisions.

The 4Cs bring joy to leadership, it brings joy to the job of being a school leader.

Luke Bristow (Deputy Principal)

I think the 4Cs are just so essential, such important elements. I think they were the missing key in our early stages of trying to transform the school. I've heard it so many times about the 4Cs, teachers saying, 'This has reinvigorated me. It's changed my outlook on what I was doing, how I was doing it and where I want to go.'

As the journey's progressed and everyone started to transform we started to 'get the 4Cs'. The 4Cs is not a thing so much as really a culture and processes. It's unlocking what are really important areas that often are the areas that get suppressed in more traditional approaches to schooling. You see that with creativity. When you talk to some of the students at school and they tell you what they're doing and where they're heading, it just blows your mind. You think wow, I would never have thought going that way. That's agency coming through creativity, through collaborative process, reflections and communication.

I was initially a quite hands-on leader but I have changed a lot because of my own learning and the agency that has been developed and built in the school. It's been really exciting to watch the rest of the staff grow and start to take things on. I don't have to direct and challenge staff because they're the ones taking us places.

> We've been transforming for three years. The first year was more around getting structures in place and then in the second year, pedagogy became the focus, which I think has been a godsend. I look at the initial staff involved in the new teaching and learning and the leadership they're providing now. I have watched other staff come in and then I just played the role of helping the initial group manage that, and then watching them lead and seeing the growth of their agency.
>
> The critical reflection element of the 4Cs is really important. Obviously, we know all the 4Cs are intertwined, but that capacity or that culture where staff will critically reflect upon performance or whatever we're looking at and will take on the reflections, work on them and come up with creative solutions is a really good thing.
>
> When we first started, we still had people having an idea or wanting victory about something and going for it. But it wasn't necessarily about the whole school direction. It was about them or what they could get. We have seen that change. When we go to leadership meetings now with something you think will be controversial and challenging, and hoping to see it head in a certain direction, they embrace the ideas, give you new ideas and make it better than you thought it could be.
>
> And like no other school I've been in, we've got more non-executive leaders who are driving things in this school. There is a general sense that they want to take things forward and want to grow things.

What is it to be a transformative leader?

Transformation means having a changed and more complex perspective and attitude, and changing your actions as a result. Transformative leaders and leadership teams develop a frame of reference that is open yet discriminating, responsive to action yet self-reflective.[43] They develop dispositions that are more critically reflective of their own assumptions and those of others, rather than continue established patterns of default thinking or sometimes 'non-thinking' in the day-to-day operations of a school. Transformative leaders develop the capacity to notice, diagnose and generate transformative action to respond to systemic issues and possibilities in schools. At the same time they notice, diagnose and realise action for the development of their own capacities as leaders.

Is Jacinda Ardern who began this chapter a transformative national leader? It was certainly something she aspired to be, but for many she has not delivered, in terms of climate change policy, the capital gains tax and the affordable housing project, Kiwibuild, as examples. Some argue she is a pragmatic idealist who has been hamstrung by accommodating her coalition partner, the conservative New Zealand First party. An oft-repeated critique is that her government does not live up to the transformative rhetoric. Transformation has constraints and restraints and takes time.

There have been achievements and Chapman argues, it is not all empty rhetoric. 'A lot happened, planned and otherwise, in Ardern's first two years as prime minister. Labour's wellbeing budget was a world first, and will undoubtedly be improved upon in New Zealand and around the world. New Zealand has also adopted a Zero Carbon Bill, setting climate change targets into law. And dangerous assault weapons have been banned.'[44] Where Chapman believes Ardern has been transformative is in:

> ... her own personal, often instinctive, conduct. While the world watched as volatile men rose to power in some of the world's most powerful nations, along came Ardern, a handbrake on the global identity car careening into the abyss.
>
> ... The simple act of wearing hijab in Christchurch united communities both in New Zealand and around the world after a terror attack. It sent a signal to leader everywhere that even the smallest acts of kindness in positions of power make a difference.[45]

Altruism and enabling others' agency are at the heart of transformative leadership. Transformative leaders can develop the processes of leadership in themselves and others, by developing the capacities in the Leadership Wheel (introduced earlier in the chapter). Through ongoing and evolving processes in critical reflection, communication, collaboration and creativity, leaders develop, and develop in others, the Leadership Wheel capacities:

- Engagement – to be bravely determined and committed to the purpose of transformation and innovation.
- Perseverance – to seek out challenges, and survive and treat difficult experiences as valuable learnings.
- Flexibility – to create agile and adaptive structures and view life with an open mind.
- Critical reflection – to honestly assess successes, mistakes and the status quo to inform future action.
- Communication – to listen to others and seek out their ideas.
- Creativity – to push thinking and actions out of the comfort zone into the unknown.
- Influence – to inspire and challenge others with vision and action.
- Altruism – to foster individual and collective efficacy in others.
- Collaboration – to build trust and co-construct ideas, actions and decision-making.

Transforming leadership

Leadership like learning is innate to all of us. Leadership can be a way of being in every aspect of school life; it means taking initiative and responsibility as an agent of positive influence and change with those around you. We recognize that there are different expressions of agency that contribute to the concept of shared leadership. Shared leadership is a combination of individual leadership (agency as self-action), distributive leadership (agency as inter-action) and collaborative leadership (agency as trans-action). In a culture of shared responsibility and endeavour, collaborative and networked teams galvanize these forms of agency to create a dynamic environment of transformation and innovation. This culture is courageously led by a guiding coalition and innovation teams working methodically, energetically and emergently to introduce and develop many of the ideas we discuss in this book.

4C transformation is not a project, programme, procedure or protocol. It is a philosophy, approach and mindset that can transform leadership and learning in a school community. As much as transformation is the reimagining of large processual and structural change in schools, it is also a deeply personal and emotional experience. For anyone leading in whatever capacity, aiming for and trying to achieve a vision is challenging, hard work. It is a rigorously difficult and creative process and there are always setbacks and obstacles. We find our individual and collective potential to enable transformation by developing capacities in the Leadership Wheel and embedding the 4Cs with others in our professional practice.

Concluding reflections

We return to Jacinda Ardern and the All Blacks to learn the wisdom of shared and transforming leadership. Ardern's leadership reminds us that connection, compassion, sincere empathy and fierce resolve are integral qualities of leadership. Leading is, however, as much in a team, as in an individual. *Legacy* author James Kerr argues that for the All Blacks, 'Shared responsibility means shared ownership. A sense of inclusion means individuals are more willing to give themselves to a common cause.'[46] Leading transformation is about finding and fostering a common cause and creating an inclusive culture of shared leadership to drive and sustain it. Finding a common cause reminds us of the legacy we can leave for the future through the education of our young people. Legacy and the traditions of Maori culture are profoundly significant to the All Blacks, as illustrated by Kerr when he recounts the tradition of the little black book.

> When a player makes the All Blacks, they're given a book. It's a small black book, bound in fine leather, and beautiful to hold. The first page shows a jersey – that of the 1905 Originals, the team that began this long *whakapapa*. On the next page is another jersey, that of the 1924 Invincibles, and on the page after, another jersey, and another, and so on until the present day. It is a visual *whakapapa*, layered with meaning, a legacy to step into. The next few pages of this All Black handbook remind you of the principles, the heroes, the values, the standards, the code of honour, the ethos, the character of the team. The rest of the pages are blank. Waiting to be filled.[47]

As members of a school community we all have pages to fill. We can make a significant contribution through leadership, for as leaders we are stewards of the future.

The next chapter concludes with how leadership with the other capabilities, values, learning, pedagogy, curriculum, teacher education and the 4Cs all work together towards school transformation and the infinite game that is education.

Transforming education
Putting the pieces together

11

Untangling infinity 228

The puzzle of transformation 228

The 4Cs enable the capabilities for transformation 230

The Transformation Tangle 231

Disorientation 233
Awareness 234
Dialogue and shared endeavour 235
Renewed perspectives and roles 235

Concluding reflections 236

Untangling infinity

Figure 11.1 The infinity symbol.

We began our discussion of transformation in chapter 1 by referring to infinite games. The object of an infinite game is to keep everyone participating and engaged in the game, no winners, no losers, just participants. We argue that even though education contains finite games, playing the infinite game is consistent with John Dewey's view of democratic education. The infinite game in education equips all participants with the capabilities, capacities and dispositions they require to survive and thrive in their present and their future. This vision for education requires teachers, students and school communities to reimagine the capabilities for transformation; values, learning, pedagogy, curriculum, teacher education and leadership. An education system that can achieve these reimaginings has potential to build a better and more equitable society. The infinite game illustrates the 'big picture' purpose of education by imagining what schools can and should be. The 'big picture' helps us reimagine what might be possible in education to make it relevant to our students in their contexts. However, there are many big picture thinkers who do not go to the next step to explain the 'how'. The mission of this book and our partnerships with schools is to explain the why and then provide the rationale, the research and some of the frameworks (coherence makers) for 'how' we might transform education.

In this final chapter, we bring together all of the pieces of the jigsaw puzzle that we introduced in chapter 2 through the 4Cs and the capabilities for transformation (values, learning, pedagogy, curriculum, teacher education and leadership). We use the metaphor of a jigsaw puzzle to show how the 4Cs connect with and enable the capabilities that help schools navigate transformation.

The puzzle of transformation

In chapter 2 we discussed transformation as a complex problem. In figure 11.2 we represent this complexity through the metaphor of a puzzle. This puzzle has three layers:

Figure 11.2 The puzzle of transformation.

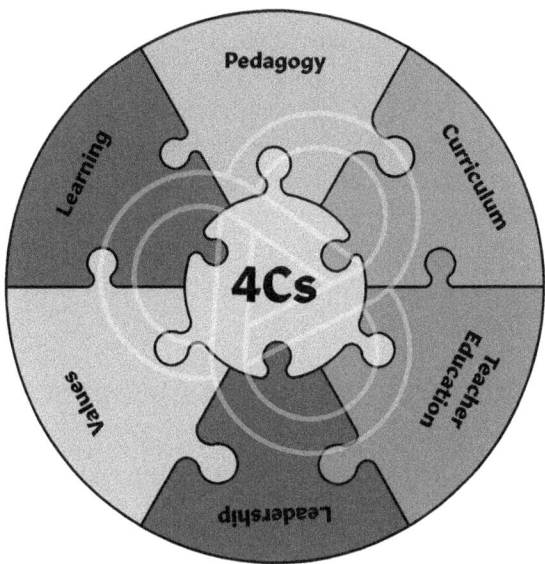

- Layer 1: The *4Cs* enable the capabilities for transformation. The 4Cs are the centrepiece of the puzzle as they provide the foundational skills, knowledge and understandings that make transformation possible through the capabilities.
- Layer 2: The *capabilities of transformation* are connected to the 4Cs and each other. The coherence makers (such as the pedagogy parachute) are not present in this figure but they are the 'how' of transformation.
- Layer 3: The *Transformation Tangle* (figure 11.3) describes the phases of transformation and links all of the pieces to each other. The tangle sits beneath the capabilities to indicate the experience of transformation that occurs as schools engage with the capabilities.

As figure 11.2 demonstrates, the capabilities interconnect with each other and with the 4Cs, begin to 'solve' the puzzle of transformation. Like a puzzle, transformation is challenging; however, when the pieces fit together a great deal of satisfaction can be derived from the successful completion of a challenge. Schools can be strategic about where they begin the puzzle and with which piece. The choice and sequence of the pieces will depend on the context and needs of each school. They may begin with the 'curriculum piece' or the 'values piece' or the 'teacher education piece'. As each piece is worked with, they inform the connection with other pieces. No piece can be fully realized in one attempt because of the influence and relationship between all the pieces. For example, changes in the learning 'piece' change pedagogy, transforming curriculum will change teacher education and pedagogy, and so on.

When we work with schools, we use the transformation puzzle metaphor to generate awareness, dialogue and action about the connectedness of the pieces, and the substance and complexity all each piece and their connections. This process of beginning and sequencing, however, always begins with the 4Cs because without the centrepiece all of the 'capabilities pieces' become untethered, incoherent and ineffective in solving the transformation puzzle.

Completing the challenge of a jigsaw puzzle might be an amusing distraction. The transformation of schools is obviously more challenging. Transforming a school is like a jigsaw puzzle where the pieces are changing shape and where they connect as you work with them. Solving the 'puzzle' of transformation is exponentially more challenging but infinitely more rewarding for our students, teachers and schools. The 4Cs are the foundational capacities that help us solve this shapeshifting puzzle. Let's consider briefly some of the ways that the 4Cs are foundational for the capabilities of transformation that make possible a reimagining of the processes and practices in education.

The 4Cs enable the capabilities for transformation

The 4Cs underpin and overarch the capabilities for transformation. We argue when transforming schools the 4Cs enable the reconsideration of assumptions and the reimagining of sometimes taken-for-granted elements of the education system. In the following precis, we have listed the capabilities that we have explored throughout this book and identified how 4C processes enable transformation in each of them.

- **Values** (chapter 3) are generated when schools *critically reflect* on their context and *collaborate* to *create* shared principles that can be communicated to the whole school community to guide and anchor transformation.
- **Learning** (chapters 4 and 5) is transformed when students and teachers have the agency to *collaboratively co-create* new understandings, skills and knowledge. Learning is transformed in intrapersonal, interpersonal and cognitive domains (identified in the Learning Disposition Wheel). *Critical reflection* provides processes to analyse and understand the impact of learning.
- **Pedagogy** (chapter 6 and 7) is a form of *communication* where educators design and enact agentic and *collaborative* learning that creates democratic self-directed learning. In the Pedagogy Parachute we have identified nine elements of pedagogy that can be curated to develop transformative learning. *Creativity* is required to curate and blend the elements of pedagogy to generate deeper learning.
- **Curriculum** (chapter 8) is the experience of learning (intended and unintended) in schools. In transformative curriculum leaders, teachers and students *collaborate* to *create* diverse learning experiences. These experiences *communicate* directly to their needs in their context. *Critical reflection* allows innovation, iteration and refinement of curriculum.
- **Teacher education** (chapter 9) is a continuum of learning that is based on reflection on experience and inquiry. *Critical reflection* enables teachers to analyse and respond *collaboratively* to experiences of learning (in themselves

and their students) through frameworks such as the DNA Eye. These reflections can *create* wise changes in pedagogy, learning and curriculum. These reflections are *communicated* and form the basis of ongoing inquiry in communities of praxis across and beyond the school community.

- **Leadership** (chapter 10) is a *collaborative* process where school communities *critically reflect* on their context, processes and assumptions before *creating* values, vision and strategies. Effective leadership incorporates multi-way *communication* that generates consensus around shared practices and through shared frameworks such as the Leadership Wheel. Creativity is required to imagine, enable and enact new leadership processes.

The capabilities help schools understand the 'how' of transformation. The transformation tangle speaks to the 'phenomenon' of transformation. That is, what do participants in transformation experience emotionally and cognitively as they engage with transformation? An understanding of the tangle will help those embarking and engaging with transformation to articulate and identify their experience of the process as they work with all the pieces of the transformation puzzle.

The Transformation Tangle

The Transformation Tangle[1] (figure 11.3) outlines the stages of transformation and provides a sense of what people might be feeling and thinking as they undertake transformation.

Figure 11.3 The Transformation Tangle.

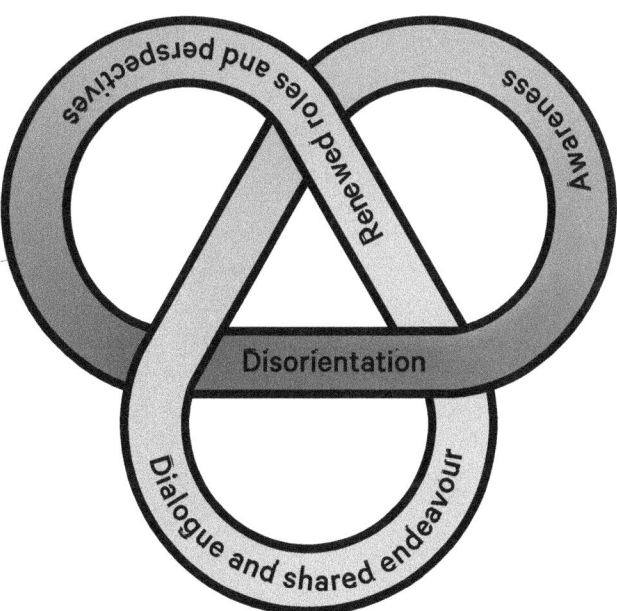

The rather puzzling metaphor of the tangle, with its twists, turns and overlaps, reflects the difficulty, ambiguity and the unpredictability of the transformation challenge. We have been inside countless transformations as observers, participants and facilitators. They are complex problems (see chapter 2) as they have many moving parts. However, if we understand the processes that enable transformation, schools can 'put the pieces together'. Effective transformations are not done *to* people, they are done *with* people. Yet no matter how collaborative the approach, transformation can lead to some disorientation.

The Transformation Tangle is not a recipe and even though it has phases, they do not all happen at the same time. In any change process, people will approach the transformation and respond differently at different times. The Transformation Tangle is based on research by sociologist Jack Mezirow.[2] In his research, he found ten phases for transformative learning. They are:

1 a disorienting dilemma,
2 self-examination with feelings of guilt or shame,
3 a critical assessment of assumptions,
4 recognition that one's discontent and process of transformation are shared and that others have negotiated a similar change,
5 exploration of options for new roles, relationships, and actions,
6 planning a course of action,
7 acquisition of knowledge and skills for implementing one's plans,
8 provisionally trying out new roles,
9 building of competence and self-confidence in new roles and relationships, and
10 a reintegration into one's life on the basis of conditions dictated by one's new perspective.

Transformation, according to Mezirow, requires deep emotional work. Transformation can only be successful when people are able to deeply consider their attitudes and practices and then work collaboratively to change culture. This approach also requires the individual to actively reflect, develop new skills, trial new approaches that respond to new internal and external pressures and demands. In our view, transformation requires a deep and active understanding of the 4Cs as the capabilities, tools and processes that navigate and sustain schools through this long and sometimes difficult process. Based on our experience of transformation and Mezirow's work, we have identified four phases that overlap intersect and recur:

- disorientation,
- awareness,
- dialogue and shared endeavour, and
- renewed perspectives and roles.

Table 11.1 How the phases of transformation are enabled by capabilities

Phases of transformation	Examples of transformative capabilities
Disorientation	Values Learning
Awareness	Leadership
Dialogue and shared endeavour	Pedagogy Curriculum
Renewed perspectives and roles	Teacher Education

To understand the experience of transformation, we will explore each one and provide examples of the ways the capabilities can help schools navigate the tangle (table 11.1). These examples illustrate the connections between transformative capabilities and the phases of the transformation tangle.

Disorientation

In this phase, participants in the transformation process may feel confused and uncertain about what change will mean for them. In disorientation, some individuals feel invigorated and inspired while others feel confused and anxious. The process of questioning deeply held assumptions may feel unsettling for some. It is, however, critical that everything is 'made strange' so the assumptions inherent in pedagogy, curriculum and schools structures (timetables, etc.) can be examined deeply.

For many educators, disorientation can be invigorating, allowing them to reimagine their school in terms of values, learning, pedagogy, curriculum, teacher education and leadership. The ambiguity of disorientation, while sometimes unnerving, allows ideas and concerns to be explored openly through clear communication strategies. Wise organizations navigate through disorientation by enabling all participants (students, teachers and the community) to engage in focused dialogue and a vision that makes the transformation a shared endeavour and not just a management-level or top-down 'adventure'. While all capabilities will be critical during this stage, the development of the creation of shared values and a commitment to explore learning deeply can support schools navigating disorientation. One of the ways schools can engage productively with disorientation is by leading a discussion around transformative *values*.

Values provide a series of parameters around the kind of change envisaged. Values will not eliminate disorientation, but they can begin a process of orientation by defining the scope and nature of transformation. In this phase, disorientation requires those involved in the transformation to reflect critically in ways that generate opportunities rather than focusing only on the difficulties and obstacles. It might be tempting to leave the disorientation phase as quickly as possible. However, schools that spend the time reflecting deeply and then collaboratively devising and communicating their developing values to their community will begin to understand the emergent nature of transformation. They will then be able to take the next steps more confidently.

Learning for teachers and students alike must be central to transformation. Inherent in the learning process is also the unlearning of practices and approaches that are no longer relevant. Learning is how people can change their practices and mindsets, leading to a change in culture. This process is made possible through the Learning Disposition Wheel and the Leadership Wheel. Disorientation allows schools the opportunity to question their assumptions, unlearn irrelevant, ineffective or damaging practices and begin the process of developing new approaches to values, pedagogy, curriculum, teacher education and leadership. After a period of disorientation, an awareness of the need for transformation and the possible solutions begin to emerge as trust and confidence in the transformation process emerge.

The experience of disorientation often leads to new awareness that practices and structures can and should change.

Awareness

As schools become aware of their assumptions and begin reimagining practices, awareness moves them from understanding to opportunity. Awareness begins to emerge as schools begin working out the details of the transformation through the process of reimagining. In the awareness phase, individuals begin to understand the need and the drivers for change. Often, they have begun to understand that transformation necessitates personal change. Many teachers and leaders begin to see the opportunities, imagining themselves in new contexts and new roles without always understanding all of the details or the implications. If the rationale for transformation is not based on research or lacks clarity, anxiety can take hold and dominate discussions. At this point, clear communication that invites questioning and constructive solution-shaping can build a shared sense of direction that leads to the next stage in the transformation process.

Leadership as discussed in chapter 10 is a quality and a process and not just a job title. In the awareness phase, leaders can enable discussions that focus on why the change is required. They can initiate reimaginings of key processes that can begin, consolidate and sustain transformation. In the awareness phase, leaders have the critical task of enabling a diverse set of views to be communicated from students, teachers and others in the school community. This broad discussion provides awareness of diverse perspectives that lead to a focus on dialogue and the design of a shared approach to transformation.

Dialogue and shared endeavour

In this phase, all of the 4Cs should be apparent in the discussions and actions. We are not referring here to the kinds of token consultation which has now become commonplace. This 'consultation for consultation sake' approach can be damaging for organizations as it generates resentment and cynicism rather than hope and optimism. As organizations collaboratively talk through the issues and concerns, shared endeavour can be developed to create transformation that is owned by everyone. The curriculum consultation process (chapter 8) is a good example of how a whole school community can work across subject and other siloes using collaborative and non-hierarchical processes to deliver meaning and sustainable benefits for students and the school community more broadly. For this stage to be successful, participants must take a part in the action (not just the discussion) of transformation in a way that enables agency.

Curriculum reimagining can crystallize how and what students learn in a transforming school in the dialogue and shared endeavour phase of the tangle. At Templestowe College (see chapter 8), the dialogue was led by the students with the school community to develop a consensus for change. The shared endeavour that emerged focused on student needs and interests. This led to a redesign of the timetable and a reimagining of pedagogy to suit a more learner-centred curriculum.

Pedagogy is essentially the way learning is structured and curated by educators. In a transforming school, a deep understanding of the elements of pedagogy (through frameworks such as the Pedagogy Parachute) can deepen the dialogue around developing transformative learning. When there is a deeper knowledge of the possibilities of a reimagined pedagogy, teachers can collaborate to design relevant learning approaches such as transdisciplinarity, collaborative teaching, place-based learning, problem-based learning, inquiry learning and experiential learning. All of these shifts in practices will give schools a taste for transformative learning that will require a reshaping of the school's organization, requiring new perspectives and roles.

Renewed perspectives and roles

This means seeing the school differently – it is a shift in the frame of reference to see the work through the frames of the 4Cs. Once the transformation strategy, approach and understanding are developed, individuals continue to develop capacities in creativity, critical reflection, collaboration and communication. This transformation creates new perspectives and new ways of working. In a way, this is the 'stuff' of 4C transformation. It is not just a case of changing job titles and where people sit in a staff room. Authentic transformation moves all participants from unfounded assumptions, irrelevant practices and problematic approaches to transformed attitudes and approaches to values, learning, pedagogy, curriculum, teacher education and leadership. These new roles and perspectives require a continuum of teacher education that focuses on experience, reflection and inquiry to build new capabilities in the school.

Teacher education is not a 'bolt on' training approach. Effective teacher education founded in reflection on experience and inquiry puts the agency to analyse and innovate in the hands of educators. This approach is best supported by expertise, mentoring and professional learning. To create renewed perspectives and roles, teachers and students can become co-creators and agents of transformative action, not just passengers. They become inquirers into the learning of their students and teacher learning. Through teacher education, educators have the opportunity to reimagine the profession by researching, creating and communicating professional knowledge rather than having it dictated to them by others.

This is a mindset and action shift to 'think and do' things differently. If educators and schools don't 'think and do things' differently, transformation is not occurring. Schools may 'improve' or have a brief dalliance with change, but this does not constitute transformation. As schools transform, they develop greater depth in the 4Cs, and embark on more journeys into transformed practice. Transforming schools understand transformation never stops. They understand that deep learning *is* transformation.

The tangle imagines transformation as a puzzle. This puzzle is often hard and requires persistence, tenacity and inspiration to navigate the process. It is, however, a puzzle that must be solved. The capabilities we identify in this book, when designed and enacted wisely, will help schools untangle the knots of transformation.

Concluding reflections

We began this book with a thought experiment which asked what a transformed education system might be like. In reality we can have schools that reflect the infinite game. These schools sustain, support and engage parents, teachers, leaders and communities to create deep, authentic and relevant learning. This may seem like a pipedream when many practices in schools reflect the past rather than transforming education for the present and the future. But the status quo is not a given. The path through the tangle of transformation is unlikely to be initiated by governments, systems or politicians. The site of change is the school. Transformation continues to emerge from inspired and wise educators collaborating to reimagine schools as inherently creative, critically reflective, collaborative and communicative spaces that focus on learners first. Transformation begins when educators collaborate and ask the simple question: what do students need to survive and thrive and how can we make that happen?

In our view, transformation happens when schools fundamentally reimagine values, learning, pedagogy, curriculum, teacher education and leadership. These are the capabilities that, when nurtured and developed collaboratively, will make a material difference for this generation of learners and the many that will follow. These are the capabilities that can make for an infinite game that strives to keep everyone playing all the time at the highest levels. If schools are to reflect and influence our society now and into the future, we must urgently transform them so we can create a more equitable, democratic and sustainable future for our communities and our planet.

Glossary

4C transformation   is the building of capabilities in creativity, critical reflection, communication and collaboration to reimagine culture, practice, approach and structures that strengthen human agency in organizations.

4Cs   is shorthand for developing the capabilities of creativity, critical reflection, communication and collaboration. The potential and capacity to transform from 'what is' to 'what could be' are developed through processes in the 4Cs.

approach   is a framework (or combination of frameworks) that determines a way of dealing with learning, situations and issues.

assessment   is a process of measuring growth in learning to support further learning.

autonomy   is the feeling of satisfaction when we experience choice and volition in our own actions.

capability   is having the freedom, opportunity and power to develop an ability to do something that achieves wellbeing.

capacity   is the human potential to function, achieve and produce through learning.

coherence makers   are schemas that organise knowledge that bring meaning and structure to critical concepts in education.

Collaborative Classroom Visits (CCVs)   are a process of noticing, where teachers collaboratively observe student learning.

competency   is the ability to learn and successfully or efficiently perform something.

complex problems   are made up of many interacting unknowns and there are very few cause and effect relationships, e.g. climate change.

complicated problems   have many difficult interacting elements that requires expertise and the ability to explore trial and error to solve that problem, e.g. the development of a vaccine.

content knowledge   is skills and understandings associated with the subject matter of a particular learning area.

curriculum   is the learning that occurs in education settings, whether intended or not.

Deep Noticing and Action (DNA Eye)   is a facilitated reflective process where teachers develop continuous perceptions into their own (and others') classroom contexts.

disposition for learning   is the inherent qualities that under the right conditions all humans possess to be able to learn.

experience   is a mix of perception, memory and embodied action for learning.

finite games   have winners and losers and clearly defined rules and objectives, e.g. football.

foundational teacher education   (also known as preservice education) forms the foundations of reflection on experience and inquiry to support a teacher's lifelong education.

framework   is a metaphorical structure that organizes concepts, knowledge or practices.

general pedagogical content knowledge   is skills and understandings about pedagogy that are applied across the curriculum.

imagine/reimagine   is to conceive of things differently to what they are or what they might appear to be.

infinite games   have no winners or losers and the rules are often unclear. The object of an infinite game is to keep everyone participating and engaged in the game, e.g. international diplomacy.

inquiry   engages with focused question to be posed, solved, challenged and re-solved by the learners.

Leadership Wheel   divides leadership into autonomy, competency and relatedness domains, and identifies the capacities for leadership that can be developed.

Learning Disposition Wheel divides learning into interpersonal, intrapersonal and cognitive domains, and identifies nine dispositions for effective learning.

lifelong teacher education (also known as in-service teacher education) is the process of professional learning that teachers undertake throughout their careers, underpinned by reflection on experience and inquiry.

pedagogical content knowledge is pedagogy specific to particular subject matter or a learning area.

pedagogy is the knowledge and skills base that connects teaching to the theories and practice of learning.

Pedagogy Parachute is a coherence maker that identifies nine interrelated elements of teaching.

praxis is the marriage of theory and practice in context.

process is a series of actions that are taken to achieve a particular experience or outcome.

reflection is noticing the perception and interpretation of an experience.

relatedness is the need to have a sense of belonging, connection and care from others.

simple problem has a clear cause and effect process to solve it, e.g. building a book case.

skill is the learning and expertise of doing something for a particular task or endeavour.

transformation is a deliberate process that moves people and organizations beyond their current realities to new practices and approaches. It involves the changing of mindsets, habits of mind and organizational culture.

transformative learning is being critically reflective of our assumptions and the assumptions of others, and to take action on that transformed perspective.

transformative values are a set of values that guide and anchor transformative action through individual and collaborative action to create transformation.

values are a set of acceptable and expected norms for the individual members of an organization.

Notes

Chapter 1

1. Elements of this chapter were first published in the following article: Michael Anderson, 'Why do we educate our children? Is why being lost in the how (all the testing and measurement) in Australia?', *EduResearch Matters* (blog), 4 March 2019, https://www.aare.edu.au/blog/?tag=michael-anderson.
2. The website for 4C Transformative Learning is http://www.4Ctransformativelearning.org.
3. James P. Carse, *Finite and Infinite Games* (New York: Simon and Schuster, 2011).
4. Simon Sinek, *The Infinite Game* (New York: Portfolio/Penguin, 2019).
5. Sanne Akkerman, 'Imagination in and beyond education', in *Handbook of Imagination and Culture*, ed. Tania Zittoun and Vlad Glaveanu (Oxford University Press, 2017), 211–21.
6. Ziauddin Sardar, 'Welcome to postnormal times', *Futures* 42, no. 5 (2010): 435–44.
7. Keith Sawyer, 'A call to action: The challenges of creative teaching and learning', *Teachers College Record* 117, no. 10 (2015): 1–34.
8. Sardar, 'Welcome to postnormal times'.
9. We mean 'learning' in the broadest sense here including processes of understanding, practising, reflecting, imagining and enabling. Learning here also relates to teacher learning, leadership learning and organizational learning. The 4C coherence makers are recursive and iterative. All of the 4Cs interact with each other. They are scaffolds intended to open new depths in learning. There is more discussion on the 4Cs and their coherence makers in *Transforming Schools*.
10. Eliot Eisner, 'What can education learn from the arts about the practice of education?' Originally given as the John Dewey Lecture for 2002, Stanford University: https://infed.org/mobi/what-can-education-learn-from-the-arts-about-the-practice-of-education.

Chapter 2

1. Jay M. Smith, *Monsters of the Gévaudan: The Making of a Beast* (Cambridge, MA: Harvard University Press, 2011), https://ebookcentral-proquest-com.ezproxy1.library.usyd.edu.au.
2. Smith, *Monsters of the Gévaudan*, 58.
3. Smith, *Monsters of the Gévaudan*.
4. Smith, *Monsters of the Gévaudan*.
5. Sally Weale, 'Top of the class: Labour seeks to emulate Finland's school system', *The Guardian*, 27 September 2019, https://www.theguardian.com/education/2019/sep/27/top-class-finland-schools-envy-world-ofsted-education?CMP=Share_iOSApp_Other.

6 Effect sizes refer to the difference in achievement between a control and an experimental group of students. So, for instance, the difference between students who do homework and those who do not. We are referring here to the work by John Hattie in *Visible Learning*.
7 Miranda Jefferson and Michael Anderson, *Transforming Schools: Creativity, Critical Reflection, Communication, Collaboration* (London: Bloomsbury Publishing, 2017), 56.
8 'SUGAR Network', last modified 2020, https://sugar-network.org; 'Change School', last modified 2020, https://change.school; 'Future Schools Alliance', last modified 2020, https://futureschools.education.
9 Albert Einstein and Leopold Infeld, *The Evolution of Physics* (New York: Simon and Schuster, 1938).
10 Adapted from Sean Snyder, 'The simple, the complicated, and the complex: educational reform through the lens of complexity theory', *OECD Working Papers*, no. 96 (Paris: OECD Publishing, 12 December 2013);
11 Sholom Glouberman and Brenda Zimmerman, 'Complicated and complex systems: what would successful reform to Medicare look like?', in *Romanov Papers: Changing Healthcare in Canada*, eds. Pierre-Gerlier Forest, Gregory Marchildon and Tom McIntosh (Toronto: University of Toronto Press, 2002), 21–53.
12 Snyder, 'The simple, the complicated, and the complex'.
13 We have adapted the features of complexity theory from an article in *Harvard Business Review* by David J. Snowden and Mary E. Boone. It can be found at https://hbr.org/2007/11/a-leaders-framework-for-decision-making. David J. Snowden and Mary E. Boone, 'A leader's framework for decision-making', *Harvard Business Review*, November 2007 issue, https://hbr.org/2007/11/a-leaders-framework-for-decision-making.
14 Sony Kapoor, 'The rising complexity of the global economy', in *OECD Insights Debate the Issues: Complexity and Policy Making*, ed. Patrick Love and Julia Stockdale-Otárola (Paris: OECD Publishing, 2017).
15 Martha Nussbaum, *Creating Capabilities: The Human Development Approach* (Cambridge, MA: Harvard University Press, 2011).
16 Nussbaum, *Creating Capabilities*.
17 Nussbaum, *Creating Capabilities*, 152.
18 Emilia Szekely and Mark Mason, 'Complexity theory, the capability approach, and the sustainability of development initiatives in education', *Journal of Education Policy* 34, no. 5 (May 2018): 669–85.
19 Seana Moran and Vera John-Steiner, 'Creativity in the making: Vygotsky's contemporary contribution to the dialectic of development and creativity', in *Creativity and Development*, eds. Keith Sawyer et al. (New York: Oxford University Press, 2003), 82.
20 National Research Council, *Education for Life and Work: Developing Transferable Knowledge and Skills in the 21st Century* (Washington, DC: National Academies Press, 2013).
21 Jefferson and Anderson, *Transforming Schools*, 39.
22 Pat Thomson, 'Ensuring and assuring an educational entitlement for the "hard to reach and teach"', *Respecting Children and Young People* (blog), 30 June 2014, https://berarespectingchildren.wordpress.com/2014/06/30/ensuring-and-assuring-an-educational-entitlement-for-the-hard-to-reach-and-teach.
23 See Jefferson and Anderson, *Transforming Schools*, 149–70; and Michael Anderson and Miranda Jefferson, *Transforming Organizations: Engaging the 4Cs for Powerful Organizational Learning and Change* (London: Bloomsbury Publishing, 2018).

Chapter 3

1. Joël de Vriend, *Extinction Rebellion*. Photograph. *Unsplash*, 2019.
2. Colin Kruger, 'Atlassian founders worth $10 billion each after record stock rise', *The Sydney Morning Herald*, 19 March 2019, https://www.smh.com.au/business/companies/atlassian-founders-worth-10-billion-each-after-record-stock-rise-20190319-p515gs.html.
3. Atlassian, 'The value of values at Atlassian', YouTube video, 4:25, 16 February 2018, https://www.youtube.com/watch?v=8xiwyk3ouuI&feature=youtu.be.
4. 'Company values', Atlassian, last modified 2020, https://www.atlassian.com/company/values.
5. John McDuling, 'For corporate Australia, climate crusading is simply smart business', *The Sydney Morning Herald*, 20 September 2019, https://www.smh.com.au/business/companies/for-corporate-australia-climate-crusading-is-simply-smart-business-20190919-p52t0n.html.
6. Katherine Murphy, 'Atlassian billionaire to announce net zero emissions target at UN climate summit', *Guardian*, 23 September 2019, https://www.theguardian.com/environment/2019/sep/23/atlassian-billionaire-to-announce-net-zero-emissions-target-at-un-climate-summit.
7. 'Company values', Atlassian, last modified 2020, https://www.atlassian.com/company/values.
8. Wulf Gaertner, 'Amartya Sen: capability and well-being', in *The Quality of Life*, eds. Martha Nussbaum and Amartya Sen (New York: Oxford University Press, 1993).
9. William Bell, 'The impact of policies on organizational values and culture', available at http://www.usafa.af.mil/jscope/JSCOPE99/Bell99.html (accessed 1 February 2007).
10. Values statement from British American Tobacco found at 'Our Vision and Values', British American Tobacco, last modified 2020, https://careers.bat.com/content/Our-Vision-And-Values/?locale=en_Gb.
11. World Health Organization, *WHO Report on the Global Tobacco Epidemic: Monitoring Tobacco Use and Prevention Policies* (Geneva: World Health Organization, 2017), https://www.who.int/tobacco/global_report/2017/en.
12. Kelly-Ann Allen et al., 'Understanding the priorities of Australian secondary schools through an analysis of their mission and vision statements', *Educational Administration Quarterly* 54, no. 2 (2018): 249–74.
13. Keith Gurley, Gary B. Peters, Loucrecia Collins and Matthew Fifolt, 'Mission, vision, values, and goals: an exploration of key organizational statements and daily practice in schools', *Journal of Educational Change* 16, no. 2 (2015): 217–42.
14. Gurley, Peters, Collins and Fifolt, 'Mission, vision, values, and goals', 236.
15. The Learning Disposition Wheel is based on research by the U.S. National Research Council (2012), *Education for Life and Work: Developing Transferable Knowledge and Skills for the 21st Century*.
16. For a full description and discussion of the Learning Disposition Wheel, see Jefferson and Anderson, *Transforming Schools*, p. 39 and Chapter 5 of this book.
17. Paulo Freire, *Pedagogy of the Oppressed* (New York: Seabury, 1970), 36.
18. Paulo Freire, *Pedagogy of Freedom: Ethics, Democracy, and Civic Courage* (Lanham, MD: Rowman, 1998), 68.
19. Devita Bishundat, Phillip Daviree Velázquez and Willie Gore, 'Cultivating critical hope: the too often forgotten dimension of critical leadership development', *New Directions for Student Leadership* 2018.159 (2018): 91–102.
20. Paulo Freire, *Pedagogy of Hope: Reliving Pedagogy of the Oppressed* (London: Continuum, 1994).
21. Robert J. Sternberg, 'Wisdom and education', *Gifted Education International* 17, no. 3 (2003): 248.

22 Anna Fahey, 'The entire IPCC report in 19 illustrated haiku', *Sightline Institute*, 16 December 2013, https://www.sightline.org/2013/12/16/the-entire-ipcc-report-in-19-illustrated-haiku.
23 National Research Council, *Education for Life and Work: Developing Transferable Knowledge and Skills in the 21st Century* (Washington, DC: National Academies Press, 2012).
24 Parker J. Palmer, *The Courage to Teach: Exploring the Inner Landscape of a Teacher's Life* (Hoboken, New Jersey: John Wiley & Sons, 2017), 11.
25 Jean Lave and Etienne Wenger, *Situated Learning: Legitimate Peripheral Participation* (Cambridge: Cambridge University Press, 1991).
26 Etienne Wenger, *Communities of Practice: Learning, Meaning, and Identity* (Cambridge: Cambridge University Press, 1998).

Chapter 4

1 Australian Associated Press, 'Scott Morrison tells students striking over climate change to be "less activist"', *Guardian*, Australian Edition, 26 November 2018, https://www.theguardian.com/environment/2018/nov/26/scott-morrison-tells-students-striking-over-climate-change-to-be-less-activist?CMP=Share_iOSApp_Other.
2 Malena Ernman, Beata Ernman, Svante Thunberg and Greta Thunberg, *Our House is on Fire: Scenes of a Family and a Planet in Crisis* (London, UK: Penguin Books, 2020).
3 Ernman, Ernman, Thunberg and Thunberg, *Our House is on Fire*, 34.
4 Organisation for Economic Co-operation and Development [OECD], 'OECD Future of Education and Skills 2030: Student Agency for 2030', last modified 2020, https://www.oecd.org/education/2030-project/teaching-and-learning/learning/student-agency.
5 Laurent Lebreton et al, eds., 'Evidence that the Great Pacific Garbage Patch is rapidly accumulating plastic', *Scientific Reports* 8, no. 4666 (2018): 1–15.
6 Jefferson and Anderson, *Transforming Schools* and *Transforming Organizations* and OECD, 'OECD Future of Education and Skills 2030: the future we want', last modified 2020, https://www.oecd.org/education/2030-project.
7 Richard M. Ryan and Edward L. Deci, 'Self-determination theory and the facilitation of intrinsic motivation, social development, and well-being', *American Psychologist* 55, no. 1 (2000): 68–78.
8 OECD, 'OECD Future of Education and Skills 2030: the future we want', last modified 2020, https://www.oecd.org/education/2030-project.
9 OECD, *OECD Future of Education and Skills 2030: OECD Learning Compass 2030* (Paris: OECD Publishing, 2019), http://www.oecd.org/education/2030-project/teaching-and-learning/learning/learning-compass-2030/OECD_Learning_Compass_2030_concept_note.pdf, 4.
10 OECD, *OECD Learning Compass 2030*.
11 OECD, *OECD Learning Compass 2030*, 6.
12 OECD, *OECD Future of Education and Skills 2030: Transformative Learning Competencies for 2030* (Paris: OECD Publishing, 2019), https://www.oecd.org/education/2030-project/teaching-and-learning/learning/transformative-competencies/Transformative_Competencies_for_2030_concept_note.pdf, 3.
13 OECD, *The Future of Education and Skills: Education 2030* (Paris: OECD Publishing, 2019), https://www.oecd.org/education/2030/E2030%20Position%20Paper%20(05.04.2018).pdf, 4.

14   Commission on Human Rights, *Convention on the Rights of the Child* (Geneva: UN General Assembly, 1990), https://www.unicef.org/sites/default/files/2019-04/UN-Convention-Rights-Child-text.pdf.
15   Caroline S. Hart and Nicolás Brando, 'A capability approach to children's well-being, agency and participatory rights in education', *European Journal of Education* 53, no. 3 (2018): 293–309, https://onlinelibrary.wiley.com/doi/epdf/10.1111/ejed.12284.
16   UN Commission on Human Rights, *Convention on the Rights of the Child*, 6.
17   UN Commission on Human Rights, *Convention on the Rights of the Child*, 3.
18   Hart and Brando, 'A capability approach to children's well-being'.
19   Richard M. Ryan and Edward L. Deci, *Self-Determination Theory: Basic Psychological Needs in Motivation, Development, and Wellness* (New York: Guildford Press, 2017), 11.
20   Ryan and Deci, *Self-Determination Theory: Basic Psychological Needs*, 11.
21   Ryan and Deci, *Self-Determination Theory: Basic Psychological Needs*, 381.
22   Christopher P. Niemiec and Richard M. Ryan, 'Autonomy, competence, and relatedness in the classroom: applying self-determination theory to educational practice', *Theory and Research in Education* 7, no. 2 (2009): 139–40.
23   Ryan and Deci, 'Self-determination theory and the facilitation of intrinsic motivation'.
24   Woon Chia Liu, John Chee Keng Wang and Richard M. Ryan, eds., *Building Autonomous Learners: Perspectives from Research and Practice Using Self-Determination Theory* (Singapore: Springer, 2016); Michael L. Wehmeyer et al., *Development of Self-Determination Through the Life-Course* (Netherlands: Springer, 2017).
25   Liu, Wang and Ryan, *Building Autonomous Learners*.
26   Ryan and Deci, 'Self-determination theory and the facilitation of intrinsic motivation'.
27   Ryan and Deci, 'Self-determination theory and the facilitation of intrinsic motivation'.
28   Ryan and Deci, 'Self-determination theory and the facilitation of intrinsic motivation'.
29   Edward L. Deci and Richard M. Ryan, 'Motivation, personality, and development within embedded social contexts: an overview of self-determination theory', in *Oxford Handbook of Human Motivation*, ed. Richard M. Ryan (Oxford: Oxford University Press, 2012, 85–107).
30   Deci and Ryan, 'Motivation'.
31   Ryan and Deci, 'Self-determination theory and the facilitation of intrinsic motivation'.
32   Mathilde Almlund et al., 'Personality psychology and economics', in *Handbook of the Economics of Education*, eds. Eric A. Hanushek, Stephen Machin and Ludger Wößmann (Amsterdam: Elsevier, 2011), 1–181.
33   National Research Council, *Education for Life and Work: Developing Transferable Knowledge and Skills in the 21st Century* (Washington, DC: National Academies Press, 2013).
34   Buckingham Shum and Deakin Crick, 'Learning Dispositions', 3.
35   Buckingham Shum and Deakin Crick, 'Learning Dispositions', 3.
36   National Research Council, *Education for Life and Work*.
37   National Research Council, *Education for Life and Work*.
38   National Research Council, *Education for Life and Work*.
39   Connect4Climate, 'Greta Thunberg, "You are never too small to make a difference"', Vimeo video, 0:28, 19 January 2018, https://vimeo.com/312281568.

Chapter 5

1   Richard W. Bulliet, *The Wheel: Inventions and Reinventions* (New York: Columbia University Press, 2016).

2 National Research Council, *Education for Life and Work: Developing Transferable Knowledge and Skills in the 21st Century* (Washington, DC: National Academies Press, 2013).
3 National Research Council, *Education for Life and Work*.
4 National Research Council, *Education for Life and Work*.
5 Norbert M. Seel, 'Metacognition and learning', in *Encyclopedia of the Sciences of Learning*, ed. Norbert M. Seel (MA: Springer, 2012), 2228–31.
6 National Research Council, *Education for Life and Work*.
7 Buckingham Shum and Deakin Crick, 'Learning dispositions'.
8 Norman Doidge, *The Brain That Changes Itself* (Melbourne: Scribe, 2010).
9 Carol S. Dweck, *Mindset: The New Psychology of Success* (New York: Ballentine Books, 2016), 7.
10 National Research Council, *Education for Life and Work*.
11 National Research Council, *Education for Life and Work*.
12 Daniel Goleman, *Focus: The Hidden Driver of Excellence* (London: Bloomsbury, 2013).
13 Carol S. Dweck and Ellen L. Legett, 'A social cognitive approach to motivation and personality', *Psychological Review* 95, no. 2 (1988): 256–73; Carol S. Dweck and Allison Master, 'Self-theories and beliefs about intelligence', in *Handbook of Motivation at School*, eds. Kathryn R. Wentzel and Allan Wigfield (New York: Routledge, 2009), 123–40.
14 Mary Niemczyk, 'Self-regulation and motivation strategies', in *Encyclopedia of the Sciences of Learning*, ed. Norbert M. Seel (Boston, MA: Springer, 2012), 3019–3021.
15 Richard M. Ryan and Edward L. Deci, 'Promoting self-determined school engagement: motivation, learning and well-being', in *Handbook of Motivation at School*, eds. Kathryn R. Wentzel and Allan Wigfield (New York: Routledge, 2009), 171–95.
16 Ryan and Deci, 'Promoting self-determined school engagement'.
17 Rosa Cera, Michela Mancini and Alessandro Antonietta, 'Metacognition, self-efficacy and self-regulation in learning', *Educational Cultural and Psychological Studies Journal*, no. 7 (2013).
18 Norbert M. Seel, 'Metacognition and learning' in *Encyclopedia of the Sciences of Learning*, edited by Norbert M. Seel (MA: Springer, 2012), 2228–31; Richard E. Mayer, 'Cognitive, metacognitive, and motivational aspects of problem solving', *Instructional Science* 26, no.1 (1998): 49–63.
19 National Research Council, *Education for Life and Work*.
20 See Logan Fiorella and Richard E. Mayer, *Learning as a Generative Activity: Eight Learning Strategies that Promote Understanding* (New York: Cambridge University Press, 2015).
21 Sukie van Zyl and Elsa Mentz, 'Moving to deeper self-directed learning as an essential competency for the 21st century', in *Self-Directed Learning for the 21st Century: Implications for Higher Education*, eds. Elsa Mentz, Josef de Beer and Roxanne Bailey (Cape Town, South Africa: AOSIS, 2019), 67–102.
22 van Zyl and Mentz, 'Deeper self-directed learning', 67–102.
23 Fiorella and Mayer, *Learning as a Generative Activity*.
24 Angela A. Duckworth et al., 'Grit: Perseverance and passion for long-term goals', *Journal of Personality and Social Psychology* 92, no. 6 (June 2007): 1087–8.
25 Duckworth et al., 'Grit'.
26 Andrew J. Martin and Herb W. Marsh, 'Academic resilience and academic buoyancy: multidimensional and hierarchical conceptual framing of causes, correlates, and cognate constructs', *Oxford Review of Education* 35, no. 3 (2009): 353–70.
27 Duckworth et al., 'Grit'.
28 Duckworth et al., 'Grit'.
29 Duckworth et al., 'Grit'.

30 Martin and Marsh, 'Academic resilience and academic buoyancy'.
31 Todd B. Kashdan and Paul J. Silvia, 'Curiosity', in *The Encyclopedia of Positive Psychology*, ed. Shane J. Lopez (Hoboken, NJ: Wiley Blackwell, 2009), 270–4.
32 Kashdan and Silvia, 'Curiosity', 271.
33 Todd B. Kashdan and Paul J. Silvia, 'Curiosity and interest: the benefits of thriving on novelty and challenge' in *Oxford Handbook of Positive Psychology*, eds. Shane J. Lopez and Charles Richard Snyder (Oxford University Press, 2009), 367–74.
34 T.B. Kashdan and P.J. Silvia (2009) 'Curiosity', pp. 270–4, in Lopez, S.J (ed.), *The Encyclopaedia of Positive Psychology*, Hoboken, NJ: Wiley Blackwell.
35 Kashdan and Silvia, 'Curiosity', 270–4.
36 John Dewey, *How We Think* (Boston, MA: D.C Heath & Co., 1910); Dewey, *How We Think: A Restatement of the Relation of Reflective Thinking to the Educative Process* (Lexington, MA: D.C. Heath & Co., 1933).
37 David Hitchcock, 'Critical thinking', in *The Stanford Encyclopedia of Philosophy*, ed. Edward N. Zalta (Stanford: Stanford University, Fall 2018 Edition).
38 Freire Paulo Freire, *Pedagogy of the Oppressed* (New York: Continuum, 1970/2006), 83.
39 Hitchcock, 'Critical thinking'.
40 Kal Alston, 'Re/thinking critical thinking: the seductions of everyday life', *Studies in Philosophy and Education* 20, no. 1 (2001): 27–40.
41 Juliana Saxton et al., *Asking Better Questions: Teaching and Learning for a Changing World* (Moorabbin: Hawker Brownlow, 2018).
42 Milton N. Campos, 'Critical constructivism', in *Encyclopedia of Communication Theory*, eds. Stephen W. Littlejohn and Karen A. Foss (London: Sage, 2009), 179–83.
43 Campos, 'Critical constructivism'.
44 Tania Zittoun and Svend Brinkmann, 'Learning as meaning making', in *Encyclopaedia of the Sciences of Learning*, ed. Norbert M. Seel (Netherlands: Springer, 2012), 1809.
45 Jerome Bruner, *The Culture of Education* (Cambridge, MA: Harvard University Press, 1996).
46 Zittoun and Brinkmann, 'Learning as meaning making'.
47 Alfonso Montuori, 'Creativity and its nature', in *Encyclopaedia of the Sciences of Learning*, ed. Norbert M. Seel (Netherlands: Springer, 2012), 837–40.
48 Lev Vygotsky, 'Imagination and Creativity in Childhood', *Journal of Russian and East European Psychology* 42, no. 1 (1998), quoted in Seana Moran and Vera John-Steiner, 'Creativity in the making: Vygotsky's contemporary contribution to the dialectic of development and creativity', in *Creativity and Development*, eds. Keith Sawyer et al. (New York: Oxford University Press, 2003), 71–90. Sternberg, D.H. Felman, J. Nakamura et al. (Eds.), *Creativity and Development*, New York: Oxford University Press, 71–90.
49 David Eagleman and Anthony Brandt, *The Runaway Species: How Human Creativity Remakes the World* (Edinburgh, UK: Canongate Books, 2017).
50 Anna Craft, 'Possibility thinking: from what is to what might be', in *The Routledge International Handbook of Research on Teaching Thinking*, eds. Rupert Wegerif, Li Li and James C. Kaufman (New York: Routledge, June 2015), 153–67.
51 Keith Sawyer, *The Creative Classroom: Innovative Teaching for the 21st Century Learners* (New York: Teachers College Press, 2019).
52 Maxine Greene, *The Dialectic of Freedom* (New York: Teachers College Press, 1988).
53 Mihaly Csikszentmihalyi, *Creativity: Flow and the Psychology of Discovery and Invention* (New York: Harper Perennial, 1996).
54 Alfonso Montuori, 'Creative inquiry', in *Encyclopedia of the Sciences of Learning*, ed. Norbert M. Seel (Boston, MA: Springer, 2012), 833–7.
55 Herbert C. Kelman, 'Compliance, identification, and internalization: three processes of attitude change', *Journal of Conflict Resolution* 2, no. 1 (1958): 51–60.

56 Wendelin Küpers and Olen Gunnlaugson, eds., *Wisdom Learning: Perspectives on Wising-up Business and Management Education* (London and New York: Routledge, 2017).

57 Makoto Matsuo, 'Empowerment through self-improvement skills: the role of learning goals and personal growth initiative', *Journal of Vocational Behaviour*, no. 115 (June 2019); Doris Fay and Michael Frese, 'Self-starting behavior at work: toward a theory of personal initiative', in *Motivational Psychology of Human Development*, Hechausen (ed.), Elsevier Science, pp. 307–24.

58 Fay and Frese, 'Self-starting behavior'.

59 Michael Mäs and James A. Kitts, 'Social influence and the emergence of cultural norms', in *Encyclopaedia of the Sciences of Learning*, ed. Norbert M. Seel (Netherlands: Springer, 2012).

60 Daniel Goleman, 'When empathy moves us to action', *SharpBrains* (blog), 11 July 2008, https://sharpbrains.com/blog/2008/07/11/when-empathy-moves-us-to-action-by-daniel-goleman; Daniel Goleman, *Focus: The Hidden Driver of Excellence* (London: Bloomsbury, 2013).

61 Daniel Batson, Nadia Ahmad and David A. Lishner, 'Empathy and altruism', in *The Oxford Handbook of Positive Psychology*, 2nd edition, eds. Shane J. Lopez and C. R. Sydner (Oxford: Oxford University Press, 2012).

62 Batson, Ahmad and Lishner, 'Empathy and altruism'.

63 Eric C. Nook et al., 'Prosocial conformity: prosocial norms generalize across behaviour and empathy', *Personality and Social Psychology Bulletin* 42, no. 8 (2016): 1045–62.

64 Fiona Kerr and Lekki Maze, *The Art and Science of Looking Up: Transforming our Brains, Bodies, Relationships and Experience of the World by the Simple Act of Looking Up* (Glider Global, 2019), http://www.gliderglobal.com/wp-content/uploads//THE-ART-AND-SCIENCE-OF-LOOKING-UP-REPORT_2019.pdf.

65 Kerr and Maze, *The Art and Science of Looking Up*.

66 Maxine Greene, *Releasing the Imagination: Essays on Education, the Arts, and Social Change* (San Francisco, CA: Jossey-Bass, 1995), 3.

67 Seana Moran and Vera John-Steiner, 'How collaboration in creative work impacts identity and motivation', in *Collaborative Creativity: Contemporary Perspectives*, eds. Dorothy Miell and Karen Littleton (London: Free Association Books, 2004), 11.

68 Lev S. Vygotsky, *Mind in Society: The Development of Higher Psychological Processes*, eds. Michael Cole et al. (Cambridge, MA: Harvard University Press, 1978).

69 Vera John-Steiner, *Creative Collaboration* (New York: Oxford University Press, 2000), 204.

70 Richard E. Mayer, *Applying the Science of Learning* (Upper Saddle River, NJ: Pearson, 2010).

71 '42 born to code?', 42, last modified 2017, https://www.42.fr.

72 Jenny Anderson, 'A free, teacher-less university in France is schooling thousands of future-proof programmers', *Quartz*, 4 September 2017, https://qz.com/1054412/a-french-billionaires-free-teacher-less-university-is-designing-thousands-of-future-proof-employees.

73 Anderson, 'A free, teacher-less university in France'.

74 Anderson, 'A free, teacher-less university in France'.

Chapter 6

1 Art Processors, interview with Jane Clark, 'How the curatorial team at Mona uses "The O"', news article, https://www.artprocessors.net/how-the-curatorial-team-at-mona-uses-

the-o. Michael Bhasker, *Curation: The Power of Selection in a World of Excess* (London, UK: Piatkus, 2016).
2. Michael Bhasker, 'In the age of the algorithm, the human gatekeeper is back', *Guardian*, 30 September 2016, https://www.theguardian.com/technology/2016/sep/30/age-of-algorithm-human-gatekeeper.
3. Bhasker, 'In the age of the algorithm'.
4. Mark K. Smith, 'What is pedagogy?', *The Encyclopedia of Pedagogy and Informal Education*, Infed.org, 2012, 2019, https://infed.org/mobi/what-is-pedagogy.
5. Basil Bernstein, *Class, Codes and Control, Volume 2* (London: Routledge & Kegan Paul, 1973), 85.
6. Brian Hudson, 'Comparing different traditions of teaching and learning: what can we learn about teaching and learning?', *European Educational Research Journal* 6, no 2 (2007): 135–46; Stefan Hopmann, 'Restrained teaching: the common core of Didaktik', *European Educational Research Journal* 6, no. 2 (2007): 109–24.
7. Sonia Guerriero, 'Teachers' pedagogical knowledge: what it is and how it functions', in *Pedagogical Knowledge and the Changing Nature of the Teaching Profession*, ed. Sonia Guerriero (OECD Publishing, Paris, 2017), 114.
8. Linda Darling-Hammond, 'Teacher quality and student achievement: a review of state policy evidence', *Education Policy Analysis Archives* 8, no. 1 (2000): 1–44.
9. Nóra Révai and Sonia Guerriero, 'Knowledge dynamics in the teaching profession', in *Pedagogical Knowledge and the Changing Nature of the Teaching Profession*, ed. Sonia Guerriero (Paris: OECD Publishing, 2017), 38.
10. David H. Hargreaves, *The Teacher Training Agency Annual Lecture 1996*, University College London, (1996), 2, https://eppi.ioe.ac.uk/cms/Portals/0/PDF%20reviews%20and%20summaries/TTA%20Hargreaves%20lecture.pdf.
11. Sonia Guerriero, 'Teachers' pedagogical knowledge: what it is and how it functions', in *Pedagogical Knowledge and the Changing Nature of the Teaching Profession*, ed. Sonia Guerriero (OECD Publishing, Paris, 2017), 114.
12. Jürgen Baumert et al., 'Teachers' mathematical knowledge, cognitive activation in the classroom, and student progress', *American Education Research Journal* 47, no. 1 (2010): 133–80.
13. Thamar Voss, Mareike Kunter and Jürgen Baumert, 'Assessing teacher candidates' general pedagogical/psychological knowledge: test construction and validation', *Journal of Educational Psychology* 103, no. 4 (2011): 952–69.
14. Guerriero, 'Teachers' pedagogical knowledge: what it is and how it functions', 109.
15. Lee S. Shulman, 'Those who understand: knowledge growth in teaching', *Educational Researcher* 15, no. 2 (1986): 4–14; and Lee S. Shulman, 'Knowledge of teaching: foundations of the new reform', *Harvard Educational Review* 15, no. 2 (1987): 1–22.
16. Shulman, 'Those who understand', pp. 4–14; Shulman, 'Knowledge of teaching', *Harvard* pp. 1–22.
17. Voss, Kunter and Baumert, 'Test construction and validation'.
18. David Charles Berliner, 'Describing the behaviour and documenting the accomplishments of expert teachers', *Bulletin of Science, Technology, and Society* 24 (2004): 200–12.
19. Mezirow's theories are influenced by the philosopher and sociologist, Jürgen Habermas and the tradition of critical theory, and by Paolo Freire and the philosophy of critical pedagogy. Transformative learning also has its roots in the pragmatist and progressive educational philosophy of John Dewey and his ideas of experience and reflection in learning.
20. Jack Mezirow, 'Transformative learning as discourse', *Journal of Transformative Education* 1, no. 1 (2003): 58–9.
21. Patrick Farren, 'Transformative pedagogy in context: being and becoming', *World Journal on Educational Technology* 8, no. 3 (October 2016).

22 Guerriero, 'Teachers' pedagogical knowledge: what it is and how it functions', 99–118.
23 Lawrence Stenhouse, *An Education that Empowers: A Collection of Essays in Memory of Lawrence Stenhouse*, Vol. 10, ed. Jean Rudduck (Bristol, UK: Multilingual Matters, 1995), 1.
24 Jack Mezirow, 'Learning to think like an adult: core concepts of transformation theory', in *Learning as Transformation. Critical Perspectives on a Theory in Progress* (San Francisco: Jossey-Bass, 2000), 13–14.
25 Michael Fullan, *All Systems Go: The Change Imperative for Whole System Reform* (Thousand Oaks, CA: Corwin Sage, 2010), xiii.
26 Donaldson, *Teaching Scotland's Future: Report of a Review of Teacher Education in Scotland*, last modified 2011, https://www.webarchive.org.uk/wayback/archive/20170401191254/http://www.gov.scot/Publications/2011/01/13092132/8.
27 Sonia Guerriero and Nóra Révai, 'Knowledge-based teaching and the evolution of a profession', in *Pedagogical Knowledge and the Changing Nature of the Teaching Profession*, ed. Sonia Guerriero (Paris: OECD Publishing, 2017), 258.
28 Yong Zhao, 'Rethinking teacher quality in the age of smart machines', in *The Wiley Handbook of Teaching and Learning*, eds. Gene E. Hall, Linda F. Quinn and Donna M. Gollnick (Hoboken, NJ: John Wiley & Sons, 2018), 610.
29 Alex Williams, 'On the tip of creative tongues', 2 October 2009, *The New York Times*: https://www.nytimes.com/2009/10/04/fashion/04curate.html?smid=nytcore-ios-share.

Chapter 7

1 National Academies of Sciences, Engineering, and Medicine (2020), *Changing Expectations for the K–12 Teacher Workforce: Policies, Preservice Education, Professional Development, and the Workplace*. Washington, DC: The National Academies Press.
2 National Academies of Sciences, Engineering, and Medicine, *Changing Expectations*, 3.
3 Zhao, 'Rethinking teacher quality', 611.
4 James R. Martin and David Rose, 'Designing literacy pedagogy: scaffolding democracy in the classroom', in *Continuing Discourse on Language: A Functional Perspective* Vol. 1, eds. Jonathan Webster, Christian Matthiessen, and Ruqaiya Hasan (London: Continuum, 2005), 273.
5 Stephen Billett, 'Situated learning: bridging sociocultural and cognitive theorising', *Learning and Instruction* 6 no. 3 (1996): 277.
6 Knud Illeris, *Contemporary Theories of Learning: Learning Theorists . . . In Their Own Words* (London: Routledge, 2009), 8.
7 Daniel Ansari et al., 'Developmental cognitive neuroscience: implications for teachers' pedagogical knowledge', in *Pedagogical Knowledge and the Changing Nature of the Teaching Profession*, ed. Sonia Guerriero (Paris: OECD Publishing, 2017), 206.
8 WordSense, 'Schema', last modified 2020, https://www.wordsense.eu/schema.
9 Jean Piaget, *Origin of Intelligence in the Child: Selected Works, Volume 3*, trans. Margaret Cook (London: Routledge, 1953/1997), 7.
10 JungMi Lee and Norbert M. Seel, 'Schema-based learning', in *Encyclopedia of the Sciences of Learning*, ed. Norbert M. Seel (Boston, MA: Springer, 2012), 2947.
11 Mark K. Smith, 'What is teaching? A definition and discussion', *The Encyclopedia of Pedagogy and Informal Education* (2018), https://infed.org/mobi/what-is-teaching; Lexico, Oxford, 'Teach', last modified 2020, https://www.lexico.com/definition/teach.
12 Allan Luke, 'On explicit and direct instruction', *Australian Literacy Educators' Association [ALEA]* (May 2014), https://www.alea.edu.au/documents/item/861.

13 John Dewey, *The Child and the Curriculum* (Chicago: Chicago University Press, 1902).
14 Dewey, *The Child*, 11
15 Logan Fiorella and Richard E. Mayer, *Learning as a Generative Activity: Eight Learning Strategies that Promote Understanding*. New York: Cambridge University Press.
16 David J. Wood, Jerome S. Bruner and Gail Ross, 'The role of tutoring in problem solving', *Journal of Child Psychiatry and Psychology* 17, no. 2 (1976): 90.
17 Vygotsky's theory of proximal development is the dynamic threshold of what the learner is capable of learning through interaction with others, rather than the capability of what they can already achieve alone. Lev S. Vygotsky, *Mind in Society: The Development of Higher Psychological Processes*, eds. Michael Cole et al. (Cambridge, MA: Harvard University Press, 1978).
18 Wood, Bruner and Ross, 'The role of tutoring in problem solving', 90.
19 Jerome S. Bruner, *The Process of Education* (Cambridge, MA: Harvard University Press, 1960), 20.
20 Shalin Hai-Jew, 'Scaffolding discovery learning spaces', in *Encyclopedia of the Sciences of Learning*, ed. Norbert M. Seel (Boston, MA: Springer, 2012), 2916.
21 Anders Ericsson quoted in Tristan Hopper, 'Malcolm Gladwell got it wrong: "Deliberate practice" – not 10,000 hours – key to achievement, psychologist says', *National Post*, 12 April 2016, https://nationalpost.com/news/canada/malcolm-gladwell-got-it-wrong-deliberate-practice-not-10000-hours-key-to-achievement-psychologist-says.
22 Richard E. Mayer (2011), 'Instruction based on visualizations', in *Handbook of Research on Learning and Instruction*, eds. Richard E. Mayer and Patricia A. Alexander (New York: Routledge; 2010), 427–45; Richard E. Mayer, *Applying the Science of Learning* (Upper Saddle River, NJ: Pearson, 2010).
23 Anders Ericsson and Robert Pool, *Peak: Secrets from the New Science of Expertise* (Boston, MA: Eamon Dolan/Houghton Mifflin Harcourt, 2016).
24 National Research Council, *Education for Life and Work: Developing Transferable Knowledge and Skills in the 21st Century* (Washington, DC: National Academies Press, 2013).
25 Paul Black et al., 'Working inside the black box: assessment for learning in the classroom', *Phi Delta Kappan* 86, no. 1 (2004), 18.
26 Susanne Narciss, 'Feedback strategies', in *Encyclopedia of the Sciences of Learning*, ed. Norbert M. Seel (Boston, MA: Springer 2012) 1291.
27 Dylan Wiliam, *Embedded Formative Assessment* (Bloomington, IN: Solution Tree Press, 2011), 132.
28 Black et al., 'Working inside the black box'.
29 Black et al., 'Working inside the black box', 19.
30 National Research Council, *Education for Life and Work*.
31 Fred M. Newmann and Associates, *Authentic Achievement: Restructuring Schools for Intellectual Quality* (San Francisco, CA: Jossey-Bass, 1996).
32 Debra Hayes et al., *Teachers and Schooling Making a Difference: Productive Pedagogies, Assessment and Performance* (Crows Nest, NSW: Allen and Unwin, 2006).
33 Hayes et al., 53.
34 Mayer, R. E. (2010) *Applying the Science of Learning*. Upper Saddle River, NJ: Pearson.
35 National Research Council, *Education for Life and Work*.
36 Stephen Billett, 'Authenticity in learning activities and settings', in *Encyclopedia of the Sciences of Learning*, ed. Norbert M. Seel (Boston, MA: Springer, 2012).
37 Jean Lave and Etienne Wenger, *Situated Learning: Legitimate Peripheral Participation* (Cambridge: Cambridge University Press, 1991), 53.
38 Paulo Freire, *Pedagogy of the Oppressed* (New York: Bloomsbury Academic, 1970/2006), 72.

39 Rebecca Wing-yi Cheng, Shui-fong Lam and Joanne Chung-yan Chan, 'When high achievers and low achievers work in the same group: the role of group heterogeneity and processes in project-based learning', *British Journal of Educational Psychology* 78, no. 2 (2008): 205–21.
40 Etienne Wenger, 'Communities of practice: a brief introduction', Office of Human Resources (Cambridge: Cambridge University Press, 2012), https://www.ohr.wisc.edu/cop/articles/communities_practice_intro_wenger.pdf.
41 Montuori, 'Creative inquiry', 834.
42 Anna Craft (2015), 'Possibility thinking: from what is to what might be', in *The Routledge International Handbook of Research on Teaching Thinking*, eds. Rupert Wegerif, Li Li and James C. Kaufman (London: Routledge), 153–67.
43 Montuori, 'Creative inquiry', 833–7.
44 Keith Sawyer, *Zig Zag: The Surprising Path to Greater Creativity* (San Francisco, CA: Jossey-Bass, 2013).
45 Adele Diamond, 'Executive functions', *Annual Review of Psychology* 64 (2013): 135–68.
46 Lawrence Shapiro, *Embodied Cognition*, 2nd edition (Oxon, UK: Routledge, 2019); Lawrence Shapiro, ed., *The Routledge Handbook of Embodied Cognition* (Oxon, UK: Routledge, 2014).
47 John Dewey, 'My pedagogic creed', *The School Journal* 54, no. 3 (16 January 1987): 79.
48 David A. Kolb, *Experiential Learning: Experience as the Source of Learning and Development*, 2nd edition (Upper Saddle River, NJ: Pearson Education, 2015), 51.
49 Arthur M. Glenberg, 'Embodiment for education', in *Handbook of Cognitive Science: An Embodied Approach*, eds. Paco Calvo and Toni Gomila (Amsterdam: Elsevier, 2008), 355–72.
50 Lawrence Shapiro and Steven A. Stolz, 'Embodied cognition and its significance for education', *Theory and Research in Education* 17, no. 1 (2019): 19–39.
51 John Dewey, *Democracy and Education* (Mineola, NY: Dover Publications, 1916/2004), 160.
52 Catriona Mackenzie, 'Critical reflection, self-knowledge, and the emotions', *Philosophical Explorations: An International Journal for the Philosophy of Mind and Action* 5, no. 3 (2002): 186–206.

Chapter 8

1 We are using the singular to denote Michael's story in this chapter.
2 For a fuller discussion of post-normality, see Jefferson and Anderson, *Transforming Schools*, 9–13.
3 Pat Thomson, 'Ensuring and assuring an educational entitlement for the "hard to reach and teach"', *Respecting Children and Young People* (blog), 30 June 2014, https://berarespectingchildren.wordpress.com/2014/06/30/ensuring-and-assuring-an-educational-entitlement-for-the-hard-to-reach-and-teach.
4 Sam Sellar and Bob Lingard, 'The OECD and global governance in education', *Journal of Education Policy* 28, no. 5 (2013): 710–25.
5 OECD, 'The Future of Education and Skills: Education 2030', *OECD Education 2030*, 2018.
6 Dominic Wyse, Louise Hayward and Jessica Pandya, 'Introduction', in *The SAGE Handbook of Curriculum, Pedagogy and Assessment* (Vol. 2), eds. Dominic Wyse, Louise Hayward and Jessica Pandya (55 City Road, London: SAGE Publications Ltd, 2016), 1–26.

7   Basil Bernstein, 'On the classification and framing of educational knowledge', in *Knowledge, Education, and Cultural Change: Papers in the Sociology of Education*, ed. Richard Brown (London: Routledge, 2018), 365–92.
8   Jung-Hoon Jung and William F. Pinar, 'Conceptions of curriculum', in *The SAGE Handbook of Curriculum, Pedagogy and Assessment*, eds. Dominic Wyse, Louise Hayward and Jessica Pandya (55 City Road, London: SAGE Publications Ltd, 2016), 29–46.
9   A Rorschach test is used in psychoanalysis. The test asks participants to identify what they see in a standard set of symmetrical ink blots of different colours and shapes, and to describe what they suggest or resemble.
10 Jerry Rosiek and D. Jean Clandinin, 'Curriculum and teacher development', in *The SAGE Handbook of Curriculum, Pedagogy and Assessment* eds. Dominic Wyse, Louise Hayward, and Jessica Pandya (Los Angeles CA: SAGE, 2016), 293–308.
11 Rosiek and Clandinin, 'Curriculum and teacher development'.
12 Erica A. Nevenglosky, Chris Cale and Sunddip Panesar Aguilar, 'Barriers to effective curriculum implementation', *Research in Higher Education Journal* 36 (2019), https://files.eric.ed.gov/fulltext/EJ1203958.pdf.
13 Rosiek and Clandinin, 'Curriculum and teacher development', 297.
14 Personal correspondence, Alison Rourke, 5 June 2020.
15 Rosiek and Clandinin, 'Curriculum and teacher development'.
16 University of Auckland, 'About Te Rito Toi', last modified 2020, https://www.teritotoi.org/about.
17 Personal correspondence, Peter O'Connor, 17 June 2020.
18 Matthew Daly, 'Learning: take control!', *Connect*, no. 229 (February 2018), 3.
19 Australian Curriculum, Assessment and Reporting Authority (ACARA), 'Templestowe College, Templestowe Lower, VIC', My School, last modified 2020, https://www.myschool.edu.au/school/45560.
20 Daly, 'Take control!', 3.
21 Jefferson and Anderson, *Transforming Schools*, 56.
22 British Columbia, 'British Columbia's new curriculum: new curriculum info', last modified 2019, https://curriculum.gov.bc.ca/curriculum-info.
23 Chloe Parkinson and Tiffany Jones. 'Aboriginal people's aspirations and the Australian curriculum: a critical analysis', *Educational Research for Policy and Practice* 18, no. 1 (15 February 2019): 75–97.
24 British Columbia Curriculum Authority, 'Aboriginal education', https://curriculum.gov.bc.ca/sites/curriculum.gov.bc.ca/files/pdf/aboriginal_education_bc.pdf.
25 Chloe Parkinson and Tiffany Jones. 'Aboriginal people's aspirations and the Australian curriculum: a critical analysis'.
26 Bob Morgan, 'Beyond the guest paradigm: Eurocentric education and Aboriginal peoples in NSW' in E. McKinley and L. Smith (eds), *Handbook of Indigenous Education*. Springer, Singapore (2019).
27 See Jefferson and Anderson, *Transforming Schools*; and Anderson and Jefferson, *Transforming Organizations*.
28 Bill Green, 'Understanding curriculum? Notes towards a conceptual basis for curriculum inquiry', *Curriculum Perspectives* 38.1 (2018): 81–4.
29 Bill Green, *Engaging Curriculum : Bridging the Curriculum Theory and English Education Divide*. New York, NY: Routledge (n.d.), 110.
30 Eunsook Hyun, 'Transforming instruction into pedagogy through curriculum negotiation', *Journal of Curriculum and Pedagogy* 3.1 (2006): 139.
31 John Dewey, *Experience and Education*. New York: Macmillan and Co., 1938.
32 Elliot W. Eisner, 'What can education learn from the arts about the practice of education?', last modified June 2019, https://infed.org/mobi/what-can-education-learn-from-the-arts-about-the-practice-of-education.

33 Pierre Bourdieu, 'Principles for reflecting on the curriculum', *The Curriculum Journal* 1, no. 3 (1990): 307–14.
34 OECD, *The Future of Education and Skills: Education 2030* (2018), 5.
35 Project Kaleidoscope, Association of American Colleges and Universities, *What Works in Facilitating Interdisciplinary Learning in Science and Mathematics?* (Washington, DC: Association of American Colleges and Universities, 2011), https://www.aacu.org/sites/default/files/files/pkalkeck/KeckExecutiveSummary.pdf.
36 Alexander Refsum Jensenius, 'Disciplinarities: intra, cross, multi, inter, trans', 12 March 2012, https://www.arj.no/2012/03/12/disciplinarities-2.
37 Norbert M. Seel (ed.), 'Cross-disciplinary learning', in *Encyclopedia of the Sciences of Learning*, Boston, MA: Springer (2012).
38 UNESCO, 'Transdisciplinary approach', International Bureau of Education, http://www.ibe.unesco.org/en/glossary-curriculum-terminology/t/transdisciplinary-approach.
39 Kathryn Paige, David Lloyd and Mike Chartres, 'Moving towards transdisciplinarity: an ecological sustainable focus for science and mathematics pre-service education in the primary/middle years', *Asia-Pacific Journal of Teacher Education* 36, no. 1 (2008): 19–33.
40 Benjamin Samuel Bloom, *Taxonomy of Educational Objectives: The Classification of Educational Goals*. New York: Longmans, Green (1956).
41 Lorin W. Anderson and David R. Krothwohl, *A Taxonomy for Learning, Teaching and Assessing: A Revision of Bloom's Taxonomy of Educational Objectives*. New York: Longmans (2001).
42 Italics in original. Veronica Boix Mansilla, Michèle Lamont and Kyoko Sato, 'Shared cognitive–emotional–interactional platforms: markers and conditions for successful interdisciplinary collaborations', *Science, Technology, & Human Values* 41, no. 4 (2016): 599.
43 See, for instance, 'Education Minister says "alarm bells should be ringing" over poor student test results', *ABC News*, 4 December 2019, https://www.abc.net.au/news/2019-12-04/alarm-bells-should-be-ringing-over-student-pisa-test-results/11764278; 'It just isn't working: PISA scores cast doubt on U.S. education efforts', *New York Times*, 3 December 2019, https://www.nytimes.com/2019/12/03/us/us-students-international-test-scores.html; Richard Adams, 'UK school reforms to come under scrutiny as world rankings released', *The Guardian*, 2 December 2019, https://www.theguardian.com/education/2019/dec/02/uk-school-reforms-to-come-under-scrutiny-as-world-rankings-released.
44 Jo-Anne Baird and Therese N. Hopfenbeck, 'Curriculum in the twenty-first century and the future of examinations', in *The SAGE Handbook of Curriculum, Pedagogy and Assessment* (Vol. 2), eds. Dominic Wyse, Louise Hayward and Jessica Pandya (55 City Road, London: SAGE Publications Ltd, 2016), 821–36.
45 Baird and Hopfenbeck, 'Curriculum in the twenty-first century', 821–36.
46 Alma Harris and Michelle Jones, 'Why context matters: a comparative perspective on education reform and policy implementation', *Educational Research for Policy and Practice* 17, no. 3 (2018): 195–207.
47 Wynne Harlen, 'Assessment and the curriculum', in *The SAGE Handbook of Curriculum, Pedagogy and Assessment: Two Volume Set*, eds. Dominic Wyse, Louise Hayward, and Jessica Pandya (55 City Road, London: SAGE Publications Ltd, 2016), 693–709.
48 Templestowe College, 'Our philosophy', last modified 2017, https://tc.vic.edu.au/our-philosophy.
49 Alma Harris and Michelle Jones, 'Why context matters: a comparative perspective on education reform and policy implementation', *Educational Research for Policy and Practice* 17, no. 3 (2018): 195.
50 Javier Fernández-Río, 'Student-teacher-content-context: indissoluble ingredients in the teaching-learning process', *Journal of Physical Education, Recreation & Dance* 87, no. 1 (2016): 3–5.

51 Templestowe College, 'Subject Selection Handbook 2020', last modified June 2019, https://static1.squarespace.com/static/57ce619237c58169970fad80/t/5d4918ecbf13a80001ba2147/1565071683153/2020+Entry+Handbook.pdf.
52 Templestowe College, 'Subject Selection Handbook 2020'.
53 Victoria State Government Education and Training, '883 Templestowe College Strategic Plan 2018–2021', March 2017, https://static1.squarespace.com/static/57ce619237c58169970fad80/t/59fa6bdc41920206984f9fb7/1509583840492/School-Strategic-Plan+2018-2021-Draft.pdf.
54 Jung-Hoon Jung and William F. Pinar, 'Conceptions of curriculum', in *The SAGE Handbook of Curriculum, Pedagogy and Assessment*, eds. Dominic Wyse, Louise Hayward and Jessica Pandya (55 City Road, London: SAGE Publications Ltd, 2016), 33.

Chapter 9

1 Jane M. Dewey ed., 'Biography of John Dewey', in *The Philosophy of John Dewey*, ed. Paul Arthur Schilpp (New York: Tudor Publishing Co., 1939): 3–45, https://brocku.ca/MeadProject/Dewey/Dewey_1939.html.
2 David Hildebrand, 'John Dewey', in *The Stanford Encyclopedia of Philosophy*, ed. Edward N. Zalta (Stanford University, CA: Metaphysics Research Lab, Winter 2018 Edition), https://plato.stanford.edu/entries/dewey.
3 John Dewey, *Freedom and Culture* (New York: G. P. Putman's Sons, 1939), 175.
4 Lifelong approaches to teacher education are well established in the scholarship of this area. See, for instance, Maria Assunção Flores, 'Teacher education curriculum', in *International Handbook of Teacher Education*, eds. John Loughran and Mary Lyn Hamilton (Dordrecht: Springer Press, 2016), 187–230.
5 Sam Sellar and Bob Lingard, 'The OECD and global governance in education', *Journal of Education Policy* 28, no. 5 (2013): 710–25.
6 Kay Fuller and Howard Stevenson, 'Global education reform: understanding the movement', *Educational Review* 71, no. 1 (2019): 1–4.
7 John Dewey, 'The need of an industrial education in an industrial democracy', in *The Middle Works of John Dewey, Volume 10, 1899–1924: Journal Articles, Essays and Miscellany Published in the 1916–1917 Period*, ed. Jo Ann Boydston (Carbondale, Illinois: Southern Illinois University Press, 2008), 137–43.
8 Andreas Schleicher, 'Reimagining the teaching profession', *Teacher Magazine*, 12 February 2018, https://www.teachermagazine.com.au/columnists/andreas-schleicher/reimagining-the-teaching-profession.
9 Maria Assunção Flores, 'Teacher education curriculum', in *International Handbook of Teacher Education*, eds. John Loughran and Mary Lyn Hamilton (Dordrecht: Springer Press, 2016), 187–230.
10 David Hansen et al., 'Reenvisioning the progressive tradition in curriculum', in *The SAGE Handbook of Curriculum and Instruction*, eds. F. Michael Connelly, Ming Fang He and JoAn Phillion (Thousand Oaks, CA: SAGE Publications, Inc., 2008), 440–59.
11 John Dewey, 'Experience and education', *The Educational Forum* 50, no. 3 (September, 1986): 241–52.
12 Knud Illeris, 'What do we actually mean by experiential learning?', *Human Resource Development Review* 6, no. 1 (2007): 84–95.
13 Gerald Burch et al., 'Do experiential learning pedagogies effect student learning? A meta-analysis of 40 years of research', *Academy of Management Annual Meeting Proceedings* 2016, no. 1 (2016): 16838.

14 Esther Cohen, Ron Hoz and Haya Kaplan, 'The practicum in preservice teacher education: a review of empirical studies', *Teaching Education* 24, no. 4 (2013): 345–80.
15 Mary A. Dyer and Susan M. Taylor, 'Supporting professional identity in undergraduate Early Years students through reflective practice', *Reflective Practice: International and Multidisciplinary Perspectives* 13 (2012): 551–63.
16 Tonya Salomons, 'Critical acceptance: a pathway to critical reflection of practice', in *Learning Critical Reflection: Experiences of the Transformative Learning Process*, eds. Laura Béres and Jan Fook (London: Taylor & Francis Ltd, 2019), 23–34.
17 Sharon Friesen and David Scott, *Inquiry-Based Learning: A Review of the Research Literature* (Calgary: University of Calgary, June 2013), https://galileo.org/focus-on-inquiry-lit-review.pdf, 1–32.
18 Lloyd H. Barrow, 'A brief history of inquiry: from Dewey to standards', *Journal of Science Teacher Education* 17, no. 3 (2006): 266.
19 Educational psychologists Ard Lazonder and Ruth Harmsen found that the following conditions contributed to successful inquiry learning: access to domain information during the inquiry, experiences and tasks that structure the inquiry process, and constraining the complexity of the inquiry process.
20 Ard W. Lazonder and Ruth Harmsen, 'Meta-analysis of inquiry-based learning: effects of guidance', *Review of Educational Research* 86, no. 3 (2016): 681–718.
21 Keith Sawyer, 'A call to action: the challenges of creative teaching and learning', *Teachers College Record* 117, no. 10 (2015): 1–34.
22 Christopher Day and Christine Grice, *Investigating the Influence and Impact of Leading from the Middle: A School-based Strategy for Middle Leaders in Schools* (Sydney: The University of Sydney, 2019), 8.
23 Helen Timperley et al., *Teacher Professional Learning and Development: Best Evidence Synthesis Iteration [BES]* (Wellington: Ministry of Education, 2007), http://www.oecd.org/education/school/48727127.pdf.
24 Margaret M. Riel and Lonnie L. Rowell, 'Action research and the development of expertise: rethinking teacher education', in *The Palgrave International Handbook of Action Research*, eds. Lonnie L. Rowell et al. (Palgrave Macmillan, New York, 2017), 667–88.
25 Alison King, 'From sage on the stage to guide on the side', *College Teaching* 41, no. 1 (1993): 30–5.
26 Linda Darling-Hammond and Nikole Richardson, 'Research review/teacher learning: what matters', *Educational Leadership* 66, no. 5 (2009): 46–53.
27 NSW Government, 'Hurstville Public School 2197: School Plan 2018–2020', April 2018, https://s3-ap-southeast-2.amazonaws.com/doe-nsw-schools/plan-report/2018/2197/2018-2020_Hurstville_Public_School_School_Plan.pdf.
28 This case study was partially based on and interview held on 28 May 2020 with Mark Steed, Jayne Muir and Alison Duff via video conferencing software. The interview was transcribed. The reflections in this case study have been edited for use in this publication and validated with the participants for accuracy prior to publication.
29 Michael Anderson and Kelly Freebody, 'Developing communities of praxis: bridging the theory practice divide in teacher education', *McGill Journal of Education/Revue des sciences de l'éducation de McGill* 47, no. 3 (2012): 359–77.
30 Etienne Wenger, *Communities of Practice: Learning, Meaning, and Identity* (Cambridge: Cambridge University Press, 1998).
31 Etienne Wenger, *Communities of Practice*.
32 Cambridge Dictionary. Meaning of Praxis. Accessed on 26 July from https://dictionary.cambridge.org/dictionary/english/praxis.
33 John Dewey. *Democracy and Education* (New York, NY: Simon and Brown, (1916/2011), 144.

34 John Dewey, *Experience and Education* (New York: Touchstone, 1938), 38.
35 Marcel Proust, *Remembrance of Things Past: The Captive*, Vol. 9. (London: Chatto & Windus, 1949).
36 See Jefferson and Anderson, *Transforming Schools*.
37 Jan Fook and Laura Béres, 'Issues in teaching and learning critical reflection', in *Learning Critical Reflection: Experiences of the Transformative Learning Process*, eds. Laura Béres and Jan Fook (London: Taylor & Francis Ltd, 2019).
38 Our emphasis, Jan Fook, 'Reflective practice and critical reflection', in *Handbook for Practice Learning in Social Work and Social Care: Knowledge and Theory*, 3rd edition, ed. Joyce Lishman (London: Jessica Kingsley Publishers, 2015), 440–52.
39 Christopher DeLuca et al., 'Collaborative inquiry as a professional learning structure for educators: a scoping review', *Professional Development in Education* 41, no. 4 (2015): 640–70.
40 Helen Timperley, Linda Kaser and Judy Halbert, 'A framework for transforming learning in schools: innovation and the spiral of inquiry', *Seminar Series Paper* no. 234 (Melbourne: Centre for Strategic Education, April 2014), https://teachingcouncil.nz/sites/default/files/49.%20Spiral%20of%20Inquiry%20Paper%20-%20Timperley%20Kaser%20Halbert.pdf.
41 Timperley, Kaser and Halbert, 'Transforming learning in schools'.
42 John Dewey, *The Early Works, 1882–1898: 1882–1888. Early Essays and Leibniz's New Essays Concerning the Human Understanding*. Vol. 1. SIU Press, 2008.

Chapter 10

1 Suzanne Moore, 'Jacinda Ardern is showing the world what real leadership is: sympathy, love and integrity', *Guardian*, 18 March 2019, https://www.theguardian.com/commentisfree/2019/mar/18/jacinda-ardern-is-showing-the-world-what-real-leadership-is-sympathy-love-and-integrity.
2 Madeleine Chapman, *Jacinda Ardern: A New Kind of Leader* (Carlton, Victoria: Nero, 2020), 242.
3 Eglantine Jamet, 'Jacinda Ardern or inclusive leadership exemplified', *Forbes*, 16 May 2019, https://www.forbes.com/sites/eglantinejamet/2019/05/16/jacinda-ardern-or-inclusive-leadership-exemplified/#47a27172384a.
4 Chapman, *Jacinda Ardern*, 241–2.
5 James Kerr, *Legacy: 15 Lessons in Leadership* (London: Constable, 2013), 5.
6 John MacBeath, 'Leadership for learning', in *Instructional Leadership and Leadership for Learning in Schools: Understanding Theories of Leading*, ed. Tony Townsend (Switzerland: Springer, 2019), 49–73.
7 John P. Kotter, *Leading Change* (Boston, MA: Harvard Business Review Press, 2012), 28.
8 Kotter, *Leading Change*.
9 National Research Council, *Education for Life and Work: Developing Transferable Knowledge and Skills in the 21st Century* (Washington, DC: National Academies Press, 2013).
10 Wendelin Küpers and Olen Gunnlaugson, eds., *Wisdom Learning: Perspectives on Wising-up Business and Management Education* (London and New York: Routledge, 2017).
11 Snjezana Kovjanic et al., 'How do transformational leaders foster positive employee outcomes? A self-determination-based analysis of employees' needs as mediating links', *Journal of Organizational Behavior* 33 (2012): 1031–52.

12 Richard Elmore, 'Leadership as the practice of improvement', in *Improving School Leadership, Volume 2: Case Studies on System Leadership*, eds. Beatriz Pont, Deborah Nusche, and David Hopkins (Paris: OECD, 2008), 38.
13 David Frost et al., 'The legacy of the Carpe Vitam Leadership for Learning project', *inFORM*, no. 8 (2008): 1–8, https://www.educ.cam.ac.uk/networks/lfl/about/inform/PDFs/InForm_8.pdf.
14 David Frost, 'The concept of "agency" in leadership and learning', *Leading and Managing* 12, no. 2 (2006): 19–28.
15 Frost, 'Agency', 20.
16 John MacBeath, 'Leadership for learning', in *International Encyclopedia of Education*, 3rd edition, eds. Penelope Peterson, Eva Baker, and Barry McGaw (Amsterdam: Elsevier, 2010), 817–23.
17 Mary Parker Follett, *Mary Parker Follett Prophet of Management: A Celebration of Writings from the 1920s* (Boston, MA: Harvard Business School Press, 1996), 119.
18 Simpson, B (2016) p. 170, 'Where's the agency in leadership-as-practice?' pp. 159–77, in J. A. Raelin (ed.), *Leadership-as-Practice: Theory and Application*, New York: Routledge.
19 Barbara Simpson, 'Where's the agency in leadership-as-practice?', in *Leadership-as-Practice: Theory and Application*, ed. Joseph A. Raelin (New York: Routledge, 2016), 170.
20 Simpson, 'Leadership-as-practice', 164.
21 Kerr, *Legacy*, 42–3.
22 Kerr, *Legacy*, 43.
23 Keith Sawyer, 'A call to action', 1–34.
24 'V is for vortex: An endangered species helps scientists to learn why migrating birds fly in a similar formation', *Nature* 50 (January 2014), 262, https://www.nature.com/news/v-is-for-vortex-1.14507.
25 Emergent systems are explained in Sawyer, 'A call to action', 16–20.
26 Miranda Jefferson and Michael Anderson, *Transforming Schools: Creativity, Critical Reflection, Communication, Collaboration* (London, Bloomsbury, 2017) quoting Vera John-Steiner, *Creative Collaboration* (New York: Oxford University Press, 2000).
27 Simpson, 'Leadership-as-practice', 172.
28 Kerr, *Legacy*, 65.
29 Matt Andrews, Lant Pritchett and Michael Wollcock, *Building State Capability: Evidence, Analysis, Action* (Oxford: Oxford University Press, 2017).
30 Ronald Heifetz, Alexander Grashow and Marty Linksy, *The Practice of Adaptive Leadership: Tools and Tactics for Changing your Organization and the World* (Boston, MA: Harvard Business Press, 2009).
31 Kotter, *Leading Change*.
32 John P. Kotter, *Accelerate: Building Strategic Agility for a Faster-Moving World* (Boston, MA: Harvard Business Review Press, 2014), 14.
33 Matt Andrews et al., 'Building capability by delivering results: putting Problem-Driven Iterative Adaptation (PDIA) principles into practice', in *A Governance Practitioner's Notebook: Alternative Ideas and Approaches*, eds. Whaites et al. (Paris: OECD, 2015), 123–33, https://www.oecd.org/dac/accountable-effective-institutions/Governance%20Notebook%202.3%20Andrews%20et%20al.pdf.
34 Kotter, *Accelerate*, 15.
35 Kotter, *Accelerate*.
36 Alison Gopnick, *The Gardener and the Carpenter: What the New Science of Child Development Tells Us About the Relationship Between Parents and Children* (London, UK: Vintage, 2016).
37 Helen Storey and Mathilda Joubert, 'The emotional dance of creative collaboration', in *Collaborative Creativity: Contemporary Perspectives*, eds. Dorothy Miell and Karen Littleton (London: Free Association Books, 2004), 40–51.

38 Vera John-Steiner, *Creative Collaboration* (New York: Oxford University Press, 2000), 204.
39 John-Steiner, *Creative Collaboration*.
40 Nóra Révai and Sonia Guerriero, 'Knowledge dynamics in the teaching profession', in *Pedagogical Knowledge and the Changing Nature of the Teaching Profession*, ed. Sonia Guerriero (Paris: OECD Publishing, 2017), 38.
41 Anne Pässilä and Russ Vince, 'Critical reflection in management and organization studies' pp. 48–62 in Fook, J., Collington, V., Ross, F., Ruch, G. and West, L. (eds.) (2015). *Researching Critical Reflection: Multidisciplinary Perspectives*. London: Routledge.
42 Kotter, *Leading Change*.
43 Mezirow, J. (1997), *Transformative Learning: Theory to Practice*, San Francisco, CA: John Wiley and Sons.
44 Chapman, *Jacinda Ardern*, 247.
45 Chapman, *Jacinda Ardern*, 248.
46 Kerr, *Legacy*, 43.
47 Kerr, *Legacy*, 183.

Chapter 11

1 Anderson and Jefferson, *Transforming Organizations*. Elements of this chapter were first published in this book and reworked for this chapter.
2 Jack Mezirow, 'A critical theory of adult learning and education', *Adult Education* 32, no. 1 (1981): 3–24.

Index

The letter *f* following an entry indicates a page that includes a figure.
The letter *t* following an entry indicates a page that includes a table.

'Aboriginal and Torres Strait Islander Histories and Cultures' 163
'aerosol' words 9*f*–10
agency 29
    Bristow Luke 221, 222–3
    children's 58–9
    classroom communication 58
    co-agency 57–8, 72
    definition 57
    4C Network workshop conferences 58
    leadership 207–14
    in learning 58–9, 72
    OECD *Future of Education and Skills 2030* project 54–7
    Self-Determination Theory 54, 59–64
    student 58, 158
    Thunberg, Greta 52*f*–4
    as transformative value 38, 40, 42, 43, 46–7
All Blacks 204, 205*f*, 209, 210–12, 225
altruism 96
amotivation 62, 63*t*
Ansari, Daniel 131
Arden, Jacinda 202–4, 209, 223–4, 225
assessment *see also* rankings
    versus curriculum 170–2
Association of American Colleges and Universities 167
Atlassian 34–5, 38, 49–50
Australia 163
authentic connections 142–3
autonomous motivation 63*t*, 64
autonomy 60, 62, 206
awareness 232–3, 234

Baird, Jo-Anne and Therese Hopfenbeck 162, 170, 171
Bandt, Adam 52
BAT (British American Tobacco) 36–7
Batson, Daniel 96
Baumert, Jürgen 110
beast of Gévaudan story 14*f*–15
behaviour 59–60
    self-regulatory 62, 63*t*
bending 92

Bernstein, Basil 107, 129, 130*f*, 156
Bhasker, Michael 106
    Curation: The Power of Selection in a World of Excess 106
Billett, Stephen 130
birds 211*f*
Black, Paul 141
blending 92
Boix Mansilla, Veronica 169
Bourdieu, Pierre 166
brain, the 78, 130–1
breaking 92
Bristow, Luke 221, 222–3
British American Tobacco (BAT) 36–7
British Columbia 162–4
Buckingham Shum, Simon and Ruth Deakin Crick 65–6
build new ideas 91–3
Bulliet, Richard W.
    Wheel: Inventions and Reinventions, The 76
buzz words 9

Canada 162–3
Cannon-Brookes, Mike 34
capabilities 16–17, 20*f*–30, 22–30, 230–2 *see also* 4C capabilities
    leadership 30
    Nussbaum, Martha 21
    Sen, Amartya 35
    transformative curriculum 30
    transformative learning 29
    transformative pedagogy 29–30
    transformative teacher education 30
    transformative values 28–9
Carpe Vitam International Leadership for Learning project 207–8
Carse, James P 4
cascading effects 220
Casula Public School 40
CCVs (Collaborative Classroom Visits) 195, 196
challenges 83–4
change 6–7, 19

Index

Changing Expectations for the K-12 Teacher Workforce: Policies, Preservice Education, Professional Development and the Workplace (US National Academy of Sciences) 125
Chapman, Madeleine
   Jacinda Arden: A New Kind of Leader 202–3, 224
Cheng Wing-yi, Rebecca 145
Clark, Jane 105
classroom communication 58
climate change 34–5*f*, 52*f*–4
co-agency 57–8, 72
co-construction (curriculum) 175–6
co-curricular learning 5–6
co-evolution 220
co-teaching 24
coactive power 208
coercive power 208
cognitive empathy 97, 98
cognitive learning domain 67–8, 80, 87*f*–93
cognitive perspectives 129–31
coherence makers. See 4C coherence makers
collaboration 11*t*, 24–5, 98
   transformative leadership 219–20
   transformative pedagogy 116–17
Collaboration Circles 11*t*, 24–5*f*, 80, 99, 117
Collaborative Classroom Visits (CCVs) 195, 196
collaborative inquiry 144–5, 197
collaborative leadership 225
collaborative partnerships 38, 39, 40, 41, 42–3, 48–9
collectivism 96
communication 11*t*, 27–8, 89–90
   transformative pedagogy 115–16
   transformative leadership 219
Communication Crystal 11*t*, 27–8*f*, 80, 90
community of practice (COP) 48–9, 145, 193–4
community of praxis 193–4
compassionate empathy 97, 98
competence 60, 62, 206
complex problems 17, 18*t*, 19, 28, 31
complexity challenges 16 *see also* complexity theory
complexity theory 17–20
compliance 94–5
complicated problems 17, 18*t*
connected and coherent learning 38, 48
connectedness to the world 142
connections 142–3
connectivity 220
consultation (curriculum) 172–3
content knowledge 110–11*f*
context (curriculum) 173–5
continuum of motivation and self-regulatory behaviour 62, 63*t*
controlled extrinsic motivation 63*t*
Convention of the Rights of the Child (CRC) 58–9
COP (community of practice) 48–9, 145, 193–4
copper 76
Covid-19 pandemic 12, 159–60

crafting (curriculum) 176–7
CRC (Convention of the Rights of the Child) 58–9
creative iteration 145–7
creativity 11*t*, 23–4, 91–3, 146
   transformative leadership 221
   transformative pedagogy 114
Creativity Cascade 11*t*, 23*f*, 46, 80, 92–3
critical hope 38, 40, 43–4
critical reflection 11*t*, 25–7, 187, 196–7
   transformative leadership 220–1
   transformative pedagogy 114–15
Critical Reflection Crucible 11*t*, 26*f*, 80, 88, 89
cross-disciplinary approach 167
culture 34, 49 *see also* values
curation 104–6, 107, 108, 118, 120–1
   pedagogy 148
Curation: The Power of Selection in a World of Excess (Bhasker, Michael) 106
curiosity 85–6, 144
curriculum 230 *see also* transformative curriculum
   assessment versus 170–2
   British Columbia 162–4
   in a complex world 158–60
   definitions 156–8
   democratic 162
   dialogue 235
   false dichotomies, unlearning 164–72
   Indigenous knowledge in the 162–4
   learning 107–8
   pedagogy 106–7
   pedagogy versus 164–6
   practice/policy gap 161–2
   'real world', and the 152–3
   shared endeavour 235
   status quo 153–6, 159, 177
   subject depth versus integration 166–70
   unlearning 164–72
Curriculum Directorate (New South Wales Department of Education, Australia) 152–3
Csikszentmihalyi, Mihaly 93

Deci, Edward and Richard Ryan 59, 60, 61
decontextualized testing 171
Deep Noticing and Action (DNA) 114–15*f*, 195–6
deep learning 38, 39, 40, 41, 43, 46
deeper learning 77–8, 177
deliberate practice 139–40
democratic curriculum 162
democratic education 181, 182–3, 190, 200
democratic learning 181
Dewey, John 136, 165, 180–3, 190
   democratic education 181, 183, 190, 200
   experience 185–6, 195
   inquiry 187–8*t*
   theory, relationship with practice 194
dialogue 232–3, 235
dichotomies, unlearning false 164–72

Didaktik 107
disciplinary learning 6
discovery scaffolds 132, 138–9
disorientation 232–4
dispositions 36
distributive leadership 210, 225
Donaldson, Graham
  Teaching Scotland's Future 117
DNA (Deep Noticing and Action) 114–15f, 195–6
Duff, Alison 194, 197, 198, 199
Dyer, Mary and Susan Taylor 187
dynamic feedback 140–2

Eagleman, David and Anthony Brandt 92
Ecole 42 100–1
education 7
Education for Life and Work: Developing Transferable Knowledge and Skills in the 21st Century (National Research Council) 66–7, 72, 78, 80, 206
effect sizes 240 n.6
egoism 96
Eisner, Elliot 12, 165–6
Elmore, Richard 207
embodied cognition 147
emergence 10, 20
emergent order 220
emotional empathy 97, 98
empathy 96–8
epigenetics 130
epistemic curiosity 84, 86
Ernman, Malena 53
existential learning 90, 91
experience 147, 185–6f, 195–6
experiential learning 186
explicit learning 38, 45–6
explicit teaching 46
external regulation 63t
extrinsic motivation 62, 63

false dichotomies, unlearning 164–72
feedback 140–1, 171
Fernández-Río, Javier 174
finite games 4–5
flexible purposing 165–6
focus 81–3
Follett, Mary Parker 208
foresight 19
formative assessment 170, 171
foundational teacher education 30, 182, 184–8, 200
4C capabilities 20f–1, 22–8, 54, 229, 230–2 *see also* capabilities
  collaboration. *See* collaboration
  communication. *See* communication
  creativity. *See* creativity
  critical reflection. *See* critical reflection
  experience 147, 185–6f, 195–6
  Hurstville Public School 190–9
  inquiry 144, 188–9, 197–8
  integrated learning 167, 168–9
  leadership 213–14f, 215–16, 217–23, 225
  Learning Disposition Wheel 67–8
  reflection 187, 196–7
  transformative teacher education 183–5
4C coherence markers 9–10, 11t, 41, 45–6, 48
  Collaboration Circles 11t, 24–5f, 80, 99, 117
  Communication Crystal 11t, 27–8f, 80, 90
  Creativity Cascade 11t, 23f, 46, 80, 92–3
  Critical Reflection Crucible 11t, 26f, 80, 88, 89
  Leadership Wheel 203f–4, 206–7, 222, 224
  Learning Disposition Wheel. *See* Learning Disposition Wheel
  Muir, Jayne 192
  Pedagogy Parachute, *See* Pedagogy Parachute
  Transformation Tangle 229, 231f–6
4C Network 42f–3, 48–9
  workshop conferences 58
4C Transformative Learning (4CTL) 2, 3, 10–12, 39f–41
  capabilities 20f–1, 22–3
  coherence makers. *See* coherence makers
  collaboration 11t, 24–5
  communication 11t, 27–8
  creativity 11t, 23–4
  critical reflection 11t, 25–7
  Hurstville Public School 190–3, 198–9
Freire, Paulo 43, 87–8, 144
  Pedagogy of the Oppressed 144
Future of Education and Skills 2030 project (Organisation for Economic Co-operation and Development) 54–7, 72, 155

games metaphor 3–5
Garnerin, André 124f
general pedagogical knowledge 110–13
general pedagogical/psychological knowledge model 112
GERM (Global Education Reform Movement) 154, 182
Gladwell, Malcolm
  Outliers 139
Global Education Reform Movement (GERM) 154, 182
Goldman, Daniel and Paul Ekman 96
Gopnick, Alison 219
Great Pacific Garbage Patch 53f–4
Green, Bill 165
Greene, Maxine 97
grit 83–5
Gurley, Keith 37–8

haiku 46
'hands up' classroom answering 44
Hargreaves, David H. 109–10
Harlen, Wynne 171
Harris, Alma and Michelle Jones 174, 175
Hart, Caroline Sarojina and Nicolás Brando 58–9

Henry Graham 209, 210, 212
Hilderbrand, David 181
hindsight 19
history 19
hope 43–4 *see also* critical hope
Howes, Peter 221–2
human behaviour. *See* behaviour
Hurstville Public School 190–9

identification 94, 95
identified regulation 63*t*, 64
imagination 6, 38, 40, 41, 45
　empathy 97
imagination experiment 2–3
in-service teacher education. *See* lifelong teacher education
Indigenous knowledge 162–4
Individual leadership 225
infinite education 5–6
infinite games 4–5, 6, 228
influence 94–6
initial teacher education. *See* foundational teacher education
initiative 94–6
'innovation' team 40
inquiry 144, 188–9, 197–8
instruction 136–7
integrated learning 5, 166–70
integrated regulation 63*t*–4
integration versus subject depth 166–70
interacting elements 19
interdisciplinary approach 168
internalization 94, 95
international testing regimes 155, 170–1
internships 186
interpersonal learning domain 67, 68, 80, 94*f*–100
intrapersonal learning domain 67, 80–6
intrinsic motivation 62, 63*t*, 64
introjected regulation 63*t*
iteration 145

Jacinda Arden: A New Kind of Leader (Chapman, Madeleine) 202–3, 224
Jensenius, Alexander Refsum 167
joint enterprises 49
Jung, Jung-Hoon and William Pinar 177

Kashdan, Todd and Paul Silvia 85, 86
Kelman, Herbert C. 94
Kerr, Fiona 97
Kerr, James
　Legacy: 15 Lessons in Leadership 209, 210–11, 225
knowledge 166
　content knowledge 111*f*
　general pedagogical knowledge 110*f*–13
　Indigenous knowledge in the curriculum 162–4
　metacognitive knowledge 82, 83
　pedagogical content knowledge 110–11*f*
　pedagogical knowledge 108–13
　teacher knowledge base 109–10
Kotter, John P. 206, 216, 217, 221

lateral thinking 194
Lave, Jean and Etienne Wenger 143
leadership 21, 30, 202–5, 231 *see also* transformative leadership
　agency 207–13
　awareness 234
　collaborative 225
　communication 27
　definitions 205–7
　distributive 210, 225
　individual 225
　as inter-action 210
　as self-action 209
　shared 204, 208–13, 225
　as trans-action 210–12
Leadership for Learning project 207–8
Leadership Wheel 203*f*–4, 206–7, 222, 224
learning 4, 230 *see also* transformative learning
　agency 54–9, 72
　build new ideas 92–3
　cross-disciplinary 167
　curiosity 85–6
　definition 147
　democratic 181
　disciplinary 6
　disorientation 234
　empathy 96–7
　existential 90, 91
　focus 81–2
　grit 83–4
　influence 94–5
　integrated 5
　interdisciplinary 168
　make and express meaning 90–1
　multidisciplinary 168
　pedagogical knowledge 110–11
　pragmatic 90, 91
　problem-based 167
　project-based 167, 169–70
　Self-Determination Theory 54, 61–2
　semantic 90, 91
　teamwork 99
　testing 8
　think why and how 87–9
　transdisciplinary 168
learning capacities 67–8
learning compass 55, 56*f*
Learning Disposition Wheel 29, 40–1, 54, 64–7, 101
　cognitive learning domain 67–8, 80, 87*f*–93
　deeper learning 77–8
　example 100–1
　interpersonal learning domain 67, 68, 80, 94*f*–100

intrapersonal learning domain 67, 80–6
inventing 76–7
metacognition 78–9
Self-Determination Theory 64–5, 67
teaching and learning 79–80
learning dispositions 29, 65–71, 78, 80
    cognitive learning domain 67–8, 80, 87*f*–93
    interpersonal learning domain 67, 68, 80, 94*f*–100
    intrapersonal learning domain 67, 80–6
learning scaffolds 112
learning schemas 135
LearnLife 118*f*, 119*t*
Legacy: 15 Lessons in Leadership (Kerr, James) 209, 210–11, 225
Leonard da Vinci 124
lifelong teacher education 25–6, 30, 182, 188–90, 200
    see also transformative teacher education
    Hurstville Public School 190–9

MacBeath, John 205–6
make and express meaning 89–91
management 206, 217
metacognition 78–9, 82, 83
metacognitive experience 82, 83
metacognitive knowledge 82, 83
metacognitive skills 82, 83
Mezirow, Jack 113, 116, 232
migratory birds 211*f*
mining 76
Miranda North Public School 68–9
MONA (Museum of Old and New) 104*f*–6, 120
monster of Gévaudan story 14*f*–15
monsters, metaphorical 15, 16
Montuori, Alfonso 146
Morgan, Bob 163
Morrison, Scott 52
motivated instruction 136–7
motivation 62–4, 81–2
Muir, Jayne 192, 196, 198
multidisciplinary approach 168
Museum of Old and New (MONA) 104*f*–6, 120
mutual engagement 48

Narciss, Susanne 141
National Research Council (NRC)
Education for Life and Work: Developing Transferable Knowledge and Skills in the 21st Century 66–7, 72, 78
Neal, Xavier 100
networked schemas 134–6
neuroplasticity 78, 130–1
Nevenglosky, Erica, Chris Cale and Sunddip Aguilar 157
New Zealand 202–4
    All Blacks 204, 205*f*, 209, 210–12, 225
    Arden, Jacinda 202–4, 209, 223–4, 225
    whakapapa tradition 212
Newmann, Fred M. 142

9/11 attacks 152*f*–3
nodes 19–20
non-regulation 62, 63*t*
noticing 92, 114–15*f*
NRC (National Research Council)
    Education for Life and Work: Developing Transferable Knowledge and Skills in the 21st Century 66–7, 72, 78
Nussbaum, Martha 21

O'Connor, Peter 159–60
OECD (Organisation for Economic Co-operation and Development) 167
    Future of Education and Skills 2030 project 54–7, 72, 155
    learning compass 55, 56*f*
    Pedagogical Knowledge and the Changing Nature of the Teaching Profession 108–9, 110, 117
Organisation for Economic Co-operation and Development (OECD). *See* OECD
Our House Is On Fire: Scenes of a Family and a Planet in Crisis (Ernman, Malena, Ernman, Beata, Thunberg, Svante and Thunberg, Greta) 53
Outliers (Gladwell, Malcolm) 139

Paige, Kathryn 168
parachutes 124*f*–5, 128, 129
Parkinson, Chloe and Tiffany Jones 163
PBL (project-based learning) 167, 169–70
pedagogical content knowledge 110–11*f*
pedagogical knowledge 108–13
Pedagogical Knowledge and the Changing Nature of the Teaching Profession (Organisation for Economic Co-operation and Development) 108–9, 110, 117
pedagogy 120, 148–9, 230 *see also* transformative pedagogy *and* Pedagogy Parachute
    affecting learning 110–11*f*
    cognitive perspectives 129–31
    content knowledge 111*f*
    curriculum 106–7
    definition 107–8
    dialogue 235
    general pedagogical knowledge 111*f*–13
    pedagogical content knowledge 110–11*f*
    pedagogical knowledge 108–13
    shared endeavour 235
    sociocultural perspectives 129–31
    teacher challenges 108–9
    teacher knowledge base 109–10
    versus curriculum 164–6
Pedagogy of the Oppressed (Freire, Paulo) 144
Pedagogy Parachute 10, 29, 80, 119, 120, 148–9
    authentic connections 142–3
    collaborative inquiry 144–5
    connections 142–3
    creative iteration 145–7
    deliberate practice 139–40

development of 125–7
discovery scaffolds 132, 138–9
dynamic feedback 140–2
experience 147
feedback 140–1, 171
imagination 45
inquiry 144
instruction 136–7
iteration 145
motivated instruction 136–7
networked schemas 134–6
practice 139–40
reflected experience 147–8
scaffolds 132, 133, 138
schema of elements 126, 127–9, 134–49
schema of elements, how they work 131–3
schemas 134–5
theoretical underpinnings 129–31
pedagogy/policy gap 16, 161–2 *see also* practice/policy gap
Peek, Kyle 101
perceptual curiosity 84, 86
periodic table 131, 132*f*
Piaget, Jean 134
PISA (Programme for International Students Assessment) 155, 170
plasticity 78, 130–1
playing with possibility 92
positional leadership 205
potential 12
power 208
practice 139–40
practice/policy gap 161–2 *see also* pedagogy/policy gap
practicum 186
pragmatic learning 90, 91
praxis 38, 40, 43, 49, 194
    Hurstville Public School 193–5
preservice teacher education. *See* foundational teacher education
principlism 96
problem-based learning 167
problem-posing 87–8
problems 17–18*t*
professional development. *See* lifelong teacher education
professional experience 186
Programme for International Students Assessment (PISA) 155, 170
project-based learning (PBL) 167, 169–70
proximal development theory 98
psychological needs 60–2
psychology 134

rankings 8, 155, 170
re-solving 88
reflected experience 147–8
reflection 187, 196–7
reflective thinking 87

reimagined pedagogy 38, 40, 42, 43, 47–8
relatedness 61–2, 206
renewed perspectives 235–6
resilience 84
responsibility 94–6
Rethinking Teacher Quality in the Age of Smart Machines (Zhao, Yong) 118
roles 235–6
Rosiek, Jerry and Jean Clandinin 156, 157, 159
Rourke, Alison 158

Sadirac, Nicolas 101
Salomons, Tonya 187
Sardar, Ziauddin 6
Sawyer, Keith 146, 188
scaffolds 132, 133, 138
schemas 134–5
Schleicher, Andreas 183
school improvement 7
schools 16
    unique factors 19
selecting and evaluating 92–3
Self-Determination Theory 54, 59–64, 72, 206
    Learning Disposition Wheel 64–5, 67
self-regulation 81
self-regulatory behaviour 62, 63*t*
semantic learning 90, 91
Sen, Amartya 35
shared endeavour 232–3, 235
shared leadership 204, 208–13, 225
shared repertoire 49
Shulman, Lee 111
silver bullet solutions 14–16, 17, 31
simple problems 17, 18*t*
Simpson, Barbara 208–9, 210, 211–12
Sinek, Simon 4
Smith, Jay 14, 15
smoking 36
social curiosity 84, 86
sociocultural perspectives 129–31
Socrates 187
status quo curriculum 153–6, 159, 177
Steed, Mark 193, 194, 195, 197, 198, 199
Stenberg, Robert 44–5
Stenhouse, Lawrence 115
student agency 58
subject depth versus integration 166–70
success
    Hurstville Public School 191–2
    measuring 8 *see also* testing regimes
summative assessment 170, 171
systems 39–40
Szekely, Emilia and Mark Mason 22

Te Rito Toi project 159*f*–60
teacher education 117, 200, 230–1 *see also* transformative teacher education

building democratic education through 182–3
experiential learning 186
foundational 30, 182, 184–8, 200
lifelong. *See* lifelong teacher education
renewed perspectives 236
roles 236
teachers
challenges 108–9
content knowledge 110–11*f*
as curators 118, 120–1
general pedagogical knowledge 110–13
pedagogical content knowledge 110–11*f*
pedagogical knowledge base 109–10, 125
pedagogy 108–9
teaching 136
build new ideas 93
challenges 108–9
curiosity 86
empathy 97
focus 82–3
grit 84
influence 95
make and express meaning 91
pedagogy 108–9
teamwork 99
think why and how 88–9
Teaching Scotland's Future (Donaldson, Graham) 117
team teaching. *See* co-teaching
teamwork 98–100
Templestowe College 160–1*f*, 162, 163–4, 235
curriculum co-construction 175–6
curriculum consultation 172–3
curriculum context 174–5
curriculum crafting 176–7
testing regimes 8, 155, 170–1
theory 129–31
Dewey, John 194
think why and how 87–9
Thomson, Pat 153, 154
Thunberg, Greta 52*f*–4, 72–3
Timperley, Helen 197–8
training 192
transdisciplinary approach 168
transformation 6–7, 16–17, 236
capabilities 22–30, 230–2
as complex problem 17, 18*t*, 19, 28, 31
complexity theory 16–17
4C capabilities 10–12, 22–8, 229, 230–2
puzzle of 228–30
successful 8–9
Transformation Tangle 229, 231*f*–6
values 23, 43–9
Transformation Tangle 229, 231*f*–6
transformative curriculum 30, 154, 157, 160
assessment 171
British Columbia 162–4
co-construct 175–6

consultation 172–3
contextualize 173–5
craft 176–7
deeper learning 177
example 160–1
false dichotomies 164
framework 172–7
subject depth versus integration 168
Templestowe College. *See* Templestowe College
transformative education 181–2
transformative leaders 223–4
transformative leadership 224–6
Bristow, Luke 221, 222–3
collaboration 219–20
communication 219
components for change 213–14*f*
creativity 221
critical reflection 220–1
example 221–3
existing operating system 215*f*, 216–17
4C capabilities 213–14*f*, 215–16, 217–23, 225
guiding coalition 215*f*–17
Howes, Peter 221–2
innovation teams 214–15*f*, 216–17
networked team structures 215*f*, 216–17
tensions 217–18*f*
transformative leaders 223–4
transformative learning 29, 181
transformative pedagogy 29–30, 113–20 *see also* Pedagogy Parachute
collaboration 116–17
communication 115–16
creativity 114
critical reflection 114–15
curating 118
definition 113
example 119
4C support 113–17
transformative teacher education 30, 182, 200
building democratic education through 182–3
4C capabilities 183–5
Hurstville Public School 190–9
transformative values 28–9, 34, 38–50 *see also* values
agency 38, 40, 42, 43, 46–7
collaborative partnerships 38, 39, 40, 41, 42–3, 48–9
connected and coherent learning 38, 48
critical hope 38, 40, 43–4
deep learning 38, 39, 40, 41, 43, 46
in education 38
explicit learning 38, 45–6
4C Transformative Learning 39–43
imagination 38, 40, 41, 45
praxis 38, 40, 43, 49
reimagined pedagogy 38, 40, 42, 43, 47–8
unlearning 38, 41, 44, 164–72
wisdom 38, 40, 41, 44–5

Transforming Organizations: Engaging the 4Cs for Powerful Organizational Learning and Change (Jefferson, Miranda and Michael Anderson) 2, 3, 161, 213
transforming school structures diagram 214–15f, 216
Transforming Schools: Creativity, Critical Reflection, Communication, Collaboration (Jefferson, Miranda and Michael Anderson) 2, 3, 10, 39, 66, 161, 167, 196, 213

understanding, depth of 168
unlearning 38, 41, 44, 164–72
US National Academy of Sciences
  Changing Expectations for the K-12 Teacher Workforce: Policies, Preservice Education, Professional Development and the Workplace 125

V-shape phenomenon (of migratory birds) 211f
values 23–4, 49–50, 230 *see also* transformative values
  British American Tobacco 36–7
  definition 36
  disorientation 233–4
  in education 37–8
  importance of 36–7
  Templestowe College 172–3

  that create transformation 34, 43–9
  that drive action 34–5
Veranzio, Fausto 1245
Vinci, Leonard da 124
Voss, Thamar 110
Voss, Thamar, Kunter, Mareike and Jürgen Baumert 112
Vygotsky, Lev 91–2, 98, 138

Walsh, David 104
well-being 58–9
Wenger, Eitienne 48–9
whakapapa tradition 212, 225
wheel, evolution of 76f, 77f
Wheel: Inventions and Reinventions, The (Bulliet, Richard W.) 76
Wiliam, Dylan 141
wisdom 38, 40, 41, 44–5
Wood, David, Jerome S. Bruner and Gail Ross 138
Wyse, Dominic, Louise Hayward and Jessica Pandya 155–6

Zhao, Yong
  Rethinking Teacher Quality in the Age of Smart Machines 118
Zittoun, Tania and Svend Brinkmann 90, 91